Absolutely Barking

Other books by Michele Hanson

ABSOLUTELY BARKING

ADVENTURES IN DOG
OWNERSHIP

MICHELE HANSON

**SIMON &
SCHUSTER**

London · New York · Sydney · Toronto · New Delhi

A CBS COMPANY

First published in Great Britain by Simon & Schuster UK Ltd, 2013
A CBS COMPANY

Copyright © Michele Hanson, 2013

Certain material in *Absolutely Barking* expands upon columns written by the author
and first published in the *Guardian* 1994–2010

1 3 5 7 9 10 8 6 4 2

Simon & Schuster UK Ltd
1st Floor
222 Gray's Inn Road
London WC1X 8HB

www. simonandschuster. co. uk

Simon & Schuster Australia,
Sydney

Simon & Schuster India,
New Delhi

A CIP catalogue record for this book is available from the British Library

ISBN: 978-0-85720-491-2
ISBN: 978-0-85720-493-6 (ebook)

Typeset in the UK by Hewer Text UK Limited, Edinburgh
Printed in the UK by CPI Group (UK) Ltd, Croydon CR0 4YY

To all our dogs: Lily, Poppy, Ziggy, Lusty, Gaddy, Milo, Caspar, Lucky, Alex, Katie, Herbie, Lettie, Harry, Gizmo, Bertie, Nala, Theo, Julius, Annie, Woody, Harry, Lucy, Trixie, Max, Navy and many more, who are gone but not forgotten.

CONTENTS

Introduction: Rude Dogs and People

Dog World is a strange and wonderful place, filled with dogs and people of every type, breed and class – some pleasantly eccentric, some fairly normal and some not pleasant at all. It is a world of charm and conviviality, but also vibrant with tensions and hatreds. I joined it 25 years ago by having my first, very own dog. I knew little about Dog World then but it looked idyllic to me. I remembered having a dog in the Fifties when the woods, fields, parks and roads were quieter, and my parents were in charge of the dog. Heaven. But now that I have my own dogs, I know Dog World is far more complicated than it seemed, and the dog population is bigger than ever before. Breeders churn the dogs out, owners care for them lovingly or tire of them and discard them, rescuers save as many as they can, and this means that once you enter Dog World, and let yourself fall in love with a dog, you are on an emotional roller-coaster – bliss one minute, worry and terror the next. So you have to be fairly robust. Not everyone can deal with it. But if you can, it will be worth it. You will have a fascinating, affectionate, loyal, entertaining and beautiful creature in your very own home, and it will change your life for the better.

And think of all that fresh air and exercise, getting up every morning to take your dog out. You'll be healthier, fitter and closer to nature and the physical world, which is vital for city dwellers, even if some of them find it difficult to cope with, like my friend Mavis.

In the carefree days when I only had one dog, she and I were having a walkie with my Boxer, Daisy, when along came Stanley. Stanley was an elderly Boxer. He hadn't much energy left, he usually plodded slowly along beside his owner, he never ran, he rarely played, he looked rather glum – until he saw Daisy, and then he came to life. He clearly thought her fabulously attractive and the minute he saw her, was overwhelmed by lust. I won't go into what he usually did to Daisy, but he did have an enormous tongue. It wasn't just the usual straightforward dog stuff. It looked frightfully rude if you weren't used to it. Stanley's owner and I had seen it so often that we tended to ignore it and just have a chat. Why not? The dogs were in heaven. They didn't meet very often, they didn't have much romance, it made them happy and at least they weren't fighting. But not everyone could deal with that sort of thing. Mavis certainly couldn't.

'Stop them,' she whispered, going red in the face. 'I can't handle this. Please stop them.'

But I didn't really want to. They were happy, I was

having a rather gripping conversation with Stanley's owner, and as we were in a busy part of Hampstead Heath, near the café, on a main path, next to a bench packed with people, the sun was shining and no one else seemed bothered – in fact they were rather cheered by the spectacle, staring and laughing in a jolly way – and so I didn't fancy wrenching the dogs apart.

But Mavis couldn't stand it. Her face went even redder and she was desperate to get away. 'I'm going. I can't stay here. I'm going to have to go.' And off she went up the path in a temper, and I had to follow her.

She had ruined the dogs' fun. But it's a difficult case to argue: one can't upset a friend just so that dogs can do that sort of thing. It's a step too far. People would say I was pandering to the dogs, or encouraging their bad behaviour, or even worse, being a voyeur. So I trudged up the hill with Mavis, feeling rather browned off.

This business of dog sex in public is rather confusing. One doesn't always know quite what to do. Ingela, another Dog World acquaintance, was on a walkie recently with her rather nervous rescue Greyhound, Milo, when along came a whacking great Pyrenean Mountain Dog, jumped on top of Milo, whose back isn't all that good, and started having its way with him. (We often find that gender is irrelevant in dog relationships.) Ingela wrenched the huge dog off, then along came its owner, and naturally my friend expected her to apologise but instead she gave Ingela a furious telling-off.

'Why did you do that?' she roared. 'You're ruining their natural pleasure.'

Personally I think that's a bit much, because it wasn't the same as the Daisy and Stanley relationship. That was at least consensual. Ingela was shocked by the woman's bonkers reaction. 'Do you know what?' she said to me after the event. 'I've never met so many mad people as I have since I started walking the dog.'

She's right. Dog World is full of odd people. Probably no more than the ratio of batty to normal among the rest of the population, but this is part of its charm. Going on dog walkies, you meet the sort of people you perhaps wouldn't normally come across in your own social circle. Fortunately most dog owners are usually a well-behaved, friendly bunch of all sorts of people who have one thing in common: their dogs, and entering their varied and colourful world can only make your life richer.

This book is not an instruction manual. I can't offer advice. It would be a bit pot and kettle, because not all my dogs' behaviour has been ideal. It is for those of you who would like to join Dog World and don't know how to go about it; those of you who are already in it and recognise the joys and perils of dog ownership, and, above all, those of you who profess to be Dog Haters but will hopefully accompany me on this journey through Dog World, come to appreciate dogs and their owners, and our unique contribution to modern life.

1. Walkies

The main route into Dog World is through dog walks. If you have a dog you must take it for walks – usually known as 'walkies' to dogs. Let's not analyse why. Could be that ending on a consonant does not appeal to a dog. Could be that I am just infantilising my pets, and so are most dog owners. I don't know, but that's what I shall call them from now on. Any dog-owner who does not take their dog out for a lovely long walkie at least once a day, and then hopefully a shorter one in the afternoon, really should not have a dog.

Walkies are not always fun. Sometimes they can be tremendously difficult and stressful, but if I am having a tough time on my walkie, I remind myself that having a dog about is usually bliss. It more than makes up for difficult walkies. Walkies only take up a couple of hours of the day, but that leaves twenty-two hours of comparative heaven. So heavenly that once you are used to having a dog in your home, it is horrible to be without one.

I wake up in the morning, perhaps thinking of global meltdown, or illness, or death or old age drawing nearer.

It may be winter, the skies may be grey or rainy, I may wonder what is the point of life. And there it is – a darling dog, in a cheery mood, wagging its tail and wanting a kiss. And a walkie or a play, or a snack or breakfast. And not only is it cheery, and it loves you, but it is beautiful. Every dog looks beautiful, especially to its owner. It is a living work of sublime art, in your very own home. You can gaze at it forever. What better reason could there be to get out of bed?

And this cheeriness and charm doesn't stop after break-fast. It goes on all day. Even when the dog is snoozing. There is nothing more relaxing than a snoozing dog. It just lies next to you, breathing gently, perhaps with the odd charming little snore, a tiny oasis of calm in a mad world, and all the tension in your body melts away. Well it does for me. It is a chum rather than a possession, which is why the term 'owners' gets up some people's noses, and although in law a dog is regarded as a 'chattel', I wouldn't dream of thinking of anyone's dog as a real 'chattel'. But I'd be in worse trouble if I called us 'parents', which is why I'm sticking to 'owners', and now that's out of the way, back to walkies.

Most dog walkers have a routine of sorts, so they take their dog for a walkie at a particular time of day. I go for my morning walkie between about 8 o'clock and 10 o'clock, and I meet all the regulars. I don't know much about the 6 o'clock to 8 o'clock lot, or the lunchtime lot, or the afternoon lot. But I have tended to avoid afternoons in the big parks, because those are the more dangerous walkie times. That is when the more irresponsible dog walkers crawl out of bed and bring their badly brought up dogs out to play: to tear at tree bark, to snatch picnics and the ice-cream from your child's little hand, to fight, jump at or chew up your dog.

Anyway, my morning lot are quite enough to be getting on with. There are dozens of them. I have made friends and enemies, I have had fun breakfasts in the dog café, I have had blood and fights on the paths and in the fields, but on the whole, things are pretty mellow, and having to go for a walkie every morning will do you the world of good – all that exercise (my bone density is perfect) and lots of people with the same interests as you – dogs.

Sometimes walkies can be solitary, giving you time for contemplation; sometimes they are like a party – friends appear, groups congregate, the dog café fills with dog-owners having morning coffee, lunch, afternoon tea. Sometimes they are almost too much of a party. I once met seven fascinating people on one walkie, had seven long and thrilling conversations before breakfast, and was completely wiped out by lunchtime. I need to try and moderate my chats, but it isn't always possible.

It is heaven to find someone who walks at the same time as you do, and follows more or less the same route, who you often meet, and find amusing. But really you know nothing of these people. They could be anything.

When I first started these walkies, with Daisy, my first own, well-behaved, benign dog, I met, among scores of others: the lady who knitted woollies from her Poodle's wool, the Whippet woman, with three Whippets, the showoff with the long, black cloak, a biblical staff and three super-obedient dogs, and a witty fellow with a pure white Samoyed, who I initially thought charming. But we all make mistakes.

Mr Fascist and his white dog

The Samoyed owner told amusing and riveting stories, a different one every walkie, but one day he somehow got onto the subject of the Jews.

'Jews are stupid and greedy,' said he, in a rather sweeping way.

'I'm Jewish,' I said. 'I'm not stupid and greedy.'

'I'm half Jewish,' said he, unashamed, 'and I'm not stupid. We're intelligent, *despite* being Jewish,' and then he warmed to his theme. 'When I walk through Golders Green,' he said airily, 'I feel like re-opening the gas-ovens.'

So that was the end of our walks together. If I saw him in the distance, I'd head off in another direction. I always avoided him if I could. But it wasn't that easy. If our dogs spotted each other before we did, they would gallop towards each other and play. Anti-Semitism meant nothing to them, so I had to talk to the fascist again, and explain why I hadn't joined him recently for another jolly walk. He was taken aback. 'I'm not a fascist,' he said. 'That was a joke.'

I didn't agree. He tried to convince me.

'I could show you a real fascist,' said he. 'He often walks around here. He wears boots and clicks his heels!' But I still didn't fancy any more walkies with this fellow.

Annoyingly the dogs still loved each other. Whenever they met in future, we would wrench them apart in silence. Which was difficult, because his dog was wild about Daisy. Physically. He blamed Daisy, of course.

'Is she on heat?' he snapped one day, after a particularly tough struggle to get his dog away from mine.

'That was weeks ago,' I said.

He wrinkled his nose with distaste. 'She's still rather high,' he said disapprovingly, as if my darling dog was somehow dirty and immoral, and it was she who had sullied his pure, white dog. I hope Daisy wasn't listening. And that really was the last time we met.

In the same club

That was the only fascist in twenty-five years of dog-walking, which is pretty good going. I met Sylvia over twenty years ago and we are still chums. We took to each other because we both had Boxers. People tend to stop and chat to another person with the same breed of dog, because they have the same looks, same charms, same behavioural and health problems. It's like members of the same footer team. You're automatically in Boxer/ Ridgeback/Yorkie/Greyhound or whatever club, and you can compare notes: does yours pull/dash/pounce to excess? Slobber? Does it have colitis and eye ulcers? Is it the handsomest, most amusing, cleverest sort of dog on earth? Of course it is.

I am in Boxer club. I blame my parents for having Boxers when I was a child. It set a pattern for the future. Having had Boxers imprinted on me from an early age, I soon learned to love them. My mother loved them, my father loved them, my auntie loved them, so I loved them. Other people love pointy-nosed dogs, long-haired and fluffy dogs, little dogs, yappy dogs, lap dogs, any dog as long as it's a dog, but I love big, squash-nosed, short-haired, muscular dogs. As I was an only child, my dog was my best friend, and a big, cuddly-wuddly, but tough and ferocious-looking dog is the best sort of friend to have. It adored me, it never shouted, argued, it never criticised or told tales. Its loyalty was unwavering. No human friend could ever maintain that standard of perfection.

Our first Boxer, Lusty, saved me from a wicked child-minder. She called me for my tea, I delayed because I wanted to finish my thrilling game of five-stones, so she rushed in, grabbed my little nine-year-old arm and started hauling me into the kitchen. But my darling dog growled a fierce warning and clamped his jaws round her wrist. Not hard enough to draw blood, just hard enough to leave some purple indentations, and she let go of me pretty sharpish.

And as well as its protection skills and caring nature, a Boxer has an adorable face, and it has a sense of humour, I swear it. Perhaps other dogs can have a laugh, I don't know. Boxers are the only type of dog I've ever lived with, but I promise you, they do jokes. They play hide and seek, they pretend to hand you a toy, then they whip it away, then they prance about, just out of reach, laughing. And they can sulk. They turn their heads aside and raise their noses up a little. The message couldn't be clearer. They're saying, 'You have upset me and are worthless. Go away.' To me, there is no dog as fabulously expressive, intelligent and amusing as a Boxer.

When we first met, Sylvia had a middle-aged Boxer and I had a puppy. Hers was the grown-up. It played very patiently with mine. Then five years later her lovely Boxer died, she acquired another puppy, and the roles were reversed. Mine was the grown-up and played very patiently with hers.

In fact mine was more or less the only dog around who could tolerate hers, because it was particularly bouncy and annoying. So we began to have regular walkies. We still do, although Sylvia no longer has a Boxer. At 85 her daughter reckoned it might be a bit much. 'What about a Staffie?' asked Sylvia. 'No,' said the daughter strictly. That might get her into trouble with the bad boys who roam about with their dreaded bull-breed crosses, looking for a fight. Or it might be stolen. Sylvia might be mugged for her dog on the way round the block, so in the end she bought a Norwich Terrier – Alfie. Alfie is perfect – small, robust, good-natured, attractive, affectionate, always in a perky mood, gets on with the cat, and with my dogs. He scuds along, never fights, and of course she loves him, but she does still miss her Boxers a tiny bit.

Two dogs at once

It is heaven to see dogs playing together. They have various games: hide and seek around the trees and bushes, bite-the-cheek, bark-at-the-crow and general running and pouncing about while growling playfully. Clearly a dog likes to have its own friends around, which made me wonder, after fifteen years of having one dog, what it might be like to have two. A good idea, I thought. A dog friend might make my dog happier, and surely a happy, well-adjusted dog is a well-behaved dog. Not everyone agreed.

'Don't do it,' says Sylvia. 'You must be mad. One dog is enough. I'm warning you. Don't do it.'

But I ignored her and went ahead with my plan.

Because at the time I didn't know that it is more difficult to train two dogs than one dog. It's not just twice
as difficult. It is ten times as difficult. And sure enough,
before the first year was up, my older dog Lily's behaviour began to deteriorate. Violet, our new dog, followed
her example, and they began to gang up and form a
vicious pack of two, rushing and pouncing at innocent
passing dogs.

Whyever did I get another dog? Because it had been a
long-term dream of mine to have two dogs. I was
convinced that Lily needed someone she could talk to in
her own language, play with, sleep next to. Someone to
keep her company when I went out. I imagined myself
out in the parks and fields with two jolly dogs gambolling along beside me, playing with each other, sharing
their toys. And for years the daughter had nagged inten-
sively for another dog. I had done my research, asking
every dog person I knew or met what they thought of
my plan. What is best? One dog or two? But the trouble
with research is that one tends to go along with the results
which agree with what you wanted to do in the first
place, like a government consultation. So I got Violet,
thinking, So what if they don't behave together? I'll just
let them off the lead one at a time.

But I hadn't thought it through. I hadn't realised
that if you let one dog off and it gets into a fight, you
can't go and sort it out, because you're hanging onto
the other dog, which is longing to join in. So you're

stymied. So I could only take them out together if I
had a friend with me, then, if the worst happened, the
friend could hold onto one, while I went and pulled
the fighting one out of its fight. It was that or take
them for walkies separately, which took up most of the
morning, and by the time one has finished buggering
around with two walkies, probably a few walkie
dramas, returning home, cooking two doggie breakfasts and having your own breakfast, it is nearly
lunch-time and you are completely clapped out and
need a little rest, so that's goodbye to most of the day,
and by the time you dredge up a little energy, it's walkies and dogs' dinner time again.

So could I advise anyone thinking of getting another
dog, to think very carefully indeed before doing so.

Two dogs?
FOR
- They will not be lonely when I go out.
- Two dogs will guard the house twice as well.
- A dog needs friends of its own sort. It may feel
  isolated when only surrounded by humans. What
  do they know of its feelings? Practically nothing.
- I like dogs. Two dogs will surely be twice as
  lovely as one dog.

AGAINST

- The dogs may not like each other.
- They may not be as well adjusted and even-tempered as I had hoped.
- They may form a pack on walkies and gang up to attack other dogs.
- Two dogs cost twice as much as one dog to feed.
- It is difficult to take one dog on holiday. It is almost impossible to take two.
- It is difficult to find a dog minder to live in your house with your dog while you go on holiday (she is too sensitive to go into kennels). It is almost impossible to find someone to look after two dogs.
- Vets' fees for one dog are high. Vets' fees for two dogs are astronomical.
- Insurance for one dog is exorbitant. Insurance for two dogs is financially crippling.
- One dog takes up a lot of time. Two dogs take up your whole life.

I found out most of the AGAINST section when it was too late. I can't quite understand why I never thought of all this while making my mind up. Probably because I had made my mind up already. But now that I have two dogs, I love them madly, so I have to cope with the problems. Anyway, on a positive note, suffering makes you a stronger person, I feel more sympathy for other people struggling with difficult dogs, and I'm hoping others might learn from my experience.

Not sorry at all

I'm just about to leave the Heath with my dogs, when two women and a white foxy-Husky type dog, just about to start their walkie, appear at the entrance. The white dog rushes at us, barking and snapping fiercely. This is no fun for me. My dogs are not pleased, they weigh eight stone between them, (something else I didn't think about when deciding to have two) they would like to retaliate, so they rear up, almost wrenching my arms from their sockets, while the white dog prances and yaps and snaps around us. I don't blame my dogs. They were behaving themselves and minding their own business, until the white dog rushed us.

Mrs Owner calls her dog, but it doesn't pay much attention. She has to call and call, while my poor little arm tendons are being ripped to shreds, and eventually she gets her dog away and secures it on a lead, but is she sorry? Does she apologise? No and no. Because this has happened before. Every time her dog sees my dogs, even just one of my dogs on its own, it rushes and yaps and snaps. I am paying a fortune in Indian head, neck and shoulder massage to repair the damage caused by this sort of incident.

But instead of a grovelling apology, she looks accusingly at me, and says, 'He only does this to *your* dogs. He doesn't do it to anyone else's!' As if it's my fault. As if my dogs are giving off some sort of poisonous vibe that forces her dog to behave so uncharacteristically badly.

What a nerve. So now, whenever I see her and her friend coming – she always has a chum with her – I try to get out of the way and turn my dogs in the other direction, but the white dog still dashes, the woman still glares crossly, and one day, my arms will snap, my dogs will escape, and all hell will let loose and of course it will be My Fault.

When it first happened I apologised. A sort of automatic grovelling that I do when my dogs misbehave, and that was probably a big mistake. Because it wasn't their fault. Sometimes it is, but this time it wasn't, so now I just glare back. I don't speak, I don't apologise, because what's the point? I like my apologies to be appreciated.

But one of the pleasures of walkies is that there is always a more charming dog-owner happy to listen to stories about ghastly dog-owners and having blabbed about the white-dog owner to scores of people, because I like to get things off my chest, I happen to tell another dog-walker who knew all about this woman and her white dog.

'She says that to everyone,' said this Pleasant Walker. 'Every dog her dog rushes at is the only dog it rushes at.'

Wait until I see that woman again.

Not sorry enough

It is a comfort to me to know that I am not the only dog-owner who occasionally has a tough time. Wei is out walking with her English Bull Terrier, Biddy, on the lead. She knows Biddy is not perfect. Biddy hates other dogs, which is why Biddy is on the lead. A friendly but rather weedy Spaniel comes wiggling up.

'I want to play,' it says. After years of observation, like most dog owners, Wei can translate their body language.

'No,' says Biddy, clear as crystal, body rigid, no playful response. But the Spaniel persists. It hasn't got the message. So Biddy whacks it hard with her paw, knocks it to the ground, pins it down and starts having a go at it. Wei hauls it off.

'I'm very sorry,' she says to the Spaniel owner, even though there's no injury and not a speck of blood. 'I'm really sorry that my dog was so horrible to your dog.'

'No you're not,' snaps the Spaniel Woman crabbily.

'Yes I am,' says Wei.

'No you're not. I don't think you're sorry enough, because if you were, you wouldn't let your dog do that.'

What? This is a bit of a shock reply to Wei, because she was telling the truth. She was profoundly sorry and wished desperately that her dog liked other dogs, and would just play normally with them, so that her walkies would be the pleasure she'd imagined they might be when she got a dog, but no, they were all too often like this. Hellish, although she did her very best to make the dog behave, and suddenly the unfairness of it hit her, and this miserable woman was the last straw, so Wei blew a gasket.

'All right then. I'm not sorry,' she shouted back. 'I'm always saying sorry, and nobody fucking believes me, and I'm fucking sick of people like you saying that I'm not fucking sorry. You lot just don't like Bull breeds, so why don't you just fuck off all of you!' and then she ran home with naughty Biddy, crying all the way. It ruined her day. Because I promise you she's a sweet, kind, usually calm person who has never screamed 'fuck' repeatedly at a stranger in a park before. But some people deserve it.

Dirty protest

It's not just fights and mean owners that can ruin your walkie. Choice of dog lavatory venue can also be a problem. This is another decision that a dog often likes to make for itself, over which the owner has little control. You can do your best: estimate likely times, get to a suitable place, take enough poo bags. But you can never be certain. Anyway, one day Wei sets off for her walkie with Biddy, she has three poo bags, which is overload, because Biddy only ever needs one, but this morning, very unusually, she needs three. Unprecedented. Wei had walked her a bit longer, hoping she might have a chance to do everything necessary, and she had. Great, because Wei needs to go to the High Street and buy a birthday present for her friend. She can now go, safe in the knowledge that the dog's toilet business is over for the day.

Off they go, through the crowded High Street to the charming gift shop, where Wei buys a present, which the assistant wraps delightfully in four layers of pink tissue and a bow, and out they come, back into the street, crowded with shoppers. It's Saturday, the road is jam-packed with traffic, they're just halfway across the zebra crossing when, yes, you guessed it – Biddy stops for a gigantic poo. Oncoming crowds of pedestrians step aside, nauseated, and Wei has no poo bags. What can she do? Panic stations. She has no choice. She must scoop it up with the four sheets of lovely pink tissue paper, and the whole High Street watching with distaste. Did Biddy do it on purpose? We think yes.

She's chosen a bad lavatory venue before. Biddy is a lucky dog. She never has to stay home alone, because her other owner, Adrian, takes her to work in his van. She sits in the front and has to wear a coat in the winter, otherwise she gets cold and shakes. She is tremendously well looked after and loved. Every now and again, Adrian pulls over, stops and takes her for a little walkie. She can't always be bothered to go. She's like a camel.

'Come on, do you want to go?'

'No.'

Adrian delivers art works all over the place, often to wealthy people with swizzy homes and gardens. One day he's delivering a work to an artist, who spots this majestic-looking dog in the front seat of the van.

'Bring your dog out,' says the artist hospitably. 'Let it come in.' He would like Biddy to join them on the patio, where everyone is having tea and scones, surrounded by a huge and delightful garden. Out jumps Biddy, runs to the patio and has a gigantic poo. The stench ruins everyone's tea and scones.

'I'm so sorry,' says Adrian, clearing it up. Shame.

Biddy was not saying sorry. She was saying 'Give me some attention.' Another bit of body language that Wei and Adrian have learned.

That dog should/shouldn't be on a lead

As my walkies with two dogs were sometimes a nerve-wracking experience, I would take them out together only three or four times a week. On the other days I took them separately. This was more relaxing, but physically more arduous. It meant two long walkies, about 2 -3 miles each, which meant 4-6 miles a day. I was 67 years old, and this was a bit much for me. But one 3-mile walkie with both dogs was mentally exhausting. Which was worse? To be mentally or physically knackered? I couldn't decide. So I did alternate days, one with the dogs together, the next with them separately. Neither option was a breeze.

Anyway, on one particular day I had them both. As usual, I let them off the lead separately, so that they didn't gang up and bomb off after some innocent dog, catch it up, pounce on it and give it the fright of its life. I reached a large deserted field. It was Violet's turn off the lead. On went her muzzle (see how conscientious I am?). Off went Violet, and then, just as she had pranced out of my range — I couldn't catch up with her and grab her — a pale, rather fluffy Lurcher emerged from a concealed entrance, with its owner.

Blast. Violet spotted it right away. Its colouring was not in its favour. Violet did not like pale Lurchers. Why? Don't ask me. If I knew, my life would be easier. Lily didn't like them either. I suspect Lily had taught Violet not to like them. There are certain breeds of dogs that my dogs didn't like — that they disliked even more than brown Labradors. Top of the hate list were pale Lurchers. Then any other Lurchers. Or any thin, bendy dog at all, or any small weak-looking versions of Lurchers. Also top of the list, about level with the Lurchers, came Wheaten Terriers. Neither of them could bear fluffy, Wheaten Terriers. Even Wheaten Terriers who were trotting along, hundreds of yards away, minding their own business. Then came brown Labradors, and they did have a short period of loathing Springer Spaniels, but that soon faded. Thank heavens.

I asked dog trainer Sue Scully why. 'A dog can't like every dog it meets,' said she. 'We don't like everyone we meet. Why should they.' Fair enough.

But knowing this didn't help matters. Violet had spotted the pale Lurcher. We had two seconds to blast-off. I could do nothing. Well I could, but would it work? I had two options. I could shout fiercely 'NO! LEAVE IT!' in a deep, authoritative voice. Or I could say 'Good girl, come,' in a relaxed way, to demonstrate that there was no need for fear and panic, that dog was harmless, Violet could approach and play, like a normal dog. I tried method number two. I thought it stood more chance of working. Apparently, method number one is dicey, because if you shout, the dog thinks that means danger and it must act to protect you, i.e. dash, pounce, fight and bite.

On this occasion, method number two did not work. Off shot Violet like a torpedo. Wham, pounce. The dogs had a short squabble. The Lurcher's mummy and I shouted at Violet. Almost immediately she came back to me, cringing with what seemed like regret. There was no blood. Violet looked deeply sorry. She sat obediently at my feet. The victim dog did not seem upset. But its mummy did. She was pink with fright and rage.

'Your dog should be on a lead,' said she. 'I could see that coming.'

'That's why she has a muzzle on.' The dog's mummy was still furious.

'What if another dog bites your dog?'

'That's my problem.'

But it was her problem too. 'My dog has never bitten another dog in its life,' said this woman crossly. 'I don't want it to start now.' She was American. And then a damning comment, with a pinched look. 'I've seen your dog do that before. That dog needs to be on a lead.'

This threw me into a glum mood. How could poor Violet spend the rest of her life on the lead? Off we went, both dispirited. This field, usually empty and a brief freedom opportunity for Violet, was now just another place of fear. Suppose the red-haired American and her curly Lurcher were to appear again? We were in big trouble. We plodded on, obeying orders, with both dogs on the lead. My day was ruined. It always is after something like this. I felt a failure. But as we trudged through some woodland, we met another woman, with a little black dog.

'Are your dogs no good off the lead?' she asked. I told her about the incident.

'Let her off,' she said robustly. 'My dog can look after herself.'

'Are you sure? My dog might pounce.'

'Just let her off. She can't do much. She's got a muzzle on.'

If only all dog-owners were so chilled. So I did as I was told. Violet did a moderate rush and pounce, but the little black dog just lay on its back. Violet had a sniff, and she and the little dog made friends. Phew. Both my dogs sat down obediently for a snack.

'That is not an out-of-control dog,' said this fabulous woman. (She was English.) 'Just take a Valium, go for your walkies, put her muzzle on and let her off.'

I thought she was definitely the more sensible of the two women and decided to take her advice. Not that I have anything against Americans. My cousin is American, some of my best friends are Americans, I love and admire many Americans, but the last time Violet rushed an American's dog – stopped short, didn't even pounce, certainly didn't bite – he kicked her. I heard her scream.

'Keep your dog away,' he roared, in front of what looked like his teenage daughter and her chum, 'Or I'll kick its fucking head in.' But I'm still not generalising. After all, Cesar Millan, the Dog Whisperer, is an American. But see what these little spats can do? They're deeply upsetting and can bring out hidden fears, prejudices and resentments, and cast you down for the day. But more often, they can perk you up. The delightful woman with the little black dog put me into a sunny mood for the whole day. Add to that the pleasure of seeing your dog frisking about happily, rolling on the sunny grass, sitting nicely for its bit of sausage, the white and golden pussy-willow almost luminous against the blue sky, and a dog walk is bliss.

The wolf pack

Among the same-dog-bonding groups in our park are some Vizsla owners, who meet in a certain field on Saturday mornings to train together. Beagle owners often have two Beagles, and stop for chats with a small cluster of dogs, and a group of Husky owners gathers daily on the top of one of the hills in a wide open space, on the Heath. We call them the Wolf Pack, because from a distance they look like wolves and are a bit scary.

John is always in the middle of them. 'If it wasn't for these dogs, I'd be six feet under,' says he. 'Honest I would. I had terrible depression. Massive, I don't care who knows it. I'm not ashamed of it. Then I started taking a dog out, then more dogs, and I got better. It cured me. I'm out here every day with the dogs, in the fresh air. And I even get some money for this!' He can hardly believe his luck. And he isn't the only one. Dogs can be an excellent cure for depression. I've heard of three dog-cures, and if I know three, there must be loads more. It's perhaps that magic trick they have for getting you out of bed in the morning – the most difficult thing to do if you're feeling terminally glum. They can wake you with a kiss, they want a walkie, and then you might notice that the sun's shining, and up you get, out of the grey blankets and into the green outdoors.

Any type of dog can do it. The Wolf Pack are not all Huskies. There's usually a selection of dogs. Various walkers pass by with their dogs and join in, to hang about and chat. But one of the Huskies is particularly keen on balls. He did once gallop over to me, knowing that I had a ball-y (another dog-friendly word ending, and it is easier to call out ball-y than ball), jumping up with its paws on my shoulders, but being used to large, jumping dogs, I remained calm.

The worry here was not that the wolf-dog would harm me, but that my dogs might take exception to him jumping up on their owner, trying to snatch their ball-y, which could have led to a big fight, which I didn't fancy. But it didn't happen. John called his dog away and it did as it was told. And then he called my dogs, who also did as they were told, because they know that he's very fond of them and knows their favourite biscuits. Violet will eat anything, but Lily will only eat donut-biscuits. She knows that he has them. She will reject his first offer of an ordinary, commonplace biscuit, and wait until he gives her a favourite donut-biscuit.

'See,' he says, holding out the substandard biscuit first. 'She won't have it. She wants her donut-biscuit. Look at that. She knows what she wants. What a clever dog.'

Absolutely. I always appreciate someone who appreciates my dog. Not everyone realises she is brainy, and when I find someone who does, then I will gravitate towards them, even if they are in the centre of the Wolf Pack. My plan is to gradually accustom my dogs to this assortment of wolf-like dogs, then they can all be friends, rather than just having Boxer friends. Dog World, I feel, should be like an ideal world – no cultural barriers, everyone mixing happily. And that's usually what it is. There are few cultural barriers in dog world. Another plus.

How to fall out with your friends

Sometimes I take a friend with me on a walkie. They used to come just for pleasure, when I had my one well-behaved dog, but now that I have two, having a friend makes things easier. We can take one dog each. If there are fights, I can leave my friend hanging onto one dog, while I dive in and separate the fighters. I know you're not meant to plunge your hands into the middle of a fight, but I have always found that hauling a dog off by its collar has always been perfectly safe for me. Well not always. I did once get my hand punctured by a Poodle when I tried to wrench two dogs apart in the bushes. But for heaven's sake don't try separating dogs on my recommendation. Your experience may be different. You may get half your hand ripped off, so be it on your own head if you want to try anything like that. There is another advantage to going walkies with a friend. It means that I only have one dog to hold onto, which doesn't play such havoc with my neck and shoulder muscles. I do my best with the walking to heel training, but while Violet is still learning, there's still rather a lot of wrenching, turning the other way, and sudden lunging, which has proved rather damaging, and so it is a tremendous relief when my friend Clayden comes too, then he can take Violet and I have a wrenching-free morning. All my torn and shredded muscles can have a little rest.

Annoyingly Clayden's methods differ from mine. He favours the harsh, dogs-don't-need-to-rush-about method. And according to him, not only do they need to be on the lead, heeling, but the lead must be so short that poor Violet often gets her little toes trodden on by Clayden's clomping great boots, which would be bad enough for a normal dog, but Violet is a bit of a cripple. She has one metal leg with stumpy toes, and one lumpy, calcified ankle, so instead of this being a totally relaxing walkie for me, I must walk in fear of Violet's poorly feet and ankles being crushed or clobbered. And worse still, Clayden believes, because he heard it from some so-called expert dog trainer, that dogs do not need to sniff the ground. They can sniff the air instead, says he. The air is also full of smells. So he schleps Violet along, no sniffing allowed, which makes it difficult for her to select a lavatory that she fancies, and when she does find one and tries to stop and use it, Clayden continues on his way, wrenching Violet along, thinking she's slowed down for a forbidden sniff, when really she's trying to go to the toilet. What torment. Both for her and for me. It's swings and roundabouts on these walkies.

Although most of my walkies are, and always have been, an absolute delight, whatever the weather, I am highlighting the difficult times, because who wants to hear about one pleasant walkie after another? I suspect it wouldn't be as fascinating as these selected tricky walkies, but don't let this put you off the idea of walking a dog. Remember, the bad walkies are the exceptions.

Dangerous neighbourhood

Once you have a dog, you can't help but notice the general dog situation. The minute you leave your house, there it is, all around you. I'm on my afternoon plod round the block and on the other side of the road are two young men with a large Staff-Pitbull cross, off the lead. It is a huge, barrel-chested, hulking, brick-shithouse of a creature. The young men are chatting away, not noticing what their dog is up to. It spots us and heads diagonally across the road, straight for my dogs, which are on the lead. It is not easy for me to hang on to two dogs weighing four stone each, especially if they're having a spat with another four-stone dog with big teeth. So I shout 'NO!!!!' because I'm terrified, am expecting a bloodbath and don't know what else to do.

Within seconds the killer-dog has reached us. All three dogs rear up snarling and snapping and batting at each other with their paws.

At last the men do something. They hear my screaming and call their dog. It returns to them immediately,
but too late. No blood, luckily, but it was a close shave.
Shall I tell these boys off for not having their dog on a
lead? Will they stab me? I don't care, because I'm so furious. So I ask, 'Shouldn't your dog be on a lead?'

'Sorry Miss.'

Which I suppose is something. An apology. It could
have been a punch in the chops or a 'Fuck off', which is
the usual response.

But when I get home I realise we hadn't got off as
lightly as I had thought. Lily's eye swells up, and the area
around it. Obviously that dog had biffed her and she had
a dog black eye. Another £100 at the vet. (It's not worth
claiming insurance, because that is the sum of my excess.)
Thank you boys.

That dog should be OFF the lead!

That's the trouble with having dogs on the lead. The
dogs off the lead don't like them. I'm walking round the
local park with my dogs on the lead, when another hefty-
looking dog – yes it's a Staffie again, but I blame the
owners – comes cannoning towards us snapping and
barking. It is horribly close. Naturally my dogs are longing to fight back, because they recognise this dog. He's
done this before, but I hang onto them for dear life,

because if I get pulled over or let go, I don't like to think what will happen. Who's dog is this? I scream for help. A chap comes running across pressing his little black button thingy, which is meant to give his dog an electric shock and stop it in its tracks. It doesn't. Eventually he gets hold of it. Phew! I am shaking, sweating and swearing horribly. I need to lean against a tree and take some deep breaths.

But he's a pleasant enough chap. He's looking after this dog for the woman who had even more trouble stopping it last time, and who also has a number of Papillon dogs, who always rush forwards in a yapping mob when they spot us, so the owner is not my favourite person. I never get near enough to speak to her, but this chap, Mike, gives me some advice.

'It's because your dogs are on the lead,' he says. 'They're giving off a bit of hostility, know what I mean? Because they're on the lead. They're defensive. If they were off the lead, you'd have no trouble.'

I've tried that, I say. 'I do have trouble with them off the lead, which is why they're on the lead.' Talk to the wall.

'Those dogs are frustrated,' continues Mike. 'They need to run about. That's going to make them worse, being on the lead.'

Round and round we go. But he's only trying to help. So why be rude? 'I bet if they were your dogs they'd be fine,' I say, 'off the lead.' I find that men always like to hear that.

The drug dealer's dog

I'm not the only person who can't quite relax while walking the dogs round the block. A neighbour, Miss Z, is so sick of having her harmless, elderly Border Collie beaten up and almost eaten for breakfast by other thug dogs when she tries walking round the local streets, that she's moved somewhere a little more genteel, nearer to Hampstead Heath. She's sure she made the right decision, because a little while after her move she was chatting to an acquaintance of hers who was a young drug addict. This girl had visited her dealer, on the street where my neighbour used to live, and just round the corner from me. Inside the ghastly dealer's home she noticed a darling little Staffie puppy tied to a radiator. Naturally she went over to give it a stroke and a cuddle, but was stopped by the dealer and told off.

'Leave it alone,' he snapped. 'I'm making it hard.'

I asked the address of this monster, I phoned the RSPCA and reported him. I don't know whether they did anything.

Wouldn't it be heaven if they could search every home in the area, find the tormented dogs and rubbish owners, and take the dogs away? But it won't happen. There's nowhere to put the squillions of rescued dogs. And life still wasn't perfect for Miss Z, even on Hampstead Heath. You can't ban foolish dog walkers from the area. So I came across Miss Z looking furious with her elderly dog hanging about and her little toddler bawling its eyes out. Why? What was the matter? Miss Z was busting to tell someone.

She'd just persuaded her toddler to get out of his push-chair and try a little walkie, when Wham! Up rushed a fat and bouncing Staffie and knocked him flat. Which is why he was screaming, inconsolable and refusing to walk another step. And did the dog-owner apologise?

No. He just said, 'It only wants to play!'

This is the worst excuse in Dog World and should never be used. But of course it will be. Over and over again. I have to admit that I've even used it myself, in the heat of the moment. I can only apologise, and hope that all the other millions of well-behaved dog-owners are not all tarred by the same brush.

2: The Professionals

For some people walkies aren't just a small part of life. Their whole life, more or less, is walkies and dogs. These people are the dog walkers. Some dog-less people view dog-walkers with horror. They see one person and a large pack of dogs and think, 'No way can one person control all those dogs.' But they can, easily. These people know what they're doing. You will never, ever hear them say, 'It only wants to play.' Relax when you see them coming. They've been practising for years. Unlike people like me, who are still learning. It's us you need to be more worried about. The dog walkers are the professionals.

How do you start being a dog walker? The idea came to Dawn about a year before she started. 'It was just a dream at the time.' She was selling tea and coffee from a tuk-tuk, and taking her dogs for walkies with friends, taking turns looking after each other's dogs, if someone was working or on holiday, but the tuk-tuk business wasn't doing that well, so she took the plunge and tried dog-walking, starting off on foot, traipsing around for miles, collecting the dogs from all over the place. Luckily her husband was working full-time, and she could just about afford to do it.

She started getting more dog clients, and after about a year her husband left his full-time job working nights, and joined in with the dog–walking. At first he couldn't walk far without wheezing, so he gave up smoking, started running everyday, began to love it, as well as the walkies, being out in the lovely fresh air, and look at him now. Glowing with health! See what dog walkies can do for you. I often bump into them both, and have never, ever seen either of them looking glum, even in the rain, sleet or freezing cold.

'It's not always easy,' says Dawn. 'It was stressful at first. I didn't worry about losing dogs, just about people moaning on about them. Because people do moan on. This man in a wheelchair comes zooming along, one of the dogs is in his path, so I call out, "Just a minute, I'll get it out the way!" But he just shouts, 'You should keep your dogs under control! Fucking dogs!"

'He's on a mobility scooter. How can I tell him to fuck off? How can people go out to such a wonderful place and be so miserable? I've said "Good morning" to some people. They just ignore it. But we're doing very well. Now we have a client list of thirty. I lose (in a business sense) some in the summer holidays, others come and stay. I started driving them around in the car, but soon there were too many to put in the boot, so we bought a van, then two vans, and I decorated them myself.'

The vans look very snazzy, with I LOVE DOGS along the sides, the LOVE is a big red heart, all in vinyl stickers, and there you go – a dog-walking business. Dawn and Mick now have a total dog life – walking dogs every day, taking in dog lodgers: some day boarders, some staying all night. They plan their timetable the night before.

'First pick-up at 8 a.m., arrive at Heath 8.30, walkies for about an hour and a half or two hours, drop off the ones who are only coming on the walk back at their homes, or bring them home if they're 'day-sitters'. Breakfast – for us and dogs, 11.30 out for a second walkie with another lot, back 1.30. Take the day-sitters out again later, if it's nice and sunny, take them home. Go home ourselves. I love it. I absolutely love it.'

The facilities at their house for dog-lodgers are excellent. I inspected them. I'd happily leave my dogs there any time, but sadly Dawn and Mick probably couldn't have them. They only take well-behaved dogs, and mine are a bit delinquent. Perhaps one day . . . because their house is a heavenly dog hotel. It's a terraced house and the dogs have their own room on the ground floor, almost the best room – downstairs front, with a bay window, with constant access to a sunny paved garden (if the weather's lovely), and how tidy it all is! There are seven dogs' beds in the dog room, different types: proper bespoke dog beds, cot mattresses with attractive coverlets, two in cages – one open, one shut (because that particular dog prefers it that way. It makes him feel secure), all spotless and tidy. How do they do it? My dogs never make their beds. I make them and they unmake them, over and over again. But these dogs have tidy beds, a radio, glamorous central chandelier and a large worktop for preparation of dogs' dinners. Perfection. And on the day of my visit, five happy dogs are milling about, with their radio tuned to Heart FM.

'Because I've been dancing with them today,' says Dawn. 'I like to have a dance with them, but usually they have classical. It keeps them calm.'

But then there's the poo. A lot of it, and it all needs to be picked up. See how robust you have to be? I have two dogs, who average three poos each a day, which makes six, and if Dawn and Mick take five dogs a day each for a walkie, that's ten dogs altogether, and let's say they have the same average number of bowel movements as mine, that makes 30, and an enormous amount of searching and picking up.

'That's all we do,' says Dawn. 'Pick up poo. I used to get free bags on the Heath, then I thought, I'm earning money doing this, so taking free bags is a bit cheeky. I started buying them, which was pretty expensive, until I found packs of 300 nappy sacks really cheap in Morrisons, so I thought, Nappy sacks is the way to go.

'We talk about it all the time. I said to Skevvy, one of the owners, "Did you have roast dinner last night?" She said, "Yes, how d'you know?" I said, "I saw sweetcorn." She has sweetcorn with her roast dinner and so do we.

[In case you want to know, dogs don't seem able to digest sweetcorn properly, so it goes straight through.] We can see if our clients have been giving leftovers. Rodan [their dog] has perfect poo – consistent, hard, because he has a good, consistent diet. We're rather pleased with ourselves about it. Sometimes we get a dog client with the runs. If they have a dodgy tummy we don't give them any treats. They get cuddles instead.'

You non-dog-owners may think it odd to talk so openly of excrement and find it fascinating, but why not? When one has something unpleasant to deal with, rather frequently, why not make the most of it, deal with it head on and have a laugh? But however jolly your approach, this excrement collection is not easy. In autumn it can get lost in the brown leaves. I have searched for ages, and sometimes had to give up, or trodden in it while searching.

Some helpful hints from Dawn: 'You have to keep your eyes on the spot, and then head straight for it. In the winter the steam can help with your search. Or it's handy if you have a dog that likes it. They like it particularly in the winter – it's chewy, like a sort of dog ice-lolly. And in the summer it's sun-dried. Just follow that dog. It will lead you to the spot. And then people let their dogs lick their faces! The dog's just eaten poo! One man I knew – I shan't say his name – came to collect his dog, picked it up and kissed it on the mouth. I couldn't tell him. It was too late anyway. Never let your dog lick your face,' advises Dawn.

'People say to me, "Aren't those people irresponsible? Why have a dog if they can't walk it?" No. They're very responsible, because they have a dog-walker. They're not leaving their dogs at home all day without any exercise.'

The dog jogger

Sometimes on my walkies, I see a rather fit and healthy-looking chap jogging past followed by a pack of lolloping dogs. It's Barry the Dog Jogger. Occasionally he's walking, but usually he's jogging along in a rather relaxed way, calling to the odd dog who's gone a bit too far off the route.

There are hundreds of dog walkers, but Barry is probably the only Dog Jogger. Why does he do it? 'It's very good for them,' he says. 'You're taking urban dogs, bred for working: herding, hunting, searching and retrieving. The ones I take jogging are all working dogs: Vizslas, Ridgebacks, an Anatolian Shepherd, Boxers, Rottweilers, Spaniels, and it's encouraging them to engage in their basic instincts – roaming in a pack. Today I was walking, because I had a new dog, a little Norfolk Terrier, with stumpy legs. You mustn't go too fast, just a steady rhythm. If they're running it's too fast – like a pack on a hunt. They all get on, they sort out the pecking order themselves, with me as the established alpha.

'But I started this because I wanted to get myself fit. It began with me and my dog, Leo the Rottweiler, going out for a run – I think Rottweilers are completely misunderstood. I can't fault him in any way. We have an open-plan house, all the dogs sleep in the same area. They come back from their walkies and they have some social contact – the family, the other dogs. And we have regular overnight dog boarders. Some dogs come for two or three months and my wife Julie does the day care. I start collecting them at 6 a. m., to get to the park before rush hour, then I take them home between 4 and 7, unless they're boarding. I use all the Royal Parks. That's what they're for – the people and dogs of London. That's why dogs are allowed off the lead in all of them.

'I've got that knack with dogs. I taught myself how to communicate with them and lead them, not to call them too often, because they then think, I can still hear him. I know where he is, I'll find him. Their sight's not that good. They live their life through their nose and ears.

'They mustn't feel that you're anxious, scared or stressed. They must know you feel confident. They must follow you because they want to. They know I'll never lead them into danger. I don't use treats. Never. I run for 6-8 kilometres, depending who's in the pack. It takes about an hour. But they have half an hour walking first, so they can sniff around and have their poos – if they stop and poo while we're jogging the whole pack will have gone ahead – then we have the hour's jogging, then another half hour's walking at the end. With a new one, if they're drifters, I sometimes hide behind a tree, so they think they've lost me and the whole pack. I let them get a bit anxious, then they're very pleased to see me when I reappear, and they don't tend to do that again.

'The jogging makes them do a bit more. It's making them do more mentally – they're focusing on what they're doing, where we're going, they're more active, it's more draining for them. It makes them so healthy – their bones and ligaments are stronger, they're less susceptible to putting on weight and, most importantly, it enhances their mental wellbeing in a highly stressed urban life. My own dog's fur's good, his running's good, his pooing's good, he's never been to the vet. I feel I've given him a good life. The dogs are all happier when they get home. A tired dog is a happy dog.

'The dogs in my life have always helped me with everything. I'm healthier, I've lost a lot of weight, look.' Barry shows me a photo of a rather podgy-looking fellow. Who can it be? Not him, surely. I would never have recognised him. It was taken a few years ago and he looks like a different man. Transformed. That one had a big round face, this one hasn't.

'I'm much happier. With a dog you can't just say, "I'll take a day off, I won't go out today." You've got to keep the momentum going, run every day. I feel healthier now than I did when I was fifteen. I used to run a restaurant, which was very stressful. But I go to work now and I love it. I can't believe I get paid for this. The dogs give me so much. They deserve the best. It's a service with a heart. We give them what they need. Not treats, not silly clothes.

'My children – I have two daughters, Lily and Scarlett – know everything through the dogs: cleanliness, discipline, not to shout, to keep calm. They see how dogs interact, they both see the dogs talking to each other with their bodies – standing over each other saying "This is my space" turning away from each other. They do it too – turn their backs if they don't want to play with them, put their hands under their chins, so that they lift their heads up when they want to talk to them, and naturally walk among the pack as little alphas.

'My enthusiasm comes from a feeling that we share this planet with a huge population of dogs without a voice, who live in cities, who should really be out working for several hours a day. People often don't realise that. They see a Weimaraner [those mushroom-grey rather tasteful-looking dogs], they think, I like that dog, I'll have one, then they stick him in a flat in Kensington and wonder why he chews on their Louboutins.'

No wonder there are rather a lot of neurotic, chubby dogs about, but luckily Barry also does a boot camp for dogs with obesity. 'They stay with me, they're checked with the vet at the beginning, to see that their hearts, legs, etc. are okay. Then they're put on a strict diet. I take them running, slowly, slowly at first –'

He shows me a photo of a Vizsla, sitting down, seen from behind. What a fatty! You're meant to be able to see the shape of their waists. No chance with this doggy. Then another picture, same dog in the same position, six weeks later. It's half the size. Miraculous. And the same with a Pug. What a transformation! And Barry has a large, spacious van to transport the dogs about. Inside are three large compartments, each with a pretend grass carpet on the floor. The carpet and whole van are absolutely spotless. Not the slightest trace or smell of dog. I can't see a single dog hair. How does he do it?

It's washed and cleaned out thoroughly every week regularly. I could learn from this. My car could be a lot cleaner. And perhaps I could start jogging, just a few yards at a time. Or perhaps I could hand my dog, the younger one, over to Barry for a bit.

3: Successes and Struggles

Another benefit to having two dogs, I'm hoping, is that when one dies, you still have the other. That hopefully helps you to carry on, which was one of the reasons which made me plump for two dogs. I remember how desolate it was having no dog at all.

When my first Boxer was getting on a bit – eleven years old – that's pretty old for a Boxer and her back legs were getting weaker, I started to get a bit worried about how much longer she would last, and began to cry on and off on our walkies, wondering how ever I would manage without her. I usually start this intermittent crying when a dog is about nine, because from that age I begin to feel that we're nearing the end. By eleven things are fairly desperate, usually, until one day, when I bumped into this woman with her Golden Retriever, who wondered what I was blubbing about. So I told her.

She thought I ought to stop worrying. She's had a Boxer who lived to fifteen. Yes, fifteen! And even more remarkable, had puppies, aged ten!! Unfortunately nobody knew who the father was. This owner went to the vet who told her not to worry. As the dog was so old it would probably only have two puppies at most, and on the day of the birth, the father would probably turn up.

She didn't believe the bit about the father turning up, but she did believe the bit about the two puppies.

Along came the day when her dog was to give birth. It all started to happen, and guess what? A dog appeared at the front gate, mixed breed, or mongrel. (You have to be careful what you call a dog. I wouldn't want to upset anyone. Apparently mixed breed means the offspring of two different breeds, but a mongrel's parents are mixed breed already.) Anyway, it was a neighbour's dog. It hung around all day until the puppies were born, and then it buzzed off. Miraculous. It must have been the father. Why else would it turn up and hang about? That vet was right. But in the meantime, puppy number one arrived looking healthy, then puppy number two arrived – presumably the last one – looking very weedy indeed. It looked almost dead. The owner did her absolute best to keep it alive, she was desperate, because this was to be her last little darling puppy, which she couldn't bear to lose: mouth to mouth, warm towel, massaging, clearing airways, and so on – and she succeeded. But it wasn't the last puppy. The vet was wrong. Out came two more puppies, both healthy. So I can stop weeping on my walkies. My dog may be here for some time yet.

A good little boy

A chance meeting on a walkie can perk you up, even if you have started off in a glum mood. Even a potential grim encounter can turn out well. I'm going round the block with my dogs, when two small boys, aged about ten or eleven, pass by with their Jack Russell. The boys are busy looking at my dogs, which they admire, because most boys admire tough and brutish-looking dogs. They're so fascinated by my dogs that the one holding the Jack Russell hasn't noticed that it's trying to poo while being pulled along. So I tell them.

'Your dog's having a shit,' I say, rather crudely. I've spoken coarsely on purpose, because I know that an old lady saying 'shit' might startle them into obedience, but an old lady saying 'your dog's going to the toilet' would only elicit mockery.

They stop pulling the dog and allow it to poo in comfort. 'That's a lot of shit for a small dog, isn't it?' I say, sticking to my method, which seems to be working. The boys go pink. My foul language has rather put them on the back foot. But then they start to leave. Without picking the poo up.

'Aren't you going to pick that up?' I ask. 'It's not nice to leave it. People will tread in it.'

'I haven't got a bag,' says the boy holding the dog.

'I have. Here you are.' For once I know I have the tone right. It's like being a teacher. I know from my experience at the chalkface. Get cross and hysterical and a boy like this will defy you cheekily, but get it right and he will do as he's told, and for once I had it right. I gave the boy the bag and he picked the poo up. A triumph. True, he did grumble a bit.

'It's not even my dog,' he said, pointing to his friend, who had cunningly gone on ahead. 'It's his.'

I thought he deserved some praise. It's now called positive reinforcement. 'That's very good of you to do that,' I say. 'Thank you very much. Shall I put it in the bin for you?' Why not? I'm going past the bin and I know better than to push my luck. He'll only drop it the minute I turn my back. And he really has been a good boy.

'Yes please.' A happy ending.

Dog-in-laws

Sophie has two Parson Russells. 'They're father and son, Navy and Blue,' says she. 'And some time ago, when I only had Navy, I left him for a moment outside the dog café in the park while I went in to get a cappuccino, came out, had a chat with a friend of mine, and by the time I got home I'd had an irate phone call from the owner of a small brown dog, now a possible mothertobe, saying that her dog and Navy had had a brief encounter in the café forecourt, and I was to take Navy to visit to see if they liked him. Would he be a suitable father? If they didn't think so, their dog would be given the morning-after pill. Luckily they approved. And Sophie approved of the daughter-in-law, and her parents. They were far more charming than her own in-laws, and her relationship with the dog-in-laws, which developed during the pregnancy and birth, was far more rewarding. So she adopted one of Navy's sons, now called Blue. To go with Navy. Another happy ending.

Babe magnets

I'm on my way home and I meet a family out with their teeny-weeny Chihuahua. Why would anyone want such a tiny dog? Its legs are like twigs. They're going so fast to keep up with a moderately paced walking human, that they're a blur. It's so tiny and twiggy it looks as if it might break. If you want such a widsy little pet, why not get a hamster? Or a pet rat? So I ask the man. His wife has gone on ahead.

'It's a babe magnet,' he says. He may be right. I've heard from another woman dog walker, that when her husband takes the dog out – it's a Lurcher called Milo – women are forever approaching him and saying 'What a lovely dog!' But if she goes out with the dog, no women approach her to say anything, even though she has the very same dog with her. So clearly dogs are not chap magnets, only babe magnets, which is fairly sickening,

especially if you are a woman who acquired a dog thinking that it might help you to find romance.

Or perhaps you don't want romance and just want to be
with your dog. Some men find it a bit of a worry that
women seem so interested in their dogs. They assume that
it's not the dogs the women are interested in at all, it's
them, which makes it tricky for the women, who may
genuinely be interested in a fellow's dog, or just wanting
to pass the time of day, and they find that the man is in a
blue funk, thinking she's after him, body and soul.

'You can bet your life,' says Sarah, who has often
spoken to men about their dogs in parks, 'that just one,
or at most two, sentences into the conversation, he will
have mentioned his wife or girlfriend.' You can look at
this in two ways: positively, because men really just like
walking their dogs, and they have no ulterior motive on
their walkies, or negatively, that they're all a bit big-
headed and can't imagine any woman could just fancy
their dog, she must be fancying them.

Life is not easy for men with dogs. Unwanted women
crowd around them, or people run away screaming with
fright. This happened to a builder chum of mine, who
used to look after my dogs when I went on holiday. As
he is a muscular, bullet-headed, Phil Mitchell type fellow,
people often assumed, seeing him out with a tough,
muscly dog, that he must have been a thug and his dog a
killer. But he wasn't. He was just a pussy-cat, tempera-
mentally, and the dog was soft as Bambi, but when the

crowds saw him coming, they parted like the Red Sea, women snatched up their children in terror, and being a sensitive fellow, he found it very distressing. Then there came a point when he was out with his family on a walkie and could bear it no more.

'You take the bloody dog,' he said to his wife. 'I can't handle this.' So she took the dog and from then on no one batted an eyelid, mothers passed by calmly, even allowing their children to approach and stroke the dog, and the rest of their walkie was all peace and harmony.

And he isn't the only one. Alex (female) walks Ike, her Rottweiler, and nobody minds, but if her boyfriend takes him out, the whole neighbourhood is on red alert. The poor boyfriend has been stopped three times by the police already, just for walking along with his dog. I promise you, both of them are as soft as butter. If only people wouldn't judge by appearances. So if you ever see a man out with a tiny, fluffy dog, you can be more or less sure that this man is as tough as you can get. He has nothing to prove.

But tough doesn't mean insensitive. Saul and his chum, both from Yorkshire, were out with their Whippets one morning, when they came across a fabulously smart woman with her Italian Greyhound. Their Whippets weren't bothered about the little Greyhound. They ignored her and just sniffed some nearby grasses, and she paid them no attention either, but her owner was rather shocked, almost disappointed, by all this.

'That's very unusual,' she drawled in a languid way. 'I've never seen anything like that before. Usually she lies down and lets them lick her!'

Saul and his chum were shocked to the core. Forthright is one thing, but this went too far. 'I don't think I could go home and tell my wife that story,' he said. A sensible decision.

4: Training

Even before you go on a walkie, you should start training your dog. You don't want it to be running away, getting lost, having fights, jumping up at passers-by or stealing picnics. Without training, walkies will be no pleasure. Training starts, if your dog is a puppy, with puppy classes. These classes will be your first introduction to Dog World – a preliminary taster, bringing you into contact with a small selection of dogs and dog people, which will show you what you're in for. Because you cannot just have a dog and live with it in isolation. With a dog comes Dog World and its people, and you must learn to live with them too. Skill in dealing with dog-owners is vitally important, if you want to have a happy life in Dog World.

Once at your dog/puppy training class, it soon becomes clear that some of us are natural-born trainers. Others are not. I am not. I have always had a bit of a problem telling people what to do. I was unable to discipline classes when teaching, my teenage daughter always tended to do as she pleased, and so do my dogs. Because in my heart I feel that I have no right to be tying something round their necks and hauling them about all over the place. What right do I have to boss them about and dictate the route on our walkies? Why should they not be free to gambol about in a natural way, frolicking after squirrels and pouncing on rats? Why should they not sniff here, there and everywhere? Why should humans dominate the planet? Dogs might have made a better job of things. Clearly I have the wrong character for a pack leader. Psychologically, I am not up to it. And the dogs know it. All dogs know a wet and a weed when they see one, and are quick to take advantage, which makes my job even harder.

Cruel Mrs Big Bum

I did take my first, own dog, Daisy, to training classes. Because that is what you're supposed to do, and as I had never looked after a dog all by myself before – my parents had done all that – I thought I might need some guidance. So I took Daisy to puppy training evening classes. But they were a bit late, I thought, for a young dog. They started at seven and they finished at nine, which was way past her bedtime, and more importantly, miles past her dinner time. That meant waiting till 9.30 p. m. for dinner, and a very late night. And the venue was a rather dismal community hall off the Holloway Road. Which was all bad enough, but on top of that, I couldn't really warm to the trainer. She was a bossy woman with a huge bum. She probably couldn't help the bum, but the bossing was avoidable, and also, she was cruel, in my opinion. Dogs were forced to wear a horrid, tight little white rope choke collar in class. So tight that you couldn't squeeze even one finger under it. So tight that I had to practically choke the dog just to get it on. Then, round and round we went in a circle. Heel, sit, heel, sit, one way, then the other way – and while we were going round, my poor dog vomited. Teacher was not pleased.

'Has your dog eaten?' she asked crabbily.

'Yes.'

'Why? You should not have fed your dog before class!' But my dog was hungry, so I fed her, so she threw up, and we were expelled. Good. Stuff the nasty training class. We didn't need it anyway. My dog's behaviour was perfect. Daisy was a saint among dogs. She did as she was told, she never fought, she never stole food or children's ice-creams, she never chewed furniture. She did no wrong. She did not need classes. I trained her myself. Remember that dog trainers are only human. They are not perfect. You may have to try several before finding the right one for you and your dog.

The shed training

It can be a bit of a shock, when you have had benign and cheery dogs for the whole of your life, to suddenly find that you have a dog with behavioural difficulties. This happened to me in my forties, when I rescued my second dog, Lily, from a cruel breeder. Heaven knows what happened to her in this woman's clutches, but by the time she arrived she had emotional problems and needed proper training. Some dogs, like Daisy, hardly need any, but Lily did. She had one particular habit that was a bit of a worry. Suddenly she would spot, in the distance, a dog she didn't like. For no particular reason, as far as I could see. The dog would be trotting along minding its own business, not snarling or threatening. Not even looking in our direction, then suddenly Bang! She was off like a torpedo.

The first dog that got this treatment was a pale Lurcher. There was a short scuffle, the poor Lurcher got a small bite on the head, the owner was surprisingly calm about it, but after that, if any pale Lurcher appeared on the horizon, bang! Lily was off again. (I suspect this set the pattern for the future, and that Violet, when she arrived five years later, learned her hatred of Lurchers from Lily.) Then it was any brown Labrador. She saw it, she rushed it, pounced on it, pinned it to the ground and bit it. I couldn't be having that. Nor could the other dog-owners. More training was imperative. More socialising with other dogs, even Lurchers.

I heard of a dog-training class for Lily, which was held every Saturday morning in a nearby park. That was my Saturday mornings down the drain. But you're not meant to think that way, so I dredged up some positive thoughts and set off. I found the dog-training area. It was raining. Nothing much was happening. Dogs and owners hung about getting wet. Where was the training? When did it start? At last some movement. New pupils had to go into a shed. It was rather dreary and damp inside the shed. Trainer gave us a lecture, while the dogs sat and sat. Mine was trembling. With cold, terror or boredom? I didn't know. Unlike me it didn't have a nice thick woolly and boots and a raincoat. It only had its own short, rather thin little brindle and white all-over outfit, which had to do for summer and winter.

According to the instructor, it was good for the dog to learn to sit still through interminable lectures. I have always had difficulty sitting about doing nothing much, especially when a long lecture could have been précised into five minutes and I could have shot home for a nice warm cocoa. And if I was longing to scream and leave in a hurry, what must the poor dog have been feeling? Soon I could no longer concentrate on the lecture. I was too worried about the dog's mental wellbeing. It must have been going through hell. At last we went back out into the sodden park. Mud and puddles everywhere. Sensibly Lily sat on my foot – the only available dry area.

'It's sitting on your foot,' said the training lady strictly. 'That dog is in control.'

Wrong. I encouraged it to sit on my foot because I didn't want it putting its poor bum in a puddle. Bad enough sitting in the damp shed for nearly a whole hour, then standing for an hour in the widdling rain with the dog shivering and whingeing beside me, without forcing it to sit in the wet. By then it was whimpering with misery. I was longing to give a big kiss, wrap it in a lovely warm towel and take it home for a hot gravy dinner, but that wasn't allowed.

'Ignore it when it cries,' instructed the dog teachers harshly. (There were two of them.) Strains of Truby King. But I stick it out, because perhaps Teacher is correct. But perhaps they were right and this is what the dog needed. I hadn't done very well on my own so far. I'd been unable to correct the terrible dashing and pouncing. Owners and onlookers had screamed and panicked, word had spread in the neighbourhood, we had become pariahs and I had been advised right, left and centre.

'Muzzle her/keep her on the lead/never take your eye off her/shout at her/don't shout at it, hit her/never, never hit her,' but worst of all, 'You have spoilt her.'

I have heard all this before. It started 20 years ago when the daughter hit nursery school, and it never let up. This is the trouble if one is a mother. Everything is your fault. And I was the dog's mother. That's what I felt like. This dog was my second baby. I only have one child, a daughter. She is rapidly growing up, and I needed another baby to fuss over. I know this sort of thing is frowned upon, I'm anthropomorphising like mad, but why not? If I want to think a dog has an emotional life vaguely like mine, then I shall carry on doing so, and stuff the anti-anthropomorphism brigade.

Perhaps I could be a better mother second time round, so I tried hard to stick at this training. Every Saturday morning. Then every other Saturday morning, because on a Saturday it is my custom to go for a heavenly dog walkie with my friend Jennifer. Why ruin every single Saturday? Why not just go now and again to dog class? There we were spending most of our time just sitting in a row, or in puddles, or in a shed, waiting for our turn to do something. Then I began to think, Why go at all? Because our big problem – the rushing and pouncing – didn't happen at dog class. Lily was overwhelmed by the dreariness of it all. She didn't want to rush and pounce. She just wanted to go home. And so did I. And seeing as she wasn't rushing and pouncing, the trainers didn't witness it, so they couldn't show me how to correct it. And Lily could do everything else perfectly well. So that was the end of our visits to the Shed Training School.

Vera, Daughter of Darkness

I should have stuck at it. Elaine and Linda did. They adopted a smooth-haired dark-grey Lurcher called Vera. What a tough time they had. They began to call Vera Daughter of Darkness. She was a difficult dog. She sounded even worse than mine, so aggressive, a snarling mass when she saw another dog – lunging, barking, snapping. 'We tried everything,' says Elaine. 'We were down in Devon in a pub, she was doing all that, I was almost in tears, but a woman said "Don't give up" and we didn't. It's taken eighteen months and about £400's worth of Red Leicester cheese.'

Now here she is in the park with Sue the trainer, and today has been a breakthrough. A first. Today Vera walked past a cat, and took no notice! Miraculous. 'Usually, if Vera sees a cat, she loses her sanity. She gets hysterical if she spots a small dog, but today she eyeballed this cat before we did, but we gave a little shake of the shake-bottle (a plastic bottle quarter-filled with gravel), just shook it very lightly, it brought her back to reality. She just walked by and ignored it.

'It's discipline via environmental corrections – a little squirt of water, a slight rattle of the shaker, and that does it,' says Sue. That is quite some achievement, because let's not forget that Vera is a Lurcher. If she spots a small fluffy thing, she'll naturally be after it in a flash, chasing.

'And she had a particular hatred for ginger dogs,' says Elaine, throwing Vera her flat, floppy squeaky toy, which they fondly call her road-kill bunny, as it's so flat. Vera trots over and pounces on it in a chilled way and brings it back to her mummy.

'Lovely, Elaine!' says Sue. 'See that?' pointing to two small, white fluffy dogs who have entered the park. Not long ago she'd have kicked off, glared, then wham! She was always looking for squirrels. Every individual dog, you have to find out what rocks their boat. Linda and Elaine have persevered. Other people would have taken Vera back, but they've stuck at it. 'We're trying to change her mind, not just come down on her like a ton of bricks.'

Vera's strolled off a little way on her extension lead; she's sniffing round a tree trunk. 'You have to look for a window of opportunity. While she's sniffing around there, it's as if she's watching a good film, and if you call her she'll go "Just a minute, just a minute", but while she's sniffing, she'll break for a second, and that's your window.' Elaine calls, and walks away, Vera comes. Amazing.

'You're training your dog from the minute you get up until the minute you go to bed, whether you know it or not. You may have a dog that just behaves itself and is no trouble, then you don't have to do all this, but Vera would jump up on the sofa behind visitors, barking and screaming.'

'We would shout and pull her off, over and over again,' says Elaine, 'but it made no difference.' Sue told Elaine to stop shouting and instead put a line (very light lead) onto Vera, and when she did her jumping on the sofa and screaming trick, to not speak to her at all, but in absolute silence, take hold of the line, gently guide the dog off the sofa and lead her up the hall, no eye-contact, no fuss, because the fuss would give Vera the attention she wanted. And it worked like magic.

'We only had to do it once. She was humiliated, being taken away from the visitors in silence. Next time I just walked towards her and she got off the sofa by herself.' Fabulous. This is why one needs a clever dog-trainer who seems to know what the dog's thinking. Sue tailors her training to the individual dog, and suspects that our expectations of how a dog should behave are now too high. 'We expect our dogs to go to the park and like every other dog they see, but they don't. And the way we live now is freer, more open-plan. During the war you had a best room with your one sofa, that hardly anyone ever used. Dogs were certainly not allowed on that sofa. Now they're allowed everywhere, all over the house, on the beds. Dogs need rules and they're not getting them, and so there are more dogs out of control.' But Vera isn't one of them anymore. She's eyeing those little dogs across the park again, her ears are flattened back, her tail's down. Does that mean she's relaxed? 'No, that's saying she's a bit anxious,' says Sue, 'and look, she's yawning. That yawn means she's a little bit stressed.' She still looked pretty mellow to me.

And remember, this morning she just walked past a cat without flinching. That is a tremendous achievement for any dog, never mind a Lurcher. Such are the rewards or perseverance, consistency, determination and love. Just like a good mother.

The Russian Dog Whisperer

My dog's rushing and pouncing, on the other hand, continued. It didn't happen very often – only when Lily spotted a dog she didn't fancy before I did – but the trouble was that I always knew, on every walkie, that there was a risk of it happening, which meant that I couldn't relax for a minute. So I tried muzzles, but none of them fitted properly, because of poor Lily's deformed, undershot jaw. That means that her lower jaw sticks out too far, and her upper jaw doesn't stick out far enough, so that her front teeth, top and bottom, are an inch apart and never meet, and that her nose is so short, a muzzle must be very tight, or it is easily pulled off. And because it had to be so tight, it rubbed and made her nose bleed, which meant that she couldn't wear it. Lily still has the scars from our attempt at muzzle-wearing. I blame the breeder, who, obsessed with creating a particular shape of dog, had only created a mutant whose jaws didn't work properly. That breeder has a lot to answer for.

So the muzzle was out. We desperately needed another method, another trainer who could solve our problem. I had heard, on the Dog World grapevine, of Dima Yeremenko, also known as the Russian Dog Whisperer, famous for training any dog to do anything, for rescuing the maddest dog from death row and turning it into a perfectly behaved pet. And he gave lessons out in the open, on the Heath, our main problem area. Was this fellow really clever enough to train Lily with all sorts of distractions and squirrels and various hated breeds of dog going by? Could he be the answer to my prayers?

Yes. This chap was a genius. In his presence, a row of up to thirty dogs would sit obediently, lie down, go and play, return at once, run around a designated tree and come back again, catch snacks, and never fight. They weren't just a pack of dogs. They were a performing circus troupe. Lily fell in love with him at once. She walked to heel, she sat, she stayed, her behaviour was perfect, and while she did so, Dima explained why. He was a dog mind-reader.

'You do this,' said he, 'dog thinks that. Dog knows that if she does the right thing, she gets reward. Look. Dog is watching you. She's waiting to see what you do, where you go.'

He was right. Dog was watching me, and waiting for clear direction. Because there's nothing a dog likes more than to have clear and consistent instructions and guid-ance. This is what she got from Dima, and she repaid him with unquestioning obedience and adoration. We would walk towards our lessons on the Heath, she would see him from afar, approach reverentially, and he would call out 'Who's my girl,' as if she was his favourite dog in the world, and to her he was a god. And while training Lily, Dima also trained the pair of nearby crows to fly down, approach and stop, play ball, and sit on a lid for a snack. In his presence, there was no wildlife, only tamed life. In his presence Lily was a changed dog. She had eyes only for Him and fawned at His feet. Had a squirrel sat on her nose, she would hardly have known it was there. She even learned to stay closer to me, concentrating on instructions and treats rather than potential victims, which minimised the risk and made our walkies more relaxing.

But not absolutely relaxing, because a) without the presence of her god, Lily's behaviour was not absolutely perfect, and b) I have always found it difficult to relax completely. Things may be going well now, but for how long? When one is up, the only way is down, and I feel that when I'm happy and think my dog training is a roaring success, it would be just my luck that things would change and all hell would suddenly let loose. So I couldn't quite stop myself looking out for pale Lurchers, and my anxiety transferred to the dog, so I'm told, then she would become anxious, and ready to pounce, and the whole thing could easily start up again. But for a while it didn't.

Anyway, I'm not sure about this 'you're-anxious-so-the-dog-picks-up-on-it-and-becomes-anxious-then-you-get-more-anxious-so-does-the-dog-until-you're-in-a-vicious-downwards-spiral idea. Because occasionally, even when I'm not at all anxious and am striding along in a sunny, carefree mood, Lily will suddenly bomb-off like a cannon-ball out of the blue and pounce and bite something that I hadn't even been aware of. Explain that, Anxiety Spiral Theorists, if you can.

Dancing with dogs

Dog trainers don't just train dogs. They're usually in Dog World up to their necks. Their whole world is dogs. They are with dogs morning, noon and night. They often have several dogs of their own, they have dog lodgers while the less dedicated owners go on holiday, they foster dogs, they rescue dogs, and as their work is dogs and their play is dogs, they also attend and organise dog events, like Mary Ray Cabaret night, set up by Dima, the Russian Dog Whisperer.

Training for these people isn't an ordeal. It is fun. They love training dogs. Why? I'd like to know. What can be so fun about repetitive, ceaseless training? So I go along to see Mary Ray, who is famous for her heelwork to music, which means dancing with dogs.

She's going to demonstrate her method and dancing in a Scout hut in Barnet, north of London. That doesn't sound like much fun, or very glamorous. The Scout hut is fairly bleak and dreary – just what you might expect from an average Scout hut – with a dull beige carpet on the floor, two rows of chairs around the edges, ordinary snacks: tea or coffee, packets of juice, biscuits, crisps and chocs. It's an usually hot, sweaty evening for the end of September. And then in comes Mary Ray with her dogs, and the place lights up. She is cheery, the dogs are cheery and the audience is cheery.

'I've been training dogs for forty years,' says Mary. 'That's about as long as I've been married. I've been married since I was six. Ha, ha!' We are in for a jolly evening. Mary has assistants. A chap who does the music, and a lady who helps with equipment and holds the dogs, because there are five of them. Only three to start with, in a wire pen, with their bedding and water, looking perky and ready to go.

'I'll start with Ozzie,' says Mary, and her assistant opens the pen door and Ozzie the Sheltie rushes out.

'I've got my clicker,' says Mary, and explains why Ozzie is staring up at her all the time, as if at the love of his life. Why? 'I've got bloody treats. That's why.' And then she demonstrates 'target training'. The dog touches her hand with its nose, she clicks her clicker, the dog gets a treat. 'Then I start moving my hand, and wherever the hand goes . . .' the dog follows it. Click for touching the hand, click for following the hand. click for twirling round after the hand, 'Weave!' says Mary. The dog weaves in and out of her legs, 'And then you add the verbal command – twist!' The dog twirls round. 'Then you change to just the verbal.' Because dogs read body language first. The words come second.

'Then you target a stick.' The dog must touch the end of the stick with its nose. Click! A treat. He'll follow the end of that stick anywhere. Then better still, a stick with food in a little bulb at the end of it. Click! A morsel of food falls out.

'He follows that stick with much more attention – 100 per cent attention.' She's right. But it looked like 100 per cent from the beginning to me. I'd rate this Ozzie as attending 130 per cent, ears pricked up, twirling, weaving, following the hand, the stick, always looking up at the beloved Mary, and while he does this, he's not just moving in a normal dog way, with both right legs and both left legs moving together. He's trotting, which dogs don't usually do – lifting his legs up high, and alternately, like a prancing horse. 'Unlike men,' says Mary, 'dogs can multi-task.' Ha. And this dog is happy doing it. It's in heaven. It finishes its turn with a bow, returns to the pen, and out bursts a second dog – Lexie the Collie.

Another happy dog, thrilled to be in front of an audience, and as well as the twirling, walking and weaving backwards, forwards, sideways, trotting, hopping, yes, hopping, it has its own speciality tricks. It can sit up on its back legs and cover its nose with a paw, looking a little ashamed. It's pretending to have been naughty. A great 'Aaaahhh!!' from the audience. More nose covering. We are all enchanted by this dog. 'Have you been naughty?' asks Mary. More charming nose covering. And it can say its prayers, kneeling on the back of a chair/pew and holding its paws up together, and hanging its head down. Another great big 'Aaaahhh.' And more treats, of course. And it will touch whatever it's told. A hand, a lid on the floor. 'If you stick the lid on a door, the dog will close your door for you.'

Is there anything these dogs cannot do? And they seem super-happy doing it: lively, busy, engrossed, playing to the audience and showing off and loving the response.

But they weren't always happy. Outside, sitting having a break, Mary says that when Lexie first came to live with her, she woke up to find him biting his tail. (He was sleeping on her bed. She doesn't seem to go in for this dogs downstairs, pack-leader/owners upstairs, business.) He'd obviously been doing a lot of tail-biting, because he'd bitten some of it off. So she immediately did a bit of clicker training with him, guessing that he'd been biting his tail because he was bored stiff. Same the next morning, and after a week he'd stopped the tail-biting altogether and was mad keen on training. Now here he was, on stage, a star performer. And his tail had even grown back a little.

Altogether, over nearly three hours, Mary had five dogs performing, who all did their turn. Pretty gruelling for her. She needed her prompter. 'What's next?' This or that action, routine, skill or the other, because with five dogs, it can't be easy to remember what you have or haven't done with which one, but the dogs remembered their own personal tricks, and they knew how to charm an audience, one by just lying on his back with his paws crossed. Aaaahhh! The audience nearly melted away. He knew that if he just lay on his back, paws crossed, with a particular look on his face, a whole room full of people would fall in love with him. And we did.

So this is the fun side of dog training. I don't want to sound soppy here, but there was something uplifting about it. I suppose there are some po-faced people who might say that the dogs were being demeaned or exploited in some way, and that I am anthropomorphising again, but to me it looked as if they were thrilled to be a part of it. Mary Ray clearly loves her dogs and they love her, and it looked like true love, even if it was intensified by snacks. There are a lot of horrible things going on in Dog World: cruelty, neglect, and selfish people who don't understand dogs at all, but this is the sunny, positive side of it. If only it was all like this.

Doggie boot camp

Once I had two dogs, the nasty incidents on my dog walkies increased and began to take their toll. An upsetting experience on a walkie can wreck one's self-confidence and crush one's spirit. I've often set out on a sunny day with my dogs, in a perky mood, only to have one or other of them involved in a nasty spat, and for the rest of the day the sky was grey, metaphorically, and I felt a failure. Lily had improved after our last lot of lessons, but now, with another dog around, her behaviour had gone down the drain again. Taking them out on a walkie together was becoming a more and more harrowing and deeply stressful experience. Taking them out separately was less harrowing, but tremendously time-consuming and exhausting. Every day I had to make the same dreary decision – together or separate walkies. Mental or physical exhaustion. It couldn't go on. So I decided to make one last huge effort to socialise Lily and Violet and improve their behaviour. I would go to a Doggie Boot Camp, run by the most effective trainer so far, Lily's hero – DimaYeremenko.

This was his ninth doggie boot camp, and this year it was in Capstone Country Park, Kent. A terrifying prospect. I have never been keen on camping. How would I be able to sleep in a tent? What if the dogs failed to sleep? Would they want to escape the flapping tent while I was asleep and roam around or run away? How would they cope with a mat on the hard ground? They were used to their own heavenly soft sofa. And the rule in camp was that they had to be hand fed with dry food, to assist with training. No lovely bowls of dinner. How would Lily and Violet cope with such a regime? Because they had delicate stomachs, they were used to their cooked chicken, with pasta (or rice and potatoes), and a variety of mashed vegetables amd drizzle of gravy, plus a little dry dog food – a dog version of chicken soup. I dared not own up to this. People would have thought us namby-pamby.

And how does one hold onto two dogs at all times?

How would they react to the other dog campers? I knew I would never manage dog-camp alone, and so I took my friend Clayden along to help, because although he had been critical of my dog-training methods in the past, he had built up a rapport with Violet. I hated camping, but he loved camping and the dogs needed camping. Here, among all the other dogs and under the supervision of Dima, who they dared not defy, Lily and Violet would hopefully learn to stop their horrible ganging up and attacking. I already knew that this was not their fault. Nothing is ever a dog's fault. It is always the owner's fault. Everything was my fault, because I'd brought them up badly. It was me who really needed the training. I accepted that. I deserved camping.

Luckily this wasn't a properly harsh boot camp. According to Dima, 'It was to have fun, while you learn a lot. Like going back to school.' To him dog training was fun, fun, fun. It was his life. He'd done it since he was a child of twelve in his homeland, the Ukraine. He trained the dogs who rescued people in the 1988 Armenian earthquake; he'd rehabilitated difficult dogs for the RSPCA; he'd trained a lost parrot which he found one day in his front garden, and those crows who were hanging about while he trained my dog; he saved his own dogs from death row, sentenced for bad behaviour, and trained them to perfection; he seemed able to train any dog to do anything. Better still, he could train them to *want* to be trained to do anything, and in his presence my dogs had never been known to misbehave. So this was the camp for us.

It was a tough first night. Singing around the nearby campfire kept me awake until 2 a.m., Then came the deluge. The rain beat down, the tent flapped wildly all night. Magically the dogs slept through it all, but I did not, until 5 a.m. At 6 a.m. the dogs woke up. They had had their sleep, now they wanted their walkie. In the rain. One cannot tell a dog to go back to sleep, so we paddled off over the sodden fields and through woods to the lavatories, the only dogs and person awake. Heaven for dogs, hell for me, after only one hour's sleep and with nowhere to make a cup of tea.

But soon the other campers were up and about, and cheery. It was like the spirit of the Blitz – everyone united by adversity, and dogs. No one whinged, and under an awning, mid-site, there was hot tea and coffee at last, and choice of cereals. Dogs and people clustered together under the canopy. We were all rather cramped together but no dogs squabbled, not even mine. Better still, everyone was tremendously kind and helpful, some-one promised to help Clayden and me move our tents to a quieter venue, away from the ghastly camp-fire and singing, and someone else – I will never forget that person's goodness – gave me two Temazepam, so that I need not spend another sleepless, tormented night like the last one.

But best of all, no one here minded if your dog

misbehaved. No one feared, or recoiled from, my dogs. I was no longer a pariah, banished to deserted areas, scowled and shouted at and shunned by normal dog-walkers. Here I was accepted, supported and understood. I was given advice, not bollockings and vets' bills. So when Violet barged into another dog's tent, starting a fight (even with her muzzle on), twice running, Eric, the dog owner, was still smiling, even with his tent door shredded, and even though his dog was blameless and only defending its own premises. Now and again a dog spat broke out. Everyone remained mellow. They understood dog behaviour.

On my way to the lavatory, having left the dogs with Clayden, I passed Bailey, a smallish Staffordshire Terrier with a bald patch on his head, with his owner Pam. Two dogs approached. Bailey's tail wagged furiously. Was he being friendly? No. 'That means two seconds to blast off,' said Pam, in a relaxed way. Blast off was somehow averted. This gave me hope. Violet was also a two-seconds-to-blast-off dog. Perhaps here Violet and I could learn to chill and not blast.

Perhaps Dog Camp wasn't so bad after all, and it was a chance to play with dogs non-stop, something I had always longed for, with no one moaning and sneering about it. Here everyone wanted to play with dogs. Everywhere we went, the dogs came too: to the breakfast tent, to lectures, to restaurants, to the barbecue, to dog-dancing demonstrations, to yoga, to bed. They took part in the egg and spoon race, fetch the biscuit race, short lead walking and to daily hand-feeding training.

I saw the logic of hand-feeding, but found it a difficult regime. No lovely bowl of dinner after the morning and evening walkie, just bits of dry dinner thrown at my darlings, and only when they deserved it. But I had to do it, at least for the duration of the camp. Why come if I wasn't prepared to do as I was told? But at first Lily and Violet weren't much good at it. Perhaps they were over-whelmed or over-excited, and had lost their appetites, Lily in particular, but hopefully they would learn from the other dogs, all chilled-out and obedient.

Easier said than done

This was not the sort of camp at which one lolls about doing nothing. There were activities − attendance was not compulsory, but advisable. Lecturers arrived daily, and specialist instructors, including two ladies demon-strating Loose Lead Walking. Wouldn't that be heaven, having your dog walk by your side on a loose lead? So I went. This is what you do:

Take your dog on a short but loose lead, arm relaxed, and walk briskly, twisting and turning in all directions (naturally the lead will tighten as you turn away), pulling the dog after you. Continue changing directions and twirling about, until the dog no longer has any idea where you're going and looks up at you to try and work out what the hell is going on. The minute it does that, praise it like mad. Soon your dog will be watching you attentively all the time, following you about like a lamb, no pulling, no sniffing, no watching the world go by. It will only have eyes for you.

Who cares if you look silly while you practice, walking all over the place in odd directions and never getting anywhere? This is dog camp. Everyone understands. Out in the park will be trickier.

Mini-dog-related-breakdown

But dog camp wasn't just about day-to-day training. It was to prepare your dog for anything, like sudden loud noise. So off we went to clay pigeon shooting. With dogs. The sun had come out. Better and better. My dogs were not keen on the shooting. Sensibly no dogs were forced to do anything that they found scary or upsetting, so at the first cringe we retired to the site café, waited for lunch with dogs, drove back to camp with dogs, called at the supermarket for supplies, with dogs, and returned exhausted to camp.

I have to admit that I had a little nervous breakdown outside the supermarket. You can't just go to a super-market with dogs. Because a) you cannot take them in, and b) you cannot leave them outside in the car. It is summer, the car will overheat, your dogs will become very distressed or even die, and c) you cannot tie them up outside the car and leave them outside the shop because a) they could easily be stolen, and b) in the case of my dogs, they will be tremendously upset, because they don't like being abandoned outside shops with doors opening and shutting, trolleys and cars rattling by and strange noises and goings-on.

So I sent my friend Clayden into Sainsbury's with a short list, and I waited outside with the dogs. But the car was boiling hot, there were no shady seats in the super-market car park and barely any shade, it was lunch-time, hottest part of the day, and annoyingly Clayden took rather a long time with the shopping, so I led the dogs into the only tiny patch of shade and we all lay on the ground, while I wept with exhaustion.

Passers-by were concerned. It isn't often that you see an elderly woman lying on the ground in a car park with two dogs, crying loudly, and they were brave enough to approach and offer assistance, which made me pull myself together. The lack of sleep had taken its toll. Like babies, dogs can put a strain on a relationship, and so when Clayden eventually got out of Sainsbury's I screamed abusively at him and nearly ruined our friendship, and we had a tense drive back to camp, and that wasn't the end of it. I still couldn't lie down and rest because I still had my babies/dogs to look after. They did not want to lie down and rest. They were not exhausted. They were thrilled by their first holiday under canvas and their new social life – getting used to other dogs milling about, and even making friends with them. And also, we had a three-hour lecture from dog behaviourist Amber Batson on dog stress to attend that afternoon. With dogs.

Nought to blast-off in two seconds

Most dogs, said Amber Batson, one of our Dog Camp visiting lecturers, give a series of little warning signs, about ten, increasing in intensity, before they do anything frightful: lick their lips, blink, turn their heads away, curl their lip a little, then a bit more, lower their ears, wrinkle their foreheads, if really pushed, and if the annoying dog or person doesn't take the hint, they may growl and bare their teeth to show that they really have just about had it. And if whoever is annoying them doesn't buzz off pretty damn quick, then there really will be some fighting and biting. And then, as an absolute final warning, they will change their body posture to furious I'm-about-to-blow mode, head and chest forward, muscles flexed, all pumped up, and then bang! You've had it.

This is what most normal, pointy-nose dogs do. My dogs don't. They just go straight to Number Ten bang you've had it. Why? According to Batson they don't have the right equipment. Their large flobby chops, squashed faces, floppy ears and wrinkles make normal dog communication almost impossible. For a start they can't curl their lips or lower their ears. But I'm not entirely convinced by this explanation. They can curl their lips a bit. I've seen them do it. But perhaps it is more difficult to get their message across clearly in the early stages. Perhaps they get sick of trying and just think, Sod it, I may as well go straight to Number Ten – FIGHT! This was their tragedy.

The very unusual bowel movement.

Luckily dogs don't seem to know about tragedy, and even if they do they just get on with life. Next morning Lily and Violet were first up again, at 6. 05. a. m. Horrid. This sounds grim, but even 6. 05 a. m. is fine, if you have had some sleep, and I had. After my heavenly Temazepam I slept like a log, awaking refreshed and ready to face the trials of dog camp. Good job too, because only five minutes into our walkie, something shocking happened. Lily stopped for a poo. But whatever was that coming out? Something smooth and pale! What could it be? A section of intestine? No. It was the finger of a latex glove, proba- bly discarded by the decorators at our house the previous week. I pulled it out carefully. As I have often pointed out, a dog owner needs to be fairly robust. You often need to pull things out of dogs' bottoms, usually grass covered in excrement, and often with the dog whirling about, panicked by something so horrid coming out of its bum, which makes it really difficult to catch hold of, and worst of all, you'll probably have to do it in public, on a pavement or in a park, with onlookers mocking or sickened, but you chose to have a dog, so tough.

It sounds vile, but this was actually a turning point for us. Until the glove emerged, Lily had been looking a bit down in the dumps and was off her food, but I'd put it all down to this being her first experience of camping. Like me, she must have been finding it difficult. But I was wrong. Once she had shit the rubber glove, she perked up tremendously. Our mood lightened. No wonder she'd been feeling peaky and lost her appetite. Soon she felt peckish again, so the morning hand-feeding session was a roaring success. Clayden took Violet, I took Lily and soon both dogs were sitting, twirling, lying down, rolling over, going backwards and forward, catching, leaving, exactly as they were told. Some sleep and the glove had worked magic for us all.

But annoyingly a new problem reared up. Violet had bonded fiercely with Clayden. Her behaviour when with him was close to perfect. With me it was hopeless. If he went out of sight she was inconsolable, staring after him in a tense way, unable to concentrate on anything else. It rather annoyed me that she would do anything for a man. Clayden isn't the only one. Once a confident chap takes hold of her lead, Violet is a changed dog, calm and a little droopy. No glaring around on red alert looking for a victim. She knows that with a man on guard, she can relax. Dima is her god, but Clayden is a tolerable substitute. I ought to be grateful to him, but it is galling to see him succeed where I have failed.

Another problem at camp was our tents. I had a wigwam, Clayden a small tent for one. All other tents were far superior. You could stand up in them. They did not flap and keep the campers awake all night. Compared to ours they were the palace at Versailles. This wasn't just envy. It affected our training. One needs to be fit and healthy to be in charge of dogs.

Luxury dog tent

Richard and Roxy, a handsome German Shepherd, have just attempted the Good Citizen Dog Obedience Test.

'Did she pass?' we ask.

'No. She was crap,' says Richard, but are they down-cast? No. How could they be, with such fabulous accommodation?

Richard's tent is the most spacious on site: living room, three bedrooms: one for him, shared with Roxy, one for storage, one for guests, awning with kitchen unit – two gas rings, and dog's swimming pool (kiddies' paddling pool). Lucky Roxy. And what does she have for dinner? A whole raw lamb shank. No dreary hand-fed dry food for her. She's on a raw meat diet. She eats her lamb shank on a comfy black and white duvet in the spacious back of a Subaru estate – her very own private banqueting hall, and I don't know how, but even with the dog gnawing at raw red meat, I swear the duvet remained almost spotless.

Dog's pyjamas

Even better than Richard's Versailles-style tent, another family had a caravan, with tent attached. Kaiser, a brown Doberman, had a darling blue velvety day bed in the outer tent-living room, in a spacious open crate, and an indoor night bed with duvet in the caravan, between the beds of Frank and Sheila. Sheila showed me Kaiser's very own black thermal pyjamas. I visited in the day, so he wasn't wearing them. How I envied him. He had the best dog accommodation in camp. It was far better than mine. Why not make your dog comfortable, if it makes him, and you, happy?

But even in my wretched tent, with my mat on the floor and primitive Primus stove, I stuck dog camp out for three nights and four whole days. Then, sadly, we had to come home. Yes, I did say sadly. Because by day three I had begun to love it. With a luxury Versailles-style tent, I could have stayed for weeks. But what sort of difference did dog camp make to me and my dogs?

'You can modify a dog's behaviour,' said Dima, 'but you can't change its character. But you wouldn't want to, would you? You just correct a problem and replace it with a good habit – get the dogs to delight children, improve your life and carry their own poo back to the bin. You can also learn to live with a dog that's less than perfect.'

That would be good enough for me. But was I getting there? The big test was when I got home and tried it when Dima was not around. So I did. My dogs seemed calmer and rather well-behaved. They had stopped lunging, pulling, dashing and growling. Big improvements from a week ago. I took them for a walkie with my friend Jennifer.

'That was almost pleasant,' she said. A result. I planned to buy a decent tent. For next year.

Saved from death row

Sitting by the doggie camp-fire, two years later, I am next to Bouncer's owner, Karen. Bouncer, the Victorian Bulldog, was here at camp when I last came two years ago, and it was in this very spot, beside the camp-fire, that he disgraced himself. He did a sudden unprovoked lunge and pounce onto the innocent German Shepherd, Max, which was lying next to him, sank his teeth into its back and wouldn't let go. Uproar and screaming, then in jumped Yeremenko and Karen and cleverly opened

Bouncer's clamped jaws. Luckily Karen had remembered a trick demonstrated by the American dog whisperer, Cesar Millan. 'You poke the jowls in from the side with your fingers, and tuck them under the dog's top teeth.'

She did it, and it worked. What a brave woman. Max was released, unharmed, no blood, but naturally in a bit of a state, and Bouncer collapsed afterwards, demure and drained of energy. The next day Bouncer and his owners, Karen and Dave, went home ashamed. They were meant to come back a day later, but they didn't.

But they hadn't given up. Now here they are again, two years later with a transformed Bouncer. He is a happy dog. He can play with other dogs, he is well-behaved, he can do fabulous tricks, he can heel, stay, dance and twirl. And he can sit about and play around without wanting to kill anything. Miraculous. What an achievement, and how lovely to see such a success story. How have they managed it?

'We had the time,' says Karen. 'I'll show you the video.'

'I've seen it,' says the lady next to me, owner of the Mitchell Brothers, two very ferocious dogs indeed. 'You'll cry.'

Back comes Karen with her laptop and on it Bouncer's story in pictures and with soundtrack. There he is when they first fostered him. What a wreck he was. Big, bloody scabby hole in his forehead where he'd repeatedly bashed himself in despair, and there he was trying to walk, his stubby white legs collapsing like jelly. They have no strength. The lady next to me was right. I have a cry. Bouncer has been kept outside, in a tiny garden for his whole life, has never been out, had any exercise or met any other dogs.

And his eyes are blank. He has a weary, joyless look. There he is, exhausted, flat out on Karen's sofa, where he would lie for hours. Then sitting up wrapped snugly in a towel, then out on a lawn, his legs are less wobbly, and he almost has a bit of bounce, then a real bounce, and then – I know some people who don't know dogs and won't believe it – he's doing what looks like a smile: ears perked up, chops flying in the wind.

And from then on it's just better and better. One day, he's out on his lead and muzzled, when a chummy black Labrador comes up wanting to play, and for the first time, Bouncer wants to play too. He has made his first friend. Here he is lying down with three friends, playing in the snow, like mad. He has become a happy, bouncing dog. It's taken two years of very hard work and huge amounts of patience and love.

'When I first saw him,' says Karen, 'I thought I could never love a dog like that. We were asked to foster him. We asked if someone else could do it. No. So we took him home. The neighbours crossed the road when they saw us coming. Only the tough boys in the park with their cans of lager and spliffs approved. 'That's a proper dog,' they said admiringly.

What a sweat it's been. Bouncer attacked everything.

'We hand-fed him, we socialised him, we saturated him with dogs, the one thing we were scared of – took him out to parks, on pack walkies, anywhere with loads of dogs. Dave had to lie on top of him in classes, to control him, but after two months he did his first sit. Just one sit, in front of all those other dogs. Our first breakthrough. One day we were invited out for a walkie with our friends with good dogs. It was very hard, because at any moment a dog could come out of the bushes and set him off, but at last we got out into the open park, lovely sunny day, all sat down for a picnic, our friends are saying, 'Wasn't that lovely! What a wonderful walk!'

'Not for us it wasn't. We were emotionally battered. We say all this, but now Bouncer is the most wonderful thing in our lives.'

And then a year and a half later, they took another dog home – Callie the Border Collie, no trouble at all, a friend for Bouncer, and then a year after that, when everything was lovely and calm, they took on another, Teddy the Terrorist. A nightmare dog. Why?

'We love dogs and we wanted a small one.' I visit and Teddy, the Miniature Schnauzer, is in his cage. Because he might bite me. 'He lived with a family at first, but bit the three children. They took him to the vet, he bit the vet. So now we've got him.'

'He's so bloody clever. He's just been spoilt and given no boundaries. I think the naughtiest dogs are the cleverest. They just get bored.'

From the kitchen window I can watch Teddy out in the garden doing his tricks. 'Look at him,' says Dave proudly. He's so wired! Look how engaged he is!' Teddy is concentrating like mad. What a cutie pie! He's staring up at Karen, riveted, he's twirling, jumping through her arms, weaving through her legs, hopping backwards, begging, gazing. She taught him all this in only eight weeks. What a dog! *Britain's Got Talent*, here's your next winner. If only he didn't bite everything. He even bites Bouncer, who has now been taught not to fight back and just sits against a wall trembling. The tables are turned. Will Teddy be allowed to stay? The jury is still out.

'Our priority is Bouncer now,' says Karen. 'The good thing about getting Teddy, is that he makes Bouncer look like an angel.' She looks at Bouncer fondly. 'He is an angel.'

Isn't that enough dogs now? Would they get another? They look at each other. Only a short pause. 'Yes.'

What sort?

'We don't know. They find us. We said we wanted a normal dog. We never got one.'

5: Risky Business

Some dogs will never will be angels, however much you train them. And dog walkers aren't the only people who use parks. There are lots of ordinary people without dogs, who just like to go for a walk. There's nothing wrong with that. But they're not all angels either. There are certain sorts of people and creatures out and about that the dog-owner should try to avoid, if possible. Sometimes there's nothing you can do, because these hazards may suddenly come upon you by surprise, from round a corner, or behind some trees, or just because they sometimes move very fast indeed. All I can say to that is 'best of luck!'

Jogger alert

There is only one Barry the Dog Jogger, sadly, and on the whole, joggers are perhaps the most common hazard for the dog walker. They are not often keen on dogs, because some dogs like to chase them. Luckily my dogs have never chased joggers. Joggers don't interest them. They prefer squirrels or cats, but my friend Sylvia's Boxer was mad on chasing joggers. When it caught up with them, it liked to run alongside, jumping up and kissing them as they sweated along. We only met one jogger who didn't mind. He wasn't going very fast and the dog had time to lick his leg. We apologised like mad. We always do, but he said he rather liked it, and jogged on in a mellow way. Unfortunately he was the exception. Usually joggers are infuriated by dogs jumping about, licking, kissing, slobbering and, with a bit of bad luck, snapping at their ankles.

I am on the dog's side here. We're walking along through the lovely parkland and Heath, the sun may be shining, the birds singing, everything's peaceful, dotted with the odd puffy white cloud, and suddenly a jogger roars past, huffing and puffing, groaning, sometimes even coughing and gobbing, shoulders tense, headphones on, ipod playing, legs like hawsers, grimace of pain on the face and giving off a general air of obsession and torment. Why do they do that to themselves? Why not get a dog and stroll along in a cheery way, as we do? But no, for them life must be all pain and no fun. And probably they smell rather sweaty, so what do they expect a dog to do, but run after them?

A dog likes to chase things that are running away. And if the thing has bits of flappy clothes to snap at playfully, then so much the better. Sylvia does her best to stop the chasing. She orders her dog to come back. Sometimes it obeys at once. Usually it doesn't. She has to bellow after it repeatedly, and eventually it stops chasing, and comes back, but if it doesn't, she gives it a telling off and says sorry to the joggers. If she can catch up with them. Because joggers often tend to make things worse by refusing to stop. If they stop, the dog will stop, then the owner can put it on a lead. You'd think they'd manage to work that one out, but they usually can't, so they just go pounding on, dog following, owner left further and further behind. Especially if, like Sylvia, the owner is in her eighties.

What fools. Apparently joggers mustn't stop running. They have to keep going. They could jog on the spot. Or they could jog back to us. But they won't, so off they go, steaming into the distance, dog yapping and snapping at their heels, sometimes shouting and kicking at the dog, which only makes it more excited. Meanwhile the poor owner is still panting along in the distance behind them, yelling after the dog, until it gets bored and comes back. Which could take ages.

Then what are you meant to do? You can't tell the dog off. It will think you're telling it off for coming back. By the time it's back, it's forgotten the jogger. Jogger? What jogger? It's a dog. It lives in the moment. It's come back, as it was told, and now it expects a nice biscuit.

My next dog, Lily, did nearly chase a jogger once, I

have to admit it. This was the only occasion upon which
any of my dogs has ever done so. She ran towards him,
then stopped a couple of feet away and came straight
back when called. I was rather proud of her. But the
jogger carried on screaming and shouting in his skin-
tight purple Lycra. 'Your dog is out of control. It should
be on a lead, I'm going to report you, blah blah . . .'

Perhaps he was frightened. It was probably fear-based
aggression, which is what my dogs suffer from occasionally. They behave badly when scared. Which is what the
jogger seemed to be doing. I could have explained it to
him, but he was in no mood to listen. They never are.

My dog only wants to play

Some people jog with their dogs. Some even jog with
their dogs on a lead. This seems a bit mean to me, because
as a dedicated jogger is not allowed to stop, it's all a bit
tough on the dog. It can't stop to have a sniff, it can't
play with other dogs, it can't even stop for a wee or a
poo, although I suppose it eventually has to and the
jogger will have to bob up and down while it does so,
which can't be very relaxing for the dog. I don't want to
anthropomorphise here, but surely it's difficult to relieve
yourself while attached to someone who's impatiently
bobbing up and down right next to you.

There's one particularly thin woman who jogs with

her dog, which is also particularly thin. They both look anorexic. I questioned her once, and she told me that it went for normal walkies in the afternoons, but it all sounded a bit Spartan to me.

There are more laidback joggers who just jog along with the dog running alongside, or ahead, or behind. But this method also has its problems. Some of these joggers tend to ignore what their dog is doing: fighting, crapping, getting lost. On they jog, leaving a trail of enraged park-users behind them. But some keep a sharp lookout for wrongdoing, especially if it isn't their dog doing it. One came jogging past with his brown Labrador one day when I was trudging along with the two dogs, me holding Violet, and my friend Jennifer holding Lily.

Up ran the brown Labrador and bounced around Lily. As brown Labradors are near the top of her hate list, this one must have rather got up her nose, so she pounced back, pretty ferociously, pinning it briefly to the ground, and at the same time, pulling poor Jennifer flat on her face.

Now Jennifer was 70 years old and had a bad ankle, which she broke ages ago, then caught MRSA in the wound, which even now still occasionally erupts and suppurates, so she wasn't the most hardy of dog-walkers, but she bravely hung onto Lily, and the Labrador escaped and bounced away, unscathed. But then up came its owner – a young, male jogger. He was in a fury.

'That dog should be on a lead,' he roared, indicating Lily.

'It still is,' I shouted back, because there was poor Jennifer, an elderly, grey-haired woman, flat on the ground, bravely clinging onto the lead for dear life. I would have thought he might at least enquire after her welfare. Something like 'Are you alright?' But no. He just went ranting on.

'My dog only wants to play. It's a very good-natured dog. It did nothing to provoke that. Your dog needs to be under control, it has no right to blah blah shout shout shout . . .'

'Is your dog injured?'

'No, but your dog blah, blah, blah . . .' But he couldn't keep arguing, because he had to jog off, of course. Idiot. And luckily Jennifer was all right. Which is partly why I am not keen on joggers. Unless it's the Dog Jogger.

Killer cyclists

Dog-owners do not own the parks. We have to share the paths with cyclists. Fair enough. Some cyclists are perfectly fine. They ride along slowly sticking to the speed limit (there is a cyclists' speed limit of 12 m.p.h. in our park), they ding their bells as they come up behind you, giving you a chance to get the dog out of the way;

they stick to the cycle paths. But this sort of cyclist is pretty rare – like a child without a mobile phone. Most cyclists are selfish, dog-hating, path-hogging, fairly murderous speed freaks who think they're always in the right. In my experience. Sometimes they come up behind you very quietly and whiz past, missing you by a whisker, nearly slicing a lump off the dog. Or you. And do they ever apologise for giving you a fright? No. Never. I admit I may be biased, because on top of all this, one of these cyclists ran over Violet when she was a bumbling little puppy.

He came bombing along a path on the Heath with his hawser legs and pointy black helmet, ran her over and then just buzzed off. Hit and run, even though Violet screamed and rolled to the edge of the path, and when I picked her up she had a tyre mark across her ribs. Nothing was broken, luckily, perhaps because puppies seem fairly rubbery, but it would have been less disgraceful if he had stopped.

Hopeless. I would never catch him or have a chance to give him a telling off, but as we were near to the Heath office, I took Violet along to report the incident. You probably have realised by now that Violet looked absolutely adorabubble, endearing and cuddly-wuddly, as all puppies do, but extra darling with her little squishy white face, brown eye patches and black nose. Aaaah!

I held her up at the window, so that the ladies in the office could see the tyre mark, and as she is white, the tyre mark was clearly visible. Ooooh! They were horrified. Their hearts melted.

'I know there's probably nothing much you can do about it,' I said, 'but I thought I'd report him anyway.' What a monster. We all agreed. And I thought that would be the end of it, but later in the day a park policeman rang me up.

'If you come back tomorrow morning at the same time, and stand in the same place,' said he, 'I'll meet you there. You never know, he may have been on his way to work, and will come by again.'

So I did, and so did he. I recognised his red and yellow outfit and his pointy nose and helmet.

'That's him.'

Mr Policeman stopped him. Because the man was cycling along a no-cycling path. 'Excuse me, sir, did you know this was a no-cycling path?'

He did. 'And are you the man who ran my dog over yesterday morning?'

Yes he was, but was he sorry? Not a bit. 'Your dog shouldn't have been off the lead,' said he, bossily.

'This lady has every right to let her dog off the lead,' said the policeman, 'but you have no right to be cycling on this path.'

'Oh tit-for-tat then,' said the cyclist, smirking. And why shouldn't he smirk? He knew he'd get away with it. The park police had no powers of arrest or even official caution. They could warn him not to do it again, but they'd done that before. They knew this fellow. He was a solicitor. He could run over dogs freely, and knew there was bugger all anyone could do.

But I could at least be mildly rude. 'What an unpleasant man you are,' I said in a restrained way, because I thought it better to stick to being Mrs Nice, which made him look more like Mr Nasty.

'What did you expect me to do?' he asked, sneering away.

'You could have got off your bike to see if she was all right. And you could have at least apologised.'

He didn't apologise, because in my experience, cyclists rarely do. You may know one who does, but I have never, ever come across one.

Silly old bag

It's nearly the end of our walkie, my friend Hazel and I are standing on the path with the dogs, chatting to another dog walker, when suddenly, whoosh! Yet another top-speed cyclist roars up behind us and belts past, nearly shaving off the older dog's bum, ringing his bell ferociously and shouting, 'Use your eyes!'

Naturally I shout back, 'Bloody idiot!' But what does he care? He's yards away by then, but he looks back, sticks up his finger rudely and shouts from a safe distance, 'Look where you're going, you silly woman!'

Silly woman. Great. He's the one going too fast on a path that clearly says 'Priority to pedestrians', he comes up from behind, we're standing still, none of us have eyes in our arses, but according to him, we're the silly ones.

I suppose it's better than 'Silly old bag', which is another favourite with cyclists, when women and their dogs get in the way of the cyclist's direct route. I find that we women dog walkers get rather a lot of uncalled-for abuse from men: cycling, jogging or walking ones. They particularly like to criticise our dogs' behaviour and training. Often we ignore them, but sometimes it all gets to be a bit much, and we answer back.

I was walking through some pleasant woodland, in dappled shade, with my friend Sylvia and our Boxers, who were playing together in a robust but benign way, when this fellow strides by with his dog and comments.

'You have no control over your dogs!'

Why? They hadn't bothered his dog. They were engrossed in their game 'bite-the-cheek' and growling playfully.

'Wank-stain!' shouted Sylvia, at the man's back. He did not respond. But I was rather shocked. Sylvia has a beautiful and rather classy voice, and it was fairly shocking to hear such filth coming out of her mouth, even if she had been provoked.

'I've never heard that before,' I said.

'You haven't lived!' said she shamelessly.

'I don't think it really rolls off the tongue,' I said. But

it was pretty effective. The man didn't turn round. Didn't he hear? Or didn't he dare? I know what I think.

Dog hater

But let's be fair. I hate to admit it, but sometimes it's the dog-owners who are at fault. I often try to convince my friend Whitwham that dogs are lovely, but things keep happening to him which prove otherwise, so I'm fighting a losing battle.

Whitwham tells me that he was out jogging in his local park and he passed a woman pushing a baby in its buggy, accompanied by her two dogs. The dogs immediately went for him, snapping and snarling and trying to bite his calves and ankles. Naturally he was furious.

How big were these dogs?

'Big as a fucking giraffe!' he says. 'I shouted at the bloody woman, "You can't control your dogs." "Yes I can," said she, so I challenged her.

"Go on," I said. "Control them," but she couldn't. She tried, "Come here. Sit! Leave him," she said, with loads of filthy words stuffed in between, but they weren't taking a blind bit of notice of anything she said.'

Was he stationary during this interchange?

'Yes, so they attacked everyone else who moved or passed by, snarling, with all that bloody saliva coming out. I rest my case!'

'How did you get away?'

'I didn't. I had to stay still till they'd gone. Idiot dog owner five points, sensitive liberal going for a run, nil.'

Screaming and swearing

What a pity there's such a lot of screeching on dog walk- ies. But when you're protecting or defending someone you love, things can get rather heated and emotional. When Sarah is out with her dogs, Oscar the Polish Lowland Sheepdog and Tess the Boxer – The biggest problem is always picnics, and she often loses her temper. Very quickly. 'Then I stamp away, realise I was in the wrong, but I can't go back and apologise. I can't be doing with toddlers and picnics.

'We came round a corner one day, and there was this young couple, picnicking with a toddler, on the edge of the park, near the road – a horrid place to picnic anyway, and the dogs went scampering over, the woman stood up, snatched up the child and started screaming her head off, the child started screaming, and the man roared, "Get your fucking dogs under control."

'But the dogs hadn't touched anyone or anything, they'd more or less lost interest before they quite got there, because there was no food laid out yet, and in the meantime, I'd called them, and they were on their way back, so I was feeling a little bit pleased with myself, and emboldened, so I said, "Keep your fucking dogs under control, *please*." The man was incensed and started towards me in an aggressive way.

'"If you come one step closer," I said, "I'll set my dogs on you!" I couldn't have done, even if I'd wanted to, and by this time the child was hysterical and will probably never dare go near another dog in its life again, or have a picnic, and so I walked off feeling rather pumped up and horrid, as you do after these things, and then a young couple, who couldn't possibly have seen anything, but had heard the screaming and crying, came round the corner.

'"You shouldn't let your dog bite little children," said the woman.

'I was furious, much more than with the picnicking man, who was at least protecting his child – a tiger protecting his cub, so I did forgive him, but not the woman.

'The trainers had warned me about this sort of thing. You must have your dogs under control, they said. It only takes one mad parent to claim that your dog bit their child, even if it didn't, and you'll have doggie social services all over you, or your doggie will be put down.

'But let's look on the bright side. These little rows are only occasional, and I couldn't be without a dog. I walked into Discover Dogs – a huge dog show at Earl's Court, and the smell! The atmosphere! I knew this was the world for me. I had to have a dog. My dogs are allowed on the sofa. Because I love to cuddle them and I can't cuddle them on the floor. Now that I'm getting older, I can't get down there.'

And the older you get, the more you may need a cuddle. Especially after screaming and shouting.

Swans

I'm just beginning my walkie and I see a drama ahead: two park police cars, a warden addressing two worried-looking people with their dogs on leads, a Greyhound and a little black Staffie, and a great scattering of swan feathers. Oh dear. What can have happened?

A dog had attacked a cygnet. It had landed and was flapping about in the grass, the little black dog had already barked at it, the owner had grabbed his black dog and put it on the lead, the cygnet tried to fly away, but hadn't really got the hang of flying yet and came floundering down again, and just his bad luck, another yellowy dog, alerted by the first dog's barking, came whizzing over the brow of a hill, spotted the poor cygnet, and jumped it – all witnessed by the Warden, who happened to be right there, on the spot.

If there's one thing a dog absolutely may not do, apart from savaging a person, or child, or another dog, it is to attack a swan. Swans belong to the Queen. They look fabulous. We are all heartbroken when rats eat the baby cygnets, and we are raging when fishermen's hooks get caught in their throats, but this year's local batch of five cygnets have all survived. Very unusual. Almost miraculous. They're now big enough to fly – well nearly, and now a ghastly dog has attacked one.

'Is it dead?'

No. It's traumatised. It's been taken away to swan hospital, and the dog owner will be prosecuted for having an out-of-control dog. A mongrel. What bad luck, because I've often met this woman. Her dogs (she has two) seem perfectly under control to me. They aren't ghastly at all. She's called them away from my dogs, they've obeyed her at once, and on this occasion she didn't call her dog in time, because she didn't know what it was up to at first, as it was out of sight over the other side of the hill, and by the time she reached the top and saw what was going on, it was too late. But luckily the chap with the barking dog had pulled her dog off.

I expect she's now at home crying. What a miserable end to a dog walk. And you'd have to have almost magical control over your dog to stop it pouncing on a lone cygnet flapping about on the grass, which is something a dog very rarely comes across. The cygnet's parents are usually about, and then your dog is in serious trouble. Any sensible dog-owner will keep his/her dog away from an adult swan, if they see it coming. Swans are famously bad-tempered, especially when protecting their babies – but some foolish dogs have been known to swim towards a swan in the pond, and been almost drowned by it. A swan is not likely to run away or remain calm. It will quite likely attack the annoying dog and push it underwater with a huge wing, and it will be goodbye dog, so I always rush my dogs away from the swans, with strict instructions to leave them alone, and show them how much better it is to turn the other way and eat a bit of sausage instead, or liver cake, or anything else supremely tasty that I always make sure to carry for situations like this.

But would even that have worked? Suppose one of my dogs had rushed off over the brow of a hill. I wouldn't have had a hope in hell at that distance, of getting them to leave a cygnet alone. Liver cake or no liver cake. Which is why Violet wears a muzzle. So although I always give swans a wide berth, especially if they're with cygnets, a swan could arrive out of the blue and attack the dog. This is what happened to John and his friends and the Wolf Pack one morning, when they were hanging about in their usual place in the middle of a large open meadow. There was a large tree nearby, the swan flew into the tree, sat there for a bit staring around, then suddenly flew down and attacked a Husky. Naturally the other dogs joined in, there was a frightful uproar, feathers scattered about, and the swan escaped and flew away. John and the Wolf Pack would have been in big trouble, but luckily for them, several passers-by saw the whole thing, and reported that the swan started it. Phew.

Anyway I asked what would happen to the poor woman with the swan-molester dog. She will have to pay a fine and will have a criminal record. Her dog will not be put down.

I should think not! That seems rather harsh to me. There was no death, not even a drop of blood. The cygnet wasn't injured, just very upset indeed. And the next week, there it was, back in the pond with its family. But the woman and her dogs haven't been seen since.

Three sisters and a bottom-sniffer

Disappointingly it isn't just cyclists, swans, picnickers and joggers that can distress a dog walker. Sometimes the problem comes from within our own ranks. It is perhaps sensible when dog-walking to bear in mind that dog relationships are not human relationships, and that dogs tend to do things in public which humans would not dream of doing, such as bottom-sniffing. To a dog, there is nothing rude about this. You'd think that any sane dog-owner would realise it, but not all dog-owners are sane. Some are utterly bonkers, like the three sisters in their fifties/sixties, who often walk their dog in our local park.

The dog is a small black terrier. That's roughly what it looks like. The poor thing is never, ever allowed off the lead. All the other dog-owners in this park disapprove. It seems so mean. The dog was good-natured. It longed to play with other dogs, but never could, and we all wondered why. One day one of the sisters told Dave, another dog-owner, the chap who made my dogs' birthday cakes, the reason why their dog was never free to run about.

She explained that she and her sisters, all devout Catholics, were worried that should the dog get near enough to another dog and sniff its bottom, it would be committing a ghastly sin and would go to Hell. Of course she didn't say the word 'bottom' or anything like that. But she made clear somehow that that was the area they were all worried about. I feel furious whenever I pass them. Why should a dog suffer for such a raving mad reason? Sometimes I glare, and they glare back, and we have a shout at each other.

'Why don't you let your poor dog off the lead?'

'Shut up you ugly old witch,' shouts the Catholic sister. Waves of hatred fill the park. From then on, whenever we spot each other, one or other of us crosses the road or goes the other way. I don't like to make sweeping statements, and there are probably millions of Catholic dog-owners who wouldn't bat an eyelid if their dog was keen on bottom-sniffing, but perhaps these three women had had a strangely repressed upbringing. What do I know? I'm not a Catholic.

I'm going to follow you home

I often meet my favourite friendly park warden on my walkies who tells me gripping stories about the odd, and sometimes frightfully rude, people he has to deal with. If you thought dogs were rude, you should hear some of his stories, which put even the rudest dogs in the shade. They don't belong in this book, because they don't concern dogs. But you do get the odd stickler warden who doesn't tell amusing stories, is never seen having a laugh, but who must have everyone obeying all the rules to the letter. And it was bad luck for John and his Border Collie, Annie, that he bumped into just such a warden.

It was a grey, drizzly November morning, he was trudging across the vast, soggy lawns that sprawl from Kenwood House down to the ponds, with his Border Collie Annie off the lead and in heaven. On these lawns, dogs are not officially allowed off the lead. But there is one plus about walkies in foul, rainy weather – there are very few people around to care whether your dog is off the lead or not. Only the most dedicated of walkers are out in all weathers, and you can almost guarantee that thugs with badly brought-up dogs will still be mouldering in bed, fights are unlikely, there are no kiddies around clutching ice-creams, and no picnics going on. So it's safe as houses to have your dog off the lead.

Unless you meet a power-crazed warden. Just John's

bad luck that he met one. This chap in a Barbour-type jacket and green wellies came striding purposefully across the empty lawns towards him, a fugitive from *Country Life*, with a folder under his arm, and questioned him strictly.

'Are you prepared to be a responsible dog-owner?'

'Why, yes,' said John. He's an easygoing fellow.

'Then put your dog on the lead.'

John pointed out that not only was his dog perfectly behaved, but the whole area was empty, not another dog in sight, apart from Annie, whose conduct was always impeccable, the odd goose, and perhaps a green parakeet.

It made no difference to the fusspot Warden. He whipped out a tabloid cutting from his folder and waved it at John. It told the story of a young boy who fell 200 feet to his death from a cliff in Cornwall, because he had been scared by an approaching dog. Then the warden asked again. 'Are you prepared to be a responsible dog owner?'

'Yes,' said John, 'but are you planning to build a cliff here?' Naturally Warden thought John was taking the piss. And worse still, he admitted that he had no lead.

'Name and address,' demanded Warden. 'You're going to be banned from here. Give me your details.' By now this was all beginning to get up John's nose. He did not wish to share his details with English Heritage, the body in charge of this area. What about his rights? His dog's rights? Fundamental freedoms?

He offered his email address, but the Warden turned it down. Then luckily, just as things were hotting up, two figures, a fellow with his Jack Russell, squelched into view. It was Brian, a gay acquaintance of John's, whose dog responded to the command 'Shopping!' rather than 'Come!'

This Jack Russell was keen on Annie. They had their usual sniff greeting, and Brian said 'Hallo' cheerily. He'd overheard a bit of the conversation as he approached, it had now reached a tedious, repetitive, stage with John and his tormentor going round in circles, John still refusing to give his details and Warden saying he would get them even if it meant following John home.

'What's going on?' asked Brian. As John told him, Brian gazed at the English Heritage fellow, then at John, then at his dog. With one deft movement, he slipped his own dog off the lead, looked appreciatively at English Heritage Man and issued an invitation.

'You can follow me home if you like.' Lengthy silence. But the walkie by now had been delayed long enough. Time to go home.

'Come on Annie,' calls John.

'Shopping,' calls Brian.

Arrest that dog!

Tanya has been out walking her three dogs: Tulip, the
Old English Mastiff, Mike the big half-Collie-half-
Sheepdog and Sheba the Scottie cross. She calls Tulip
a couple of times, and then up comes a furious chap,
and berates her.

'You're calling your dog too loudly,' says he in a bate.
'People are trying to sleep.' This is late morning in the
middle of Hampstead Heath. 'I'm going to take a photo
of you and your dog on my mobile phone, and report
you to the police.' And off he goes and does just that.

The police come round and question Tanya. They
think the whole business ridiculous, and go away laughing. Tanya thinks her troubles are over. They are not. A
couple of weeks later I meet her again. This time she is
not so cheerful. The dogs are in trouble again. For nothing. Mike has stolen some bread which a father and his
children were feeding to the ducks. The father has again
reported Tanya and her dog to the police. Round they
come, looking crosser. The duck-feeder man has told
them that if the dog was capable of stealing the ducks'
bread, then it was capable of biting children, and the
police believed him.

I don't understand this link. Pinching bread and biting
children. Neither does Tanya. Her dogs have never, in
their whole lives, shown the slightest hostility to children
or to any other human. Or dog. But they are now in

serious trouble. Tanya is no longer allowed to take her
dogs out for a walkie together. They may not play in the
lovely meadows, fields and woods together; they may
not paddle or swim in the ponds like other dogs, which
they love. They must stay on a dismal side path, or go
out separately.

What bad luck! And they haven't done anything
wrong. Anyway, bread is not good for the ducks, especially white, processed bread, but try telling the public
that. They don't give a toss. But that isn't the end of
Tanya's problems. Things are going to get far worse. I'm
out a few weeks later and I come across the favourite
warden. 'Have you heard about this Mastiff?' he asks.

'Yes I have,' Good. I've been wanting to see this
warden, so that I could speak to him on Tulip's behalf,
and tell him to disregard any horror stories about this
pleasant woman and her dogs, because they are not justi-
fied. Tulip may be huge, but he is good-natured, like all
Tanya's dogs, and has never harmed anything or anyone,
ever. So I start telling him this. The Mastiif, I remind
him, is 'revered for both its protective abilities and its
extraordinary gentleness'.

'Oh really,' says Warden, looking grim. 'Well that
Mastiff attacked one of our police dogs, and we're going
to make an example of it.'

What? Can't be true. I feel very sorry for Tanya. She
was very busy working, so her cousin often took the
dogs for their walkie. I often meet the cousin and the

dogs seem under control to me. They've always been pleasant to my dogs – not a single hackle raised, or the slightest growl, even from Tulip. Their behaviour seems exemplary. Until this latest ghastly bit of news. So the Warden and I have rather a heated chat about it.

'That dog went for our police dog,' says Warden, trying not to get agitated. 'I saw it. I had a distress call on my radio, I'm just across the field, so I drive straight over to see what's going on, and there's that Mastiff going mad, running round and round, I've never seen anything like it. There's this poor man with a Doberman on a lead, then the Mastiff bites the Doberman, and our policeman is in attendance. He says to the woman, three times, 'Put your dog on the lead.' Did she do it? No. Did she buggery, so he gets out his baton and says to the woman, 'If your dog bites that Doberman again, I'm going to hit it on the head with my baton.' It does and he does, and we're going to make an example of that dog,' says Warden, looking very determined.

The sensitive Pug

While Favourite Warden and I are getting rather hot under the collar about Tulip, along comes this woman with her two darling Pugs, Betty and Bosco. Bosco is standing a few yards away staring at us anxiously. Its owner comes nearer.

'Excuse me,' she says, indicating the staring Pug, 'my Pug's getting upset because he thinks you're having an argument.'

'We're not,' I say. 'We're friends. We're just having a heated discussion.'

'Could you both please reassure him?'

Of course we could, so this lady picks up her Pug and carries him over to Warden and me in turn, and we both assure it that we're not having an argument and stroke him. He's then put down and is able to carry on with his walkie. Which just goes to show how sensitive dogs are. I always knew it.

So that was the Pug sorted out, but Tulip's troubles were to go on for some time.

I come across him months later with the cousin again. What a tragic sight. He is trussed up like a Christmas turkey: harness, short lead and long lead, and black muzzle. Lumps of his squashed-up chops are drooping out of the gaps in the muzzle. He's so browned off he's standing still, can't be fagged to walk along and is too big to pull. He perks up a little when he sees Violet, and trudges along with us for a while, but what a sad dog he is – a shadow of his former self.

There's no happy ending here. All Tanya's dogs have been to six months' enforced training at group classes and she's been driving her dogs miles away to a distant park for their walkies. And she's been to court. £220 court cost and a £35 fine for having a 'dog out of control'.

£35 is the minimum amount anyone can be fined for this misdemeanour. It can't have been a very serious crime. But it hasn't done Tanya much good. She ended up in the Priory, is now scared stiff of our heath and wardens, can't go out for walkies without a Valium, and a year later barely goes for walkies at all.

'Anywhere I walk,' she says, 'my heart is in my mouth. I've become a mental wreck.'

As my mother used to say, 'The world is not fair.' Even Dog World.

6: Clever Dogs

Luckily not all clever dogs go mad with boredom. John Brown has two Border Collies: Charlie, the mother, and Maisie, the daughter, who he thinks are remarkably clever. The cleverest sort of dog going. 'They understand and can act on more commands than any other dog, are extremely beautiful, they're multitalented: hunting dogs and herding dogs, and are the most popularly kept dogs in Britain. There's a wide spectrum of Border Collies, ranging from mad, nervy, dangerous farm dogs – it's wise to stay well away from some of those – to domestic ones, which are OK, but it's still wise to be cautious. As a breed, they're nervy and unpredictable. A working Collie on a farm does about twenty or thirty miles a day. Domestic ones also like to be busy and interested; they watch things most intently. Maisie barks at everyone going past. Charlie only does it if someone comes onto the premises. They're petite, graceful, girly, feminine. They chase my chickens, but don't eat them, because they know what's good for them.'

JB also discovered that his dogs had a surprise talent.

They protected him, on their own initiative, when he was in a tight corner. Sometimes he patrols the local river banks looking for poachers, with his dogs. (He is a keen fisherman himself.) One night he came across four men poaching. They were big blokes. 'It is always wise not to go in confrontationally,' said JB sensibly. 'I was very polite, saying, "How are you doing? But I think you've made a mistake, etc."' They agreed to leave, then one of the older ones asked for a lift, approaching JB in a menacing way, but his dogs just dropped to the ground in front of him and growled. The large fellow backed off, threw his rod into the river rather dramatically and disappeared. JB was thrilled. Charlie and Maisie got extra treats that night.

Clever dogs, silly scientists

John Brown is right that his dogs are clever. But all dogs are clever. Probably far cleverer than most people think. Sometimes it even looks as if people wilfully refuse to accept how clever dogs are. Especially some psychologists. The trouble with dog psychologists is that they often seem to be behind the times. After years of study at the University of the Bleeding Obvious and £squillions of research grants, up they come with something that most sensible dog-owners were already aware of decades ago.

'We are learning that dogs, horses, and perhaps many other species are far more emotionally complex than we ever realised,' said Dr Paul Morris, psychologist at the University of Portsmouth, in 2008. '*Are* learning?' Didn't he know already? I did. So did everyone who ever watched *The Dog Whisperer* or *Lassie* or owned a dog, and so did my friend Sylvia, whose dog died of misery decades ago when Sylvia had her baby. It must have had a broken heart. The vet could find nothing else wrong with it. The poor dog had been cast out of paradise. Usurped by a newcomer. It looked desolate, wouldn't eat and would barely move. For months Sylvia and her husband had to carry it outdoors to go toilet, until it gave up the ghost. Most dog-owners know that you have to watch out if you have the dog first, then the new baby. Sylvia was lucky that her dog only moped soundlessly. Others have tried to murder the baby. And succeeded. Dogs do not always like to share love, or snacks and treats. Most of us know that it isn't always sensible to offer a strange dog a snack in front of our own dog, from its own snack selection. That would be asking for trouble. You wouldn't give your child's sweeties away to a strange child, just because it happened to turn up. Why would you do that to your dog? Nor would you embrace a new partner and expect the dog to mind its own business. It loves you. Why should it want some other creature to come between you and steal its place on the sofa?

Psychologist Dr Friederike Range, of the University of Vienna's neurobiology department, worked out, several centuries later than your average dog-owner, that dogs feel intense jealousy. They 'show a strong aversion to inequity', said she. I am rather jealous of these doctors. If only I could just flop about at home observing the dogs, noting down what they did, having a little think and get paid for it, but no such luck. Ages ago I proved that dogs think sequentially, but nobody believed me and my research has never been adequately funded. It wouldn't be expensive, and only requires a favourite chewy, a watering can and two dogs. No psychologists needed. But I am prepared to share it with the world, free of charge. Here it is.

This little experiment/observation proves that not only is my dog pretty clever, but it also thinks ahead and has plans. Scientists have been puzzling over this for years. Do dogs think sequentially or not? I could have told them without any further research and this is the proof. One sunny day I'm sitting in the kitchen, looking out at the dogs in the garden. Violet has Lily's favourite chewy. I know this because Lily is whimpering in an agitated way, ignoring the other chewy, and staring at Violet. But I do nothing. I don't think it would be fair to take Violet's chewy away, just because Lily fancies it. She does, after all, have an identical one. Then Lily comes up with a better idea. She goes over to the watering can, taps it with her paw, looks at Violet, then me, and whimpers again. She does this repeatedly. Because she knows that there is one thing that Violet loves doing more than anything else, even more than eating a chewy. Violet loves drinking water pouring from a watering can. Lily continues to tap the can, glare at Violet and cry at me. She is clearly asking me to go out, water a plant, distract Violet from the chewy, and then she can get it.

If that isn't sequential thought, I don't know what is. I feel she deserves a bit of help here. So I go out, pick up the can, water a nearby plant, and sure enough, Violet drops the chewy, rushes to the watering can for a drinkie, Lily nips over and grabs the chewy.

This forward planning is common among dogs. A couple who owned two Pugs and a Border Collie confirmed my theory. Their Collie used the same technique. 'The Pugs had the chewies,' they reported, 'the Collie wanted them, so she went and barked at the door, pretending someone was there. The Pugs ran to the door to see who it was, and the Collie whizzed over to the chewies and snapped them up. Clearly dogs thinking sequentially again. Scientists eat your hearts out.

A bit too clever

Some dogs have a long-term strategy. They use a mixture of charm, patience, cunning and understanding of the person who's meant to be in charge of them, to get what they want. This can easily happen without you being aware of it, and it took me some time to realise that the dogs had cleverly manipulated my reward system. I had begun it correctly, rewarding my dogs for going into the garden for a poo or wee. This is one of the first things one has to train a dog to do – go to the lavatory in the garden, and not in the house. They learned this quickly, receiving a treat when, having done what they were meant to do, they came back into the house.

But what if they'd gone out, been unable to go to the lavatory, and come back without doing anything? Surely they still deserved a reward? They'd tried to go, they'd tried in the right place. It wasn't their fault if they could do nothing, so I gave them a treat anyway. No one can control their bowels to that extent. Perhaps they knew that I knew that, because they then seemed to realise that going into the garden and coming back, poo or not, would get them a treat, and as I've already proved, they are fabulously clever and think sequentially. So they perfected this method of obtaining a reward and could soon get one by just going outside, taking a few steps, and coming back in again. Or perhaps just putting their two front paws outside, sniffing the air, returning for the treat. Which even I could see was pushing it a bit, so I've cut down on those rewards. They now don't get one unless they've made at least a small tour of the garden and some effort to go to the lavatory, or at least given them-selves the chance to do so. Unless it's raining heavily, and then I feel that it's quite brave of them to go out at all, and if they don't fancy going too far in such vile weather, then why punish them? They gave it a try, they got a little wet, they deserved a biscuit, which makes one wonder who is training who.

What do the dogs think?

People have been trying to work this out for centuries, and, a few years ago, scientists at Bristol University discovered that some dogs were optimistic, and others pessimistic. Examining the behaviour of dogs when separated from their owners, the scientists found that some dogs seem gloomier than others. I already want to bang my head against the wall. Did the scientists expect all the dogs to behave in the same way? Do they have dogs of their own? Have they not noticed that dogs each have their own little foibles? All dogs are different.

Dogs that are calm when left alone have an optimistic attitude, suggest the scientists, but dogs performing 'undesirable separation-related behaviour (SRB) . . . vocalising, destruction and toileting' while alone, have a more 'pessimistic cognitive bias'. Well you would have, wouldn't you? If you were a dog. Imagine it. You've been living in a dogs' home (all twenty-four dogs in the experiment were in animal re-homing centres), you're taken into a strange room where a person hides behind a screen with you, then you're allowed to come out and find your dinner in a bowl. The bowl could be anywhere in the room, some days it's here, some days it's there. Some days it's full, some days it's empty. You may keep optimistically dashing to the bowl hoping your dinner's in it. You may get hacked off with being jerked about and decide not to bother. Either choice is reasonable, for a dog.

It's the owners who sound barking in this study. Some apparently think a dog that shreds their sofa, craps on their carpet or barks incessantly while they're out is 'fine' or 'happy' or even spiteful; some get rid of the dog, a 'few seek professional help'. The scientists have concluded that the dogs' behaviour and underlying emotional state . . . requires elucidation. Are they concentrating on the right group here? Perhaps another study is in order — observing the humans.

But I am cheered, in some ways, by these findings, because they prove me right. They show that a) dogs have 'emotional states' and that b) many dog-owners are fairly brainless and unfit to have a dog at all. They don't understand their doggie, they can't be fagged to keep it if it's trouble, and they don't even know that dogs prefer not to be left alone for too long in a boring house, unable to snack, play or relieve themselves. They are naturally scavengers and parasites. They need to be busy doing their job, scavenging or parasiting: begging for food, waiting for treats. If there's no one around, they're unemployed, which is no good for anyone.

We did once have a dog which was very upset by the sight of suitcases. He knew that they meant we were going on holiday and abandoning him. Even though a kind and familiar friend came to stay with Lusty in his own home, nothing could relieve his 'pessimistic cognitive bias'. He pined, was despondent, ate hardly a scrap and was always skeletal by the time we returned. Luckily my two current dogs do not pine or perform undesirable SRB when left alone (not that they're left alone for very long – four hours at the most). They remain calm and asleep. They are an optimistic pair, always expecting the next happy event: dinner, a snack, walkies, an adoring visitor, a brush, a lie in the sun. Sometimes they are overly optimistic. They think they will catch that squirrel, or that crow that is taunting them from the tree, or that they will dig fast enough to catch the vole. A million futile attempts have taught them nothing. They live in hope, that one day the bird will not fly away, the vole, squirrel, rat or cat will not escape. They even look forward to visiting the vet. They forget the pain and just anticipate the liver treat. Sometimes they look a little glum, if their dinner's late, if their walkie is postponed, and of course if they're left alone. But they just accept it and have a kip.

I realise how tremendously lucky I am.

Nowhere dogs

Haven't some people had odd ideas about dogs? A few years ago the Chief Veterinary Officer, Fred Landeg, commenting on research commissioned by DEFRA, announced that we should keep dogs out of bedrooms and kitchens because they may transmit disease. Luckily Mr Landeg was about to leave his job. No more scare-mongering from him. But I would liked to have asked where the dogs are allowed to be. Hall? Bathroom? Lavatory? Tied up on the pavement? And what if you brush against them in these places? Will the diseases not transmit? What if you kiss or play with your dog in the garden or on its walkie? Will the germs be off duty? Are we allowed to touch the dogs at all, and if so, how much? And another important question for Mr Landeg. Where are all the dog-owners with the 'new and emerging [zootic], unknown and exotic diseases' that the dogs are meant to be transmitting? The MRSA, campylobacter and salmonella that he predicted? I haven't heard of any. So far.

I haven't caught any of these diseases yet, although I do kiss two large dogs daily, and have them dribbling, fiddling, eating and sleeping in the kitchen. They don't sleep in the bedroom or on the bed, but for behavioural rather than health reasons, and they have their dinner in the garden – unless it's raining, then of course they dine indoors – but we do sit in a pile on the sofa together, and in less fun times I have to stick pills down their throats and clear up shit and vomit, or wipe their darling little faces and clean the muck from their eyes, ears and wrinkles and sometimes, my least favourite task, remove long grasses from their bottoms, but my health is still all right, and as Mr Landeg had to admit, I may even be healthier than your average person, because I have to go for marathon walkies every day, rain or shine, and the dog presence does wonders for my blood pressure.

Of course I know this all makes non-dog-owners feel a bit queasy, but that's because their environment is sterile and dog-free, they've lost their connection to nature and are no longer very robust. They perhaps obsessively wipe their kitchen surface with anti-bacterial this or that, and should a germ break through and enter their home, the family would go down like ninepins. But the dog-owner, accustomed to filth, may well have built up a resistance to dog and any other germs. Unfortunately, like everybody else, we have to go out in the streets and down into the crowded, fetid tube or onto the packed buses and get up close to the coughing, sneezing, spluttering, sweating public, with their unwashed hands, nits, flus, new drug-resistant TB, impetigo and heaven knows what else. It's much safer in bed with the dogs.

Dog dreamers

I do get rather sick of people telling me not to anthropo-morphise my doggies. Why not? Why should they not share some attributes with us? I know why. Because these people cannot bear to think that we might be a bit like animals and not their superiors in every possible way. Well I'm very sorry, you people, but I suspect that we're not as superior as you think. Dogs have emotions: fear, anger, happiness; I've already proved that they plan ahead – all right, they may not have very complex plans, but they have short ones: if I do this, she'll do that, then I can have this. They empathise, they learn, they remember, and they have a subconscious. They must have, because they dream.

How can anyone argue with that, once they have seen a dog sleeping, with its eyes flickering, legs jerking about, lip curling, making little yelps and cries? Quite clearly it is having a thrilling dream. Or a nightmare. Perhaps something's chasing it or telling it off. What else could be going on? I can't ask them, annoyingly, because they can't tell me, but you never know. Perhaps one day. If I could learn their language. I'm getting there. I know a certain bark which says, 'Would you please move my bowl, because it's up against the wall and I can't reach the bits of food which are stuck behind it.' They some-times shout/bark from the living room to say, 'She (the other dog) is taking up the whole sofa. Please come and move her across to make room for me.' So I do.

I can also recognise 'Hurry up with the dinner,' and 'Let me in (or out),' and 'Somebody's at the door,' and 'Somebody's creeping around upstairs and shouldn't be,' and 'I'm bored.' And I'm not the only one. I heard some people on the radio who were being played sounds of their dogs barking. Each person correctly identified, through differences in sound and tone, what that particular bark was saying, without even seeing the dog! They recognised: 'I want to play with my ball,' 'The postman's here,' 'I'm hungry,' 'There's a squirrel in the garden,' and loads more. I rest my case.

Read to the dog

Not all dogs get the chance to show quite how clever they are. Danny the Greyhound did. His is a rags-to-riches story. Found homeless, wandering the streets and scavenging for scraps in Cork, Ireland, he rose to fame as a Reading Education Assistance Dog (READ), won International Fund for Animal Welfare (IFAW) dog of the year Amazing Animal award, which he received at the House of Lords, presented by Brian May, followed by lunch, biscuits and a goodie bag. A meteoric rise, from homeless indigent to Westminster, and even 10 Downing Street, star of TV, doggie magazines and newspapers. Still the same modest creature, he now visits libraries and schools, where he listens to children reading. He's a big, white springy dog with a grey patch on his face, grey, perked-up ears, bright, intent eyes and a chirpy look, and now he's visiting Maplefields School in Corby with his owner and trainer, Tony Nevett.

Maplefields is a brand new academy for children with special educational needs, surrounded by a high wire fence, every gate or door needs a special security pass, but what does a dog care about all that? He's got his own security pass and everyone's pleased to see him – most of all, the children.

Tony has a degree in Animal Assisted Therapy and trained the first READ dog in England. Danny is the third.

'He's a very special dog,' says Tony. 'People say to me "Why do the kids like him?" I say, "Because he doesn't judge. He builds a bond, he gives them confidence. He's never hurt the children [as some adults have]. Their shouting and kicking-off doesn't bother him, or the tail and ear pulling. He doesn't respond to that at all. Look at him. He wouldn't hurt a fly. The children love Danny to bits. They know when he's due in.'

We have a little stroll around the school, around the curvy corridors, in and out of the classrooms and gym, past the Time Out rooms (for children who need to be out of class for a bit), the soft play rooms (where they can't hurt themselves), everyone saying 'Hallo Danny!'

Terrible roaring and screaming comes from one of the Time Out rooms. In go Danny and Tony. The screaming stops. After a few minutes, out they come.

The screaming starts again. Nothing fazes this miraculous dog. A boy asks to take his lead in the corridor. He looks like a good boy, holding the dog's lead. 'If you tell them they won't see the dog if they misbehave, then they behave.'

'Danny works wonders,' says one of the teachers. 'As soon as they see him, their faces change. He calms them down.' And he does. Up comes a cross little boy with a tight, red face. He strokes the dog, and hey presto, a smile and the angry red flush disappears. Children call out to Danny as he passes, and rush over to stroke him. The mood lightens. Another boy takes him by his lead going along the corridor. Tony asks where he's going. 'I'm going to heaven,' says he.

It's in the library that Danny gets really clever. He sits on some cushions and in come the children, one at a time, they choose a book, sit down next to the dog and start reading out loud. Danny gets no instructions, but he knows exactly how to treat each one of them – dances and twirls around to perk up a sad one, lies down to calm down a jittery one, kisses a peaky looking tatty one who probably badly needs a kiss ('His home life is crap. See his shoes? They're all busted. His mother has a different 'Uncle' round every night'). He keeps away from a nervous one, gets close to the one that needs a cuddle, and they all look angelic in his presence, some leaning on him, and start reading – no hesitating, no self-consciousness. Do they like reading to Danny more than

the teachers? Yes. 'Other dogs bark when you're reading. Danny just listens,' says one little boy. 'We had a
Jack Russell and a St Bernard. We had to get rid of the
St Bernard, because he dribbled and punctured our
footballs.'

It can be a tough world for dogs out there, but here in
the library Danny is king: he has his own bed with
Danny-print cushion, Danny photos on the wall with
various smiling, cuddling children, a painting of Danny
– done by a lady who paints with her mouth – and on
the shelves a book about Danny, 'Danny goes to London',
the story of his Amazing Animal award.

In comes a seven-year-old boy. Danny kisses his hand.
'He's your friend,' says Tony. 'He likes you.' Danny
gives the boy another kiss. 'That's how much he loves
me,' says the boy, and starts reading straight away. In
comes a small girl. She's not so keen on dogs, so she sits
a little way away. Danny stays where he is. No kissing.
She reads non-stop and very well. They don't read like
that in class, but are model children with the dog.
Impeccable behaviour from all of them. But through the
wall you can hear loud screaming and banging coming
from one of the little Time Out rooms outside. Danny's
not bothered at all by screeching and banging. 'If they
kick off, he just lies on the floor.

'He used to be very aggressive if you went near his
dinner, because he'd been living on the streets. Out there
he had to protect his own food. The vet told me to run

my fingers through his food, so that it smelled of me. Then he didn't mind anymore. He has Weetabix and milk for breakfast. And whatever we're eating – beef, Yorkshire pudding. He has some dry dog food. I add other things to it. Look at his dirty face! He's had spaghetti bolognese.'

This dog is a saint. He also donates blood to a dog blood bank every six months. He just lies down, they give him a biscuit afterwards. No tea. He doesn't get paid for it. The vets pay, and that covers the costs. And the Kennel Club funds his work reading with children. It's free to the schools. 'It works well, why don't they do it more?' asks Tony, 'with a barrel of brandy round their necks for the teachers. Ha ha.'

Dog chats

At home, when nobody is looking, I often talk to my dogs, in what those critics call a 'silly' way. We have little conversations. Sometimes the dogs speak first. I hear a little whimper, I ask, 'What is it?' If someone else was present you can bet your life that in their opinion, the dog should be ignored. To them the dog is attention-seeking, and if I pander to it, I'll be making a rod for my own back. But over the years, my dogs and I have learned to communicate rather well. They have their own ways of making a request, and clearly if one of them is whimpering, then I know that it wants something. My dogs hardly ever whimper for nothing. The whimpering dog may feel poorly, it may want to go out to the lavatory, it may have a tummy ache. It may just be being greedy and want another biscuit or some of my baked potato, but sometimes it may want something specific, so I still like to answer it.

'What do you want?' I ask. Do you feel poorly? Are you bored? Do you want to be a clean girl?'

It doesn't always seem to know. I suspect it just wants some attention. And why not? One walkie, then a day stuck at home doing nothing much for hours except breakfast, fiddling about the garden and snoozing until the second, shorter afternoon walkie, is not good enough. And its demands are reasonable. It usually just asks for its basic requirements. If it wants to relieve itself, it will go to the back door and stare longingly at the garden. If it wants a biscuit, it will stare at the biscuit tin. If it wants its bone back, it will stare at the fridge. If it wants to leave the room but the door is shut, it will stare and point at the door. If it wants to play, it will bring me its rubber piggy, or favourite toy of the moment. But sometimes its desires are more vague. It may just feel lonely, unloved or listless. It may be worrying about something, it may feel that something is missing in its life. It may be feeling the old call of the wild. I don't know. Who does know how a dog thinks? Some people refuse to believe that a dog thinks at all. They don't believe that it thinks ahead, dreams or has little schemes or a wide spectrum of emotions. Mine clearly do.

Extreme dog communication

Sometimes a dog needs to use extreme methods to get its message across. The normal forms of communication are not adequate. Facial expressions, sounds and body language are just not up to the job. So the dog uses excrement. Of course they use it sparingly, and only in response to extreme provocation.

My dog Daisy used it to deal with a rather unpleasant lodger who we had at the time. He would hide the dog's snacks and toys and treat her as a health hazard. When Lodger began to wear white towelling and search obsessively for dog hairs and I was just about to ask him to leave, Daisy speeded things up by expressing her own opinion.

Lodger had begun to throw her into the air, which she didn't like, then catch her and pretend to drop her, which she liked even less. I told him repeatedly not to do this. You could see that Daisy was upset by it. She tried all the usual signals: running away, cringing under the table, fur standing on end, but Lodger wouldn't stop, and so Daisy took drastic action.

One day, when she had a tummy upset, instead of running into the garden for her poo, which would have been the quickest and most convenient option, she ran all the way up to the second floor and shat all over Lodger's carpet. I don't know how she managed it, because she must have been in a frightful hurry, but she did, which was something of an achievement.

Naturally I knew nothing of this until I heard a terrible scream from upstairs when Lodger came home from work and went up to his room. Not expecting a sea of diarrhoea, he walked straight into it, and trod it all over his paperwork, which was spread over the floor.

Now this could have been coincidence, but I don't think so. I think Daisy was paying him back for terrifying the life out of her. Why else would she want to contain herself while running all the way up three flights of stairs, when she could have just nipped into the garden? It must have been revenge. And it worked. Lodger was apoplectic with fury. We had a tremendous row, and out came the truth. It was *me* who Lodger couldn't stand, but you can't throw your landlady up in the air. He left at once.

I should have evicted him the minute he started throwing the poor dog into the air, but instead I let him get away with it, and allowed her to suffer, for weeks. I'm ashamed of myself, forcing the dog to go to such extremes to express herself, and to bring about a solution to our domestic problems, which I had been too weedy to sort out myself.

This is only a theory of mine, but I have two more examples of similar behaviour, which proves me right.

Rebellion

I need to go away for a day and a night, so I ask my friend
Jed to look after the dogs. He kindly moves in, and sleeps
downstairs on a divan bed, in which I sometimes sleep,
in the same room as the dogs. They sleep on their sofa.

They know Jed. They like his dog, Caspar the
Weimaraner. We have been for walkies together, he
has looked after them in the day. But he's never stayed
the night. This time he does. He awakes to a horrid
sight. And smell. The dogs have relieved themselves all
over the floor. And it isn't the tidy sort that you can
easily pick up. Worse still, they could have done it on
the wooden boards, but they chose the rugs. Why?
They have never in their lives done such a thing,
however desperate they were. If they want to go to the
lavatory in the night, they always wake me and tell me,
by crying, or by stamping their feet until I wake up.
Why suddenly do it all over the floor, very quietly so as
not to wake Jed up? They must have been awfully careful, because he's a light sleeper.

My theory fits the bill here. I think they were upset
that not only had I left them for the whole night, but
another person was sleeping in my bed. I'm not quite
sure what to do the next time I need to go away.

And just in case you were thinking that it's just my
dogs, they suffer from colitis, it must have been an accident, I am being over-imaginative and my dogs are

particularly neurotic, just think again, because other dogs
do it too.

Extreme Pug

I'm on my walkie and I meet a woman with her Pug.
We often meet and chat about our dogs, which we can
do in a relaxed way, because Violet and the Pug are
friends. The weather is cold and rainy, and we are not
having a pleasant time.

'I'm never having another dog!' says this woman
crossly. 'I can't leave it, I can't go away anywhere, I'm
sick and tired of going for walks every day, and it isn't
even my dog. It's my daughter's dog, she can't be bothered to take it out, so I have to!'

What about a dog walker? Why doesn't she try that?

She tried it five years ago, handed the dog over to the
walker, Dima, the Russian Dog Whisperer, who had
trained it and who it knew and trusted. But when it came
home after the first two walkies with him, it looked very
grumpy, and after the third it had had enough.

'It came home and pooed all over the house, even in
my daughter's bedroom! And I was expecting six house
guests at any minute.' Panic stations. Her dog had never,
ever done such a thing before. Dima suspected that the
Pug was punishing her for sending him off for walkies
without her.

That means it's not only my dog and not only my theory. It's now been corroborated. So I am right again. As usual.

Or am I? There are different theories about a dog's choice of lavatory. This is the trouble with Dog World. Everyone has a different theory for everything. Why did one of my current dogs also run upstairs and relieve itself all over the wooden bedroom floor and upstairs hall, when I would have thought downstairs on the kitchen lino would have been more convenient for both it and me?

'Bedrooms are usually a protest,' says the vet.

I was only out for three hours. Couldn't it have been the dog thoughtfully using an area that we don't often use? The spare bedroom? That's what I thought.

And why a rug, on the last dirty protest occasion? Was that just to annoy? A protest because I stayed away all night? Even though a friend stayed with them who they love?

'No,' says the lady with the Pug in the park. She reckons they do it on rugs because rugs are soft, like the grass.

Why Pugs?

'What is so special about pugs?' Clearly they're very sensitive, but they're also very tolerant of humans, not snappy, happy to be picked up, held and petted,' says Suzanne,

Bosco and Betty's 'human'. Suzanne prefers this to 'owner', which sounds rather bossy and proprietorial, and you can't really feel like that about Pugs. Or probably any sort of dog. They have too much character.

'They love children, but they do squeal with excitement, run round them and lick them, which occasionally frightens the children. They're good with other dogs, usually couldn't care less about dominance. We used to walk them once with a naughty Alsatian, to calm him down and get him used to walking with other dogs. Betty is not quite so calm as Bosco. She thinks she's leader of the pack. She has a go at other dogs, tells them off, but that's all. You can have a whole lot of Pugs together, because they hardly ever fight. That's why you can have Pug gatherings, and there are Pug Parties in the park. Regent's Park every third Saturday in the month, Green Park every first Saturday. They just like to run about together, often in figures of eight, and as they like to be chased, you get outbreaks of Pugs running after each other.

'They sleep in our bedroom and they do snore at night, but that's a good thing, because you know they're alive. They get hot quicker than other dogs, they need lots of water and to keep their weight down. They're the perfect size for cuddling and kissing. Mmm! Kiss, kiss.'

Quite right. They fit beautifully on a lap, light enough to pick up easily, but solid, furry, warm and of course, beautiful. That's why their photos are all over the walls and mantelpiece, and why they look so fabulous in red bows and golden bell collars for Christmas, or lying back to back, or on birthday cards, and that's why there are ornamental Pugs on most surfaces: a plain standing Pug, a Jewish Pug in a yarmulke, Pugs in fancy dress, a library of Pug books, Pug this, Pug that, because they look so endearing, to the Pug-lover.

'They like to suckle the thighs of women, and of men who are in touch with their femininity,' says Suzanne. 'I often have wet patches on the thigh bit of my trousers. And they suckle on their bed, lifting their paws up and down like suckling kittens. But they hate mud and puddles, like Poirot in the country. It's the same look. We have to airlift them out.

'We escape the usual horrors. They don't get into trouble in the park, we avoid picnickers, but they wouldn't help themselves anyway. They just stand looking. At Bosco's first birthday we had thirty humans and one Pug. We played pin-the-tail-on-the-Pug and pass the parcel. Every time the parcel stopped, the person and the Pug got a present. At his second birthday party we invited dog friends, but a Labrador invaded, and took all the biscuits. It tore open the cardboard and plastic wrapping and demolished the lot. And another Pug – Humping Henry – kept humping Bosco and made the party a misery for him. His own party! He only had two parties.

'They have very strong characters. Bosco gets a bit

stubborn, and they have a strong sense of humour. We had a big, fluffy slipper and Bosco chewed a hole in the middle of it and used to stick his head through the hole to make us laugh.

'Like all dogs, they look at the right side of the face, because it shows the truest side. The emotions. Bosco is more empathetic. I got into the car once,' says Velo (co-human), 'feeling very angry, I said to Bosco "I'm really mad, but don't worry, it's nothing to do with you." He put his paw on my thigh and looked up at me, sympathetically.' When Suzanne had chronic fatigue syndrome Bosco moderated his behaviour accordingly, demanding very little attention. 'When my cousin stayed the night before flying out of the country,' says Suzanne, 'she felt ill the night before because she was terrified of flying. Bosco insisted on sleeping in her room. She went to the bathroom to be sick, heard him scratching at the door, let him in and he sat next to her the whole time she was throwing up, and stayed with her all night.

'They also have a job. They work as companions to an elderly lady. She used to live above us in a block of flats, she'd collect the dogs after she'd done her shopping and they'd stay with her, keep her company and sit on her knee. They're very calming. A dog releases the same chemical that mothers release to their babies. But now we've moved away and the elderly lady has dementia. We still take them to stay with her twice a week and we take a litter tray. Bosco will use it, so he can stay all day, but Betty won't, so a dog walker has to take her out, but they cheer her up and make her laugh.'

Velo tells a Navajo story about dogs. Animals and man used to all live together, but man became more and more evil. Eventually the Great Spirit separated us all – animals on one side, humans on the other. Before the divide became too great to cross, he asked the animals, 'Do any of you want to join them?' Only the dogs said yes. I suspect that for these Pugs, it was the right decision.

7: Dogs Indoors

Just because I adore my dogs, it doesn't mean that my visitors do. Some are frightened, some are sickened by the dribbling, the general smell of dog, the hairs which may stick to their clothing, the germs which I may be transferring from the dogs to the visitors' dinner, and some resent the attention, which I'm giving to the dogs instead of them.

Frankly, I think they're making too much fuss over nothing. I can attend to people and dogs at the same time, or at least I can distribute bits of attention fairly among them all. Once visitors have got used to the smell, they will barely notice it, hairs and dribble can be brushed and wiped away, and if a visitor is really scared, then all they have to do is say so and I will put them in a safe corner barricaded by chairs, and order the dogs to leave them alone.

Sometimes it isn't the dog who needs to be told how to behave, but the visitor. If you are visiting and don't want a fuss and kiss from someone's dogs, then all you have to do is ignore the darlings and turn away. Do not speak to the dog. Do not look it in the eye. If you do, it will think you expect it to respond.

'What does that person want me to do?' the dog will wonder, and will fuss about waiting for a straight answer. 'It wouldn't be looking at me if it didn't want something. Does it want me to fetch my squeaky duck? Does it want to give me a snack? Why doesn't it give me a sign? I'd better hang around, just in case, making sure that I am noticed and waiting for instructions.'

I do have a friend, Clare, who once arrived at the door and greeted my dogs in what I thought was the perfect way. She didn't speak to me at first, just to the doggies, saying clearly, 'Widgy, widgy, widgy-woo!'

They were thrilled to bits. And so was I, to see them so happy, and to see my visitor so happy to see them. But I have never dared to tell the rest of the world about this little event until now. Clare and I will only be criticised for being silly, treating my dogs like babies and bringing them up badly. Ideally, they should bark to alert me to a visitor, then back away from the door and allow the visitor to enter into the empty hall.

When I first started having problems with my dogs' behaviour, the pack leader theory was popular. I was to behave like pack leader, my family and friends were to be the next most important creatures in the hierarchy, and the poor darling doggies were to be at the very bottom of the list. The last to be spoken to or receive attention. The last to get their dinners. And they must sleep below me. On the floor. If possible, I should sleep upstairs, and never, ever allow them on my bed.

My mother would have preferred this method. When living with me, she always complained that I put the dogs first. It wasn't true, but she did rather go on about it. But I wasn't keen on this tough, put-the-dogs-last method. I couldn't get it to work. And luckily for me the pack leader theory is now being discredited. Even newer theory suggests that dogs know we are not pack leaders, because we're not dogs. They are not idiots. But what do I care? In the privacy of my own home, I ignore the rules and am thrilled if my visitors talk pleasantly to the dogs. Only yesterday I was playing the piano – a Beethoven sonata, my visitor joined in, improvising on the flute, and then Lily, my older Boxer joined in, singing. It was a fun trio. What's wrong with that? Why insist that dog is bottom of the pile and not allowed to join in, when it can sing so well?

But to shut all the critics up, I am often strict in front of visitors, ordering the dogs about, refusing to allow them snacks from table, keeping them away from guests. They can do what they're told if they sense that they must.

Offensive visitors

Sometimes, however, it is the visitors that get out of hand and need to be reprimanded. My friend Nova was once at home with her dog – an English Bull Terrier – when a friend of hers came visiting with his new girlfriend.

'Erk,' said the girlfriend when she spotted the dog. 'What an ugly dog!' Nova was furious, and pointed out that when visiting someone's house you would never dream of saying 'What an ugly sofa' or 'What an ugly child', so how dare anyone say 'What an ugly dog'. She ordered the visitors to leave at once. Good for her.

So can I advise visitors, that however unattractive your host's dog may seem to you, never criticise it. Unless, of course, its behaviour is beyond the pale: growling, snarling and generally terrifying visitors. None of my dogs have ever done this. But they, and I, still come in for harsh criticism. Particularly from the sort of visitor who thinks he/she knows better than I do, how to bring up my dog.

My friend Clayden is one such visitor. Annoyingly, even though he treats her harshly in the house and on walkies, Violet is still rather fond of Clayden. Ever since Dog Camp, his harsh, masculine treatment of her has created a bond between them. Why? Is it terror? Is it love? Is Violet that desperate for consistency and guidance? At home she quietly admires Clayden, and sometimes he gives her a brisk, dismissive pat. But it is his behaviour towards darling Lily that I find most callous. He ignores her. She brings him her favourite toy, she dances in front of him, she whimpers and twizzles about, and eventually, feeling desperate, she kisses him. The other day he responded particularly harshly, saying 'Go away, you smell!'

Unbearable. I had to tell him off seriously. Because I know that she understood – perhaps not the vocabulary, but the tone of rejection and dislike. And if he thinks he knows so much about dogs, then he ought to know that they are sensitive creatures, able to detect a mood from a single word, or even a look, or the tiniest bit of body language. And if one has two dogs, one may not have a favourite. We are friends, but for how long if this goes on?

Clayden is also one of many visitors who are critical of my methods. I shouldn't let my dogs sleep on the sofa, I shouldn't speak to them in a silly way, or keep kissing them, or feed them at table. Blah, blah blah. If people like him hope their criticism will make a difference, they can keep hoping. I find that when people tell me that I'm wrong and they're right, I tend to stick to my guns. Even if, in my heart, I know that they may be partly right. I don't care.

Bichon Frises. A love affair

'The current king of my castle is a somewhat moody, always ravenous and rather high maintenance Bichon Frise called Hugo – "Hugs"', says Jill Dawson. 'My dogs

have always slept on the bed, and Hugo sleeps on the end
of it with a pile of fluffy things: his sheepskin, his koala
and other cuddly toys. He nestles in them. In the morning he sneaks up and gets under the duvet. That's my
special five or ten minutes with him before I get up. I
have a very high mattress and so Hugo either slides off
the bed, or he calls for help from the bedroom. My
Yorkies always slept *in* the bed. My husband didn't like
it at first, but he got used to it, and luckily neither Yorkies
or Bichons shed hair.

'Visitors all fall in love with Hugo. My main piece of
furniture is a chaise longue-type sofa. It's Hugo's, with
his accoutrements. No one may sit there. I often think
we might have named him Arlecchino since he's very
much like a character straight out of an Italian restoration
comedy. Before he was castrated (which had to be done
at around 7 when he got ill) his whole being was focused
on sex. Gizmo, my Yorkie, was alive then, and the poor
thing was always available and got used to the constant
attention. Weirdly he put up with it. When Giz wasn't
around, people, table legs, lampposts, etc. were all fair
game for Hugs. But since the big day when he lost his
masculinity, it's been almost as if a new switch was
installed – from that moment on his entire being has
been focused on food. Hugo is greedy. He shouts for his
food. He will sing for his every meal – a terrible wailing
sound. People ask "Have you got a baby in the house?"
He knows what time it is: dinner times are at 8 a.m., 12

noon and 4 p.m., and his singing builds up into a resound-
ing crescendo as we reach the hour – it's Caruso-like by
the time we get there. It's better for him to have three
small meals a day than one big one, then he doesn't
scream all the time.

'My youngest son (who at 26 still lives with me) and I
were recently chatting about my love for dogs. I said that
I couldn't help myself, I'm sorry, I just love dogs a little
bit more than I love people – for your information, I do
love people – and my son chipped in with a comment
that I thought summed me up. He said "It's not that you
love dogs, Mum. It's that loving dogs is who you are."

'I judge the sons' girlfriends by their reaction to the
dog. The latest, a vegan, went up to Hugs on his sofa,
knelt down next to him, at [dog's] eye level and touched
his back. He rolled over and obviously loved her. A pass.

'Gizmo the Yorkie used to attack every dog in sight
when he went out, and once bit my son's nose. The son
came to me with blood dripping from his nose, saying
"Mum, Gizmo's bitten me."

'"What the hell did you do to the dog?" was my first
question. But my son is still understanding. We have an
overfed goldfish in our house, so he explains to any new
girlfriend, "As long as you realise that the goldfish is a
dog and the dog is a person, you'll be all right."

Darling little fluffies

Jill continues, 'I had bought a Yorkie, Bertie, seriously undershot, from a pet shop, soon after I got married. He was my child for a couple of years, until my oldest son came along. I was so worried, panic-stricken, about Bertie while I was giving birth to my son, that my husband had to smuggle him into the maternity hospital inside his coat. Once I'd seen him, I was all right. My kids have always accepted that the dogs come first. Husband asked, "Do you love the dogs more than me?" I said, "Don't ask questions if you already know the answer."

'Bertie died aged five of pancreatic cancer. I was devastated. He had come from a puppy farm and pancreatic disorder is a classic puppy farm illness, from being taken away from his mother too young.' Never, ever buy a puppy from a pet shop. They have usually come from a puppy farm.

After the heartbreak of Bertie's death, Jill didn't want another dog at first, but after a couple of years with no dog, found herself shooting a documentary for the BBC on breed standards, puppy farms and odd, misshapen breeds.

'We were filming at a British Bulldog breeder's home and this moving, white topiary hedge with a long tail came rushing out of the house, a perfectly formed white fluff – so full of character. I had met my first Bichon Frise, and I fell in love. I knew I had to have one of these wonderfully vibrant little topiary hedges.

'When Theo was ten we got another Yorkie – Gizmo, my soulmate, the love of my life, and that includes men. Gizmo was to keep Theodore company. This pocketsized macho man made all around think he was some kind of Tasmanian Devil. He went for the jugular every time we saw another dog. But with me - I could have pulled his teeth out and he wouldn't have minded. Hugo, my second Bichon, moved in with us when Theo died. So now we had a Yorkie and a Bichon again – but the Yorkie was the senior in the team. When he died two years ago I was too devastated to sleep in my own bed (his bed too) for two weeks. Now Hugo and I share it and we miss him still. Hugo is now my partner in life. My fluffy angel.

'Bichons are never all over you whatever happens. They're more choosy. They want something in return. Unlike the Yorkie – which says, "I'm yours. I love you always anyway," the Bichon will be, "How many treats am I going to get? What's in it for me?" But Hugo is so cuddly, looks and feels so gorgeous, I could forgive him anything. Bichons are laid back. "I can't help it if you think I'm beautiful," they say, "but don't touch me. I'm not in the mood. I would rather (if it's a stranger) that you don't prod me." He's very independent. He'll come over, put one paw across you, which says, "I'm available now."

Anyway, I must stop going on about my fluffies. I could ramble on forever . . .'

Dog table manners

I'm pleased to note that in our house, the dogs at least respect age. The old lady dog has her dinner first. I didn't realise how strict the dogs were about it, seeing as the humans in the house didn't observe this rule. Sometimes it was children first, grown-ups next and sometimes the poor grandma last. Shame.

I used to think, although I usually put the old dog's dinner down first, that it was the position of her dinner – on a step by the door – which was important. The younger dog had hers on a large, flat log a few feet away. Until I accidentally put the young dog's dinner down first, on the log. The old dog went straight over to it, the young dog waiting for the bowl on the step. They didn't care which bowl it was, or where, but they did care about the order of starting. And because one dog had medicine in its dinner and the other didn't, I had to swap the bowls round again pretty sharpish, but it was no good. The old dog still followed the first bowl that had been put down, and the young dog followed the second, so I had to start again, taking the bowls back into the kitchen, coming out into the garden and putting the bowls down in the right order.

Once more, I wouldn't mind a fee for this fascinating bit of research. Or perhaps a grant for more. Then I can just spend my days staring at dogs. Bliss. And my research is fairly thorough. I don't just observe my own dogs, much as I would love to do nothing else all day. I also tear myself away from the gorgeous creatures and investigate other dogs, like Wei's dogs – Biddy the Bull Terrier and Jonah and Riley, the Patterdale Terriers. Jonah and Riley arrived when Biddy was nine, and people told Wei to feed all the dogs together. People in Dog World do tend to offer advice, even if you don't need it or ask for it, and as there was a lot of it coming at her, Wei took it. She fed the dogs all at once.

Biddy was a bit grumpy. 'I thought I was top dog!' she thought. Then Jonah, the older Patterdale, thought the same and started to get cocky and began to pick on his little brother. And not just indoors. They had horrid fights even when they went out for walkies, which meant disapproving glares from the public and other dog walkers, who often offered more advice, if they could get near enough.

So Wei and Adrian tried a new plan. In the natural hierarchy, they thought, it would be the oldest first, then the next lot have the leftovers, so they gave Biddy hers first, saying, 'Sit! Wait. TAKE!' And she did. Then the juniors, saying Sit! 'Wait. EAT!' So that there wouldn't be any confusion, they wouldn't TAKE Biddy's and she wouldn't EAT theirs, and after about three months of this rigorous regime, it all worked like magic. No more fights, indoors or out.

The dog who likes to join in

An open-plan flat is not ideal for a dog. Zara and her husband Mark live in one, but they never intended to get a dog. Then Mark's mother died. 'She had bred Vizslas for forty-five years. She was a top breeder, she'd written books about them. When she died there were five left. One very old. We found them homes but Skye didn't get on well in his home, so we had him, in the flat. My mother would never have allowed that – a dog in a flat. But I'd fallen in love with him anyway, six months before my mother died. His father's a champion who had 566 offspring.'

'Mark loved him first,' says Zara. 'He loved him straight away, when he was still with his mother, then Skye came here and I fell in love with him after five days. I caught up. When we got him he was frightened of water. Mark's mother used to work dogs. She did HPR, Hunt Point and Retrieve. Vizslas are pointers. They pick up pheasants. For them to do that they have to cross water and rivers. But Skye was frightened of water.

'It was weird for him, moving from the country to Belsize Park. At first he was frightened of town noises and sights: traffic, prams, umbrellas, big red buses, mopeds, even postboxes.'

'He suddenly got frightened of your stilettos,' says Mark. 'You weren't wearing them. They were just standing on the floor in the bedroom. And then he was frightened of the hair-dryer. He'd never slept on his own, always with other dogs in a kennel. In the kennel he had all his siblings, aunts, uncles. At first we were going to let him sleep downstairs. We thought he wouldn't be able to get up the spiral staircase to the bedroom, but he cried to get upstairs, and tried to get through the side of the staircase, so we taught him to climb up the spiral.'

'We couldn't let him be on his own on his first night. He likes to be part of the game. If we're having a cuddle in the kitchen, or if we're dancing, he wants to join in. As far as he's concerned, we're all in the kennel together. He always wants to join in the action. When Mark's away he keeps waking up wondering where Mark is. He looks for him. Last time he got on the bed and sat on my head. The bathroom is the only room with a door on it. Mark goes in there sometimes to read.

'Everyone's got an opinion. Everyone tells you the dog's got to know you're the boss. You've got to say "No!" So I did at first, but if I shouted he'd start to shake. So I thought, "I'm never shouting at him again." I read Cesar Millan's book. He said not to speak to your dog in the morning. I threw it straight in the bin. Men like to dominate, but not my husband. He's the gentlest man.

'This is a studio flat. We were fine just the two of us, but with the dog we're all on top of each other. Skye's not a problem at home. He can sleep all day, he likes a lie-in. He's got the best bit of the sofa. The corner section, but it was never right for us anyway. It's a very posh sofa – Roche Bobois. That's a bit of a change from bales of hay and paper in the kennel, to the high life.

'And luckily, my mother has a swimming pool in the country. Skye used to stand at the poolside crying and whimpering, pawing at the water, but he wouldn't get in. So Mark coaxed him into the swimming pool. My mother wouldn't let him use the pool, so we taught him while she was out. He could get in at the shallow end, down the steps. Then he got to love it. He'd get to the park and jump in the pond and wouldn't get out for an hour and a half. Then he jumped into Mark's bath.

'He makes us happy. He's changed our lives, he's very soothing. After he's eaten he likes a cuddle. He sighs, we sigh, we're all relaxed in each others' arms.'

New baby dog

What a darling widsy-didsy, squidgy little thing a puppy is. Why bother to have a baby, when one can have a dog-baby instead? It's the same thing: sleepless nights, incessant cleaning up of sick and poo, potty training, permanent exhaustion and anxiety, displacement of the older siblings, doting grandma, passers-by saying 'Aah', obsessive interest and comment on the tiny one's progress and bored friends glazing over.

'Take that stupid look off your face,' my friend Jennifer

used to snap at me, when baby Violet arrived. 'It is sick-making.' She preferred human babies. But a baby-dog brings the same old problems. When other people spot a new arrival they tend to a) give advice to the new mother/owner, and b) they will not follow her instructions or chosen regime, but will switch to theirs, which they feel is right. I tell my immediate family and friends all about diet, training and dog behaviour, based on my years of dog experience and research, but do they listen? No. They do exactly as they please.

Daughter was desperate to bottle-feed puppy Violet. I had told her not to but she defied me and bought a bottle. I came home to find her and her boyfriend bottle-feeding the baby dog at the kitchen table. It was their baby. They cuddled it, gooed over it, took photos and competed for position of Best Parent. They had forgotten that the dog was meant to be *being weaned*. This meant coming off milk and going onto solids. Daughter and I had a little row about upbringing, routine and consistency. What luck that this was not a real grandchild. Imagine the tempestuous squabbling that could go on. No wonder the family is often a fairly hellish unit. And worse still, everyone was ignoring Lily, the first born, who was being pushed out of paradise.

I'd been warned about this by many dog persons: it was vital that we always attend to the older dog first. Say hello first, dinner first, lead on first, out the door first, unless we want bloody fights over position of top dog in future. I passed on this information to my family. Did anyone pay attention? Fat chance.

It was a bit of a relief taking the new baby/puppy out for a walkie. There was no arguing or defiance, just general adoration from passers-by and other dog-walkers, who all gathered around to worship the divine tiny one. They saw its little wibbly legs, its darling dinky face and their hearts melted. I felt a sort of expectancy – that my baby ought to be worshipped. How could anybody not think it exquisite?

On one of my walkies I met a woman with twin babies (human) in a double pushchair, and one Boxer puppy. Scores of people stopped her to ooh and aah and have a soppy look, but at who? The puppy, of course. No one seemed bothered by the baby twins. But at least out on a walkie, people are not in competition with the new arrival. Research (mine) has shown that family members will still be jealous, and resent the attention your baby dog is receiving, even though they adore the puppy themselves.

But to make up for all this family rubbish, there are the thrilling developmental milestones that the darling puppy is reaching, like going toilet outdoors in the garden! Rejoice! No more stinky carpet or acres of newspaper. I remembered my human baby crawling about searching for rusty nails, cigarette ends, stones or anything life-threatening to stuff into her mouth and swallow. Same again. I was back to the old meticulous and incessant

sweeping, tidying and hoovering to prevent the new
baby from swallowing dangerous rubbish, and costing
me a fortune at the vet.

But it was all worth it for me, and for my elderly
mother. She adored having Baby Violet sat on her knee,
or plonked on her bed, so that she could coo over her
and cuddle her, and in return Violet would shower her
with kisses and love. Violet was so rewarding – someone
to babysit, show off to visitors and worry about. Would
Violet fall off the bed/run away/die/escape on a walkie,
drown in the pond? Hopefully not, but one thing she did
do – improved my mother's health beyond measure. My
mother was 98 at the time, very poorly and fed up and
longed to drop off her perch. She could barely eat, speak
or move. She had nothing left to live for. Then we
plonked the darling, sweetie-pie puppy on her bed.
Within days she was a new woman: laughing, cheery and
eating up her dinners, and the biggest surprise of all – a
few days cuddling our new puppy brought to an end my
mother's forty-year battle with miserable, immovable
constipation. Miraculous. I swear it's true. Who would
have thought a baby-dog could bring back someone's
appetite and get her bowels in order? I'm pretty sure that
the puppy extended my mother's life for several months.
Dogs are obviously good for health, and my mother had
always wanted another grandchild. This was the best I
could do.

Lifesaver dog

A dog doesn't care what age you are. It is oblivious to wrinkles. It will still want to kiss you, which is perhaps why dogs are so good at perking up the elderly. Janice's elderly mother, like mine, also lived with her family: Janice, husband Andy, two teenage daughters and large Poodle Arthur. One night her mother had a dreadful nightmare, woke up feeling desperate and longed to drop dead. She couldn't stand another day of it.

'I want to die,' she moaned. 'You're going to have to finish me off. Will you? Would you do that for me?'

Janice wasn't sure. 'I could go to prison for that,' she said, but her poor mother was beyond caring about repercussions. Then in came Arthur with his squeaky monkey and she perked up at once. The dog was a lifesaver. And not just regarding her mother's life. When one is trapped in the stew of family life, when family members are sulking and rowing, when the household is throbbing with resentments and hatreds, a dog will diffuse the tension. A dog will provide distraction and continue to kiss everyone. It is a lifeline out of there – into the garden, out for a walk, an ally when the rest of the family is intolerable. Arthur provided support for all of them, always, any time, day or night. He never took sides. He was never annoyed by teenagers, never criticised their outfits, and would always cuddle them. When there was no one else they could bear to kiss or speak to, and no one else could bear to speak to them, then every-body could always kiss and speak to the dog.

But a dog is a sensitive creature and sometimes the domestic uproar gets it down. It may be so upset by the ghastly rows, that it will cower under a table like mine do, trembling and distraught, with their hair on end, and if that doesn't shame a family into shutting up and calm-ing down, then probably nothing will. It worked in Janice's house. The dog stopped her shouting over lost keys, or lost anything. At the sound of the words 'Where's my . . .' uttered in a crabby tone, Arthur would cringe and tremble, although they couldn't tell whether his fur was on end or not, and it is unbearable to watch a dog suffer like that, just because you have lost your keys. And so Janice controlled herself and learned to search quietly and calmly for lost items, and even the girls followed her example. A miracle.

Family interference in the training process

Training is difficult enough if you are left to get on with it yourself, but in Dog World people tend to have strong opinions and like to give advice on how you ought to bring up your dog. Family members are particularly prone to this, and if they don't agree with your method and rules, and can't make you change them, then they will just ignore them and do as they please. Especially mothers and daughters. Even in her nineties, feeble, speechless and almost completely bedridden, Jacqueline's mother was still defying her instructions and sabotaging her efforts to train Bonzo, her Bulldog. It is essential that Bulldogs do not become obese, it makes their lives even more difficult, but Jacqueline's mother would not stop feeding the dog dangerous snacks. And Bonzo had a delicate stomach, but the mother would stuff him with ginger-nuts, sweeties, lumps of fat and gristle, cakes and anything that her false teeth couldn't quite manage.

Time and time again Jacqueline begged her not to do it, made sure that there was a supply of approved dog snacks on her tray, showed her the vet's bills, described the terrible consequences of her actions: the mopping up of vomit, blood and excrement, but would she stop it? No. Down went the hand with the poisoned snack the minute Jacqueline's back was turned.

Every scrap on her plate may have gone, but down whose throat? Jacqueline would question her.

'Did you give him your dinner? Or any fat? Crusts with butter on?' There she sat, a little old lady with pale blue eyes in pastel bed jacket affecting innocence. She shook her head sweetly. Visitors gazed at her soppily and thought her adorable. How could Jacqueline imagine that such a person would knowingly poison a dog? But downstairs the kitchen floor was often awash with crap and sick, the garden spattered with puddles of heaven knows what, even when her mother had sworn blind that not a morsel of lamb chop/Turkish delight/tortilla chips had passed the dog's lips.

This is clearly a favourite wheeze of elderly relatives. It brings them love and adoration from the dogs, while simultaneously providing opportunities to defy and enrage their bossy sons and daughters. But it isn't just wilful defiance. It is difficult for anyone to resist a begging dog, especially Bulldogs or Boxers, which have perfected an expression of such heart-rending longing, that only the most steely-hearted diner can resist them. Jacqueline's mother is far from the only one. My friend Mavis' mother-in-law is forever slipping their Golden Retriever dicey treats, although she is also forbidden to do so. Last week Mavis noticed Mother-in-law's hand down by her side, trailing the golden syrup spoon. She is the dog's favourite person in the world, because she drips snacks and sweeties. Everyone loves to be a dog's favourite person.

Terrifying foam-flecked beasts

Perhaps that was rather a sweeping generalisation. Some people couldn't care less about being the dog's favourite person. They would prefer to never even encounter a dog, and if they must meet one, then they would prefer the dog to completely ignore them. My friend Whitwham is one such person. I suspect this is because a dog tried to bite his face off when he was a little boy, and he still has not overcome his fear. I suppose this is understandable, but I still think he's a bit wet. And unfortunately his fear has turned to aggression. If only he could calm down, he might realise that he and Violet have something in common – fear-based aggression. But he hasn't yet reached that mature stage, so this is what he feels when visiting my house. I'm letting him have his say, because I think it may help dog-owners to understand strange people like Whitwham. It's the fear speaking. Here goes:

'I don't know whose house it is,' he says. 'Their house or yours. I arrive, then there's that awful howling, like the Baskerville, then you open the door ajar, but I never see your face, just these two terrifying, foam-flecked beasts, peering out at calf level, then the medieval chain on the door is released and you say, "They're saying hallo. They're pleased to see you, but don't look them in the eye." So I have to go along looking at the ceiling, I can't see where I'm going, so I often fall down the stairs. I hate that first five minutes. I don't know why I bother to visit. And then I'm encouraged to admire their beauty. "Look at Lily! Look at her darling little face." Eurghh!'

Whitwham does try hard to cope with my dogs, and once he bravely came for a walkie. I had hoped that a glimpse of Dog World would encourage a more positive attitude, but it did no good. 'Oh that was vile and horrid,' he said afterwards. 'As far as I could see your dogs did three things. First they went into the undergrowth and chased out some terrified smoking teenagers, then they approached a pram and frightened its contents, then thirdly, I was sitting near a wooden park table, and one of them, I can't remember which, they're both so horrible, jumped up at me, in that pleasing friendly violent way, and thumped me on the chest, and then like all bloody dog-owners, you said, "They only want to play."

'No they didn't. They wanted to terminate my life. I've got high blood pressure, for Christ's sake; then one of them starting mating with my knee. And this also happened every time I sat and had a cup of tea in your kitchen. One of them's wiggling against my leg in a most distasteful manner. For an otherwise intelligent person, when you're with your dogs, your IQ plummets. You become an idiot. A completely sentimental idiot, and you keep saying, "Look at them, they're sitting so nicely in their baskets, don't they look sweet. Look at those faces!" Or some rubbish like that. Or they'd be playing with that bloody rubber thing that squeaked, while I'm trying to conduct a serious conversation, or they're fornicating with my legs. So in conclusion, your dogs have turned you into a dimwit, and you keep going "Widgy-widgy", and then they'll do something terrible, and at the end, when it's over, you always go, "But I LOOOOVE them." It's quite sickening. You declare your love for them at least every ten minutes. Yuk.'

Oddly enough, we are still friends. And he is not alone with these feelings. Many visitors probably feel the same, but they don't express their opinions quite so strongly, which is why I felt that it's only fair to let Whitwham express himself, on behalf of dog-phobics everywhere. Not many people would dare to be so offensive, but I think it helps us to cope with them? And fair enough, my control of the dogs when visitors arrive is not always perfect. They should back away from the door and visitor when told to, but they often like to stick around, twirling about excitedly. Must try harder.

Who do you love best?

David has a darling Whippet called Max. He is the only creature in the house who seems really pleased to see him when he comes downstairs in the mornings. He kisses the dog's head. It's quite happy about that. Then his son comes downstairs, not particularly happy to see his father, but David loves his son, so he kisses him. He was aiming for his cheek, but as the boy was moving, he didn't quite hit the target correctly and almost touched his mouth.

'Erk!' says the son, jerking away. 'You kissed my mouth! Weird!'

'It's not weird,' says David. 'You're my son, I love you.'

'You love the dog more than me,' says the son. He often says it.

'I love the dog more than anyone, in the way you love

dogs. I love you more than anyone, in the way you love sons. It's a different thing.'

'Grunt.' The son doesn't get it.

'As you get older you have to be more serious,' says David. 'But you can still be silly with a dog. I was in the pet shop and this woman says, "I know you. You're that man who jumps with your dog." I can do that because a dog doesn't say, "Dad! You're so embarrassing." You're proud of your dog and you're proud of your son. My mother was proud of me, even just for breathing.

'At first having Max was like having a little alien in the house. Whippets have a slight alien look about them. I can't quantify whether it makes me a better person, but it takes away my inhibitions. I can still show it the love I used to show my three-year-olds.'

Why a Whippet, anyway? They don't look very cuddly.

'Max finds a way to cuddle. He puts his chin on you. Sometimes it's just bony, other times it's wonderful. He cuddles our rabbit. The rabbit feels more comfortable with him than with me. Isn't that bizarre? In the park today he wanted to put his chin over some puppies and be loving. I could fault him for wanting to roll in fox poo, but that's all. He's wonderful to watch. Whippets are majestic when they run, like speeding gazelles or jaguars, or ancient Egyptian sculptures.

'When I'm with him, I talk dog language. I use a special grunting noise to tell him to drop his Frisbee. He has a different greeting for each member of the family.

He jumps up at them in a different way. Right now he's stretching out on the sofa in the sun, as if he's sunbathing on a beach. I would think similar things about my children, but it's easier to say these things about a dog, especially as the child gets older. This creature says, "Just love me," so it makes you more loving.

'Some people say to me, "You humanise your dog." It's odd how they want to judge you. Others look at my dog in the street, and if they have a nice crinkle round their eyes and a smile, I think, that's a nice person. The dogs socialise humans. If you have a dog, people stop and talk. If you don't have a dog, they don't.'

Dog kissing

You have to be careful who you kiss in front of who. While Whitwham, our anti-dog friend, was visiting the other day, despite dog-walker Dawn's warning, Daughter and I absolutely couldn't resist kissing the older dog. I know she has a deformed, undershot jaw, but to us she still looked so exquisitely beautiful that we both fell upon her, cuddling and cooing over her as she lay on the bed, in front of Whitwham, which made him feel horribly sick. To him, dog kissing is a form of depravity.

I can sort of forgive him, because he is scared to death of dogs, and obviously his revulsion is tinged with fear. But we both know that there isn't the remotest chance that the dog would bite us while we were showering her with kisses. She does get a bit bored with it, and turns her head away wearily, but bite? Never.

My friend Tanya is also frightened of dogs. She too was bitten as a child, but she bravely tries to stifle her fear and loathing. I sit her in a corner, behind the table, or some such barricade, and then she can relax. But Jennifer has no such excuse. She isn't frightened of dogs. She just doesn't like them much. She appears at the front door, the darling dog wiggles up to greet her. It is even carrying its squeaky monkey as a welcoming gift, but she only shouts, 'Get that wretched dog out of the way!'

Her attitude is almost ruining our dog walkies. If I stop for one minute and chat to other dog-owners, about diet, or diarrhoea, or fights and other little habits, or just general dog-chat, she stamps off ahead in a bate. Because she doesn't realise that this is my Other Life. It has always been my way of escaping the housework, my mother, partner and daughter, my computer and domestic dramas. Out with the dog I have only the natural world and dog people. It is absolute heaven, stops me from going raving mad, and keeps me healthy, because without the dog, I would never go walking outdoors or take any exercise. I am not one to exercise voluntarily. The dog is saving my sanity, and should be appreciated, especially by someone who calls herself my friend.

And the dog has helped her in her hour of need. A dog can understand a person's state of mind and behaves appropriately. I think Jennifer could have been a little more grateful. Even though she sometimes treats the dogs rather callously, in my opinion, Jennifer does appreciates this particular dog skill. After a fashion. 'When I'm very depressed, I love your dogs,' she says. 'Lily was so nice to me when I was depressed, and she still brings me her toys. But now I'm not so wild about her. She's served her purpose. Although I do still say hallo.'

The desperate shepherd

The dog really deserved more respect and gratitude. Again research (mine) shows that dogs do seem to know when a person particularly needs someone/somedog to be nice to them. Lily wasn't the only dog who honed in on someone desperate for affection.

Daisy, the Boxer who was cruelly treated by the lodger, also came to the aid of someone in trouble. One day, that same lodger brought an Italian shepherd to stay in our house. Lodger's sister had visited Italy, fallen in love with the shepherd, and brought him back to England. Within days she had fallen out of love with the poor shepherd, whom she abandoned in a bleak bed-sit in Earl's Court. Imagine the culture shock. One day he's in the beautiful sunny Umbrian hills with his sheep and dog, then suddenly he's all alone in ghastly, dreary old Earl's Court.

As Lodger wasn't a totally heartless man, he took pity

on the shepherd, and brought him to our house. He led him up to the spare room, where the poor fellow sat mutely on the bed, with his small, inexpensive suitcase, looking rather desolate, and as he spoke no English and our Italian was poor, nobody quite knew what to do.

But the dog did. Daisy went straight up to the spare room, fussed around the shepherd and kissed him repeatedly. The shepherd burst into tears. He wailed and sobbed loudly in a heart-rending way, clinging onto the dog, while she kept kissing him and stayed with him until he'd calmed down. She then kept him company until he left a couple of days later, and flew back to Italy. To his own dog.

Hairs in your yoghurt

Stephanie loves Newfoundlands more than any other dogs. Why? 'Because they're so lovely. We first got one because they're good with children and naturally protect them. [She has four children.] They've been known to stop children going into ponds and their own paddling pools – they put themselves between the child and the water – nothing aggressive, they don't pull them, push them or lead them, they just stand in their way. I couldn't live without a Newfoundland. I'll always have one. They're lazy dogs – don't eat much. Poppy's a great big bear of a dog, never goes too far away on walkies, runs ahead a little, rushes back like a big fat nanny to see if we're still there and we're all right, very loyal, looks after the baby, she wouldn't let him get too near the gate – a little nudge – "You're not going too far that way."

'Our first Newfoundland, Nala, died of liver failure, only two and a half. The baby jumped on her when she was nearly dead – but still able to get up and walk – and she still didn't get cross. After that I did lots of research. I was terrified of getting another that would die young of the same thing. She wasn't a Kennel Club dog – I'd thought that would be better, because she wouldn't be inbred – but this time, before I got another one, I phoned everybody in the Newfoundland club, any number on the website, anyone I could speak to. I didn't care, I just rang them all up and asked, "Is liver failure something NFs die of?" But they said not really. They have bad joints, because they're so big, and heart trouble. And the Kennel Club dogs all have health checks, so that's safer. Anyway one person happened to know about this seventy-year-old lady in Devon who had twelve Newfoundlands and needed to downsize. Five of the dogs were teenagers – eighteen months to two years. And there was this one that the others didn't like – she'd been re-homed for eight months and then sent back, but then was no longer part of the family.

'I went down there to see this woman. She lived in a caravan with a bit of fenced-off decking around it, with Newfoundlands, a Whippet and a Cocker Spaniel. There was a bedroom, but she slept on a couch in the caravan living-room with her dogs around her. It was a mess, piled high with bits and pieces – carpet sodden in August, because of the wet dogs coming in and out. I took the baby and it got its jeans wet crawling on the floor – no poo in the house, but a bit on the decking, which the lady scraped off with a trowel when we arrived.

'"Come in," she said. So we went in. "Hallo. Just a minute, I'm watching the athletics." The dogs were all lying around, a couple of very old ones who stank, and she hardly talked to us for the first hour, because of the athletics. I don't think she liked people very much – she was what I call a real animal person – used to be a very prolific breeder, but it was getting too much for her. It was pretty smelly in there. She had grown-up children who brought her food, but there wasn't much there. She didn't seem to eat or drink much. "Can I have one of your cigarettes?" she asked. "I don't think my daughter's going to bring any shopping today." She kept asking for cigarettes, so I left her the packet when we went.

'It was perhaps getting to be a bit much for her. The dogs often knocked her over, running through the garden. She was on remote farmland – the nearest neighbour about a mile away. They'd complained about the barking at night. "I won't pester you," she said when we left with the dog, "but it would be nice to know how she's getting on." I do write to her now and then, with a progress report.'

'Dogs are incredible. I think Newfoundlands think they're people. Poppy got up on a garden bench, she sat up on it with Graham [Stephanie's partner], leaned back saying. "Yes, I'm like you. I'm a person." They don't seem to know how big they are. They try and get through small gaps.

'Big fat dog, we call her. I've had rabbits, ducks, cats, a giant millipede. Now it's just dogs.'

Dogs lounging around and sleeping. Stephanie's four children, aged two, seven, ten and thirteen, and two dogs – Poppy the Newfoundland and Dylan the Lurcher/Pointer cross. Imagine that, but she's cleverly divided the garden up – one third fenced off for the dogs, two thirds left for the children, which means no poo in the children's area, and a bit of peace for the dogs.

'Look.' She pulls at Poppy's thick black fur fairly gently. Huge tufts come out in her hand. She throws them absentmindedly into a tub of spinach growing by the kitchen door. 'See? You get hairs everywhere. I find them at work. I can always recognise them. Newfoundland hair is slightly crimped when wet. If you completely brush it out at moulting time, you can end up with a pile as big as the dog. If I brush it out for five minutes at moulting season I'd have a carrier bag full. I've spent £100 on brushes to find the best one. On a Newfoundland website it says, "Don't ever expect to eat a yoghurt again without a hair in it." The woman I got Poppy from was worried that I might be too house-proud – you can't have a Newfoundland if you are. And the fur's water-proof. They have webbed feet, because they were used to do sea rescue and pull the boats in.'

During my stay with Stephanie, it's my dog Lily's birthday, so we have a dog party. Home-made dog liver cake with a candle on it. I blow out the candle, then we sing happy birthday – children and grown-ups, then the dogs have their cake – one's in its bed, two standing in the kitchen, the Newfoundland outside. Then they have gravy-bone biscuits to follow. A brief but thrilling little celebration. And the dogs are all fairly mellow. No rows over the cake. I had worried about this stay in advance. How would the dogs get on? My dogs' behaviour is not ideal. How would they cope with four children and two dogs? Play or fight? And what would the two resident dogs think of two rather ill-mannered visitors in their home?

They didn't seem to mind. They were tremendously tolerant, and all had a little introductory play on the lawn, but it did heat up a bit, because somebody made a fuss of one dog rather too close to another, which felt left out, and then it was nearly blood on the grass, but we averted it, by being calm. And with the large dog pen, we could have two dogs in it and two dogs out. Luckily Stephanie is a bit of a dog whisperer, and she took Violet in hand. Violet likes a fight, but Stephanie just walked her backwards and forward, along the side of the pen past the other dogs, and every time Violet does the slightest glare, then Stephanie makes a quick hiss and jerk on the lead, and after a few minutes of that Violet is completely chilled out and you wouldn't know there was another dog in sight. Success.

But what with four children and an early morning job, Stephanie doesn't have as much time to play with dogs as she would like. More in term time when all the children except baby are at school. She must wait until they all grow up a lot more.

'I want to be an old lady living in a caravan with dogs,' says she wistfully. I can understand her dream.

Love rivals

Living with only dogs sounds like a breeze compared to living in some families. In a family like ours, you can't really win. The dog's popularity only causes more problems. It leads to dog-love-rivalry. Well not for me, because I'm the main dog-owner and their very favourite person, so I'm fairly secure, but the other resident humans tend to resent my close relationship with the dogs. Who does the dog love most? They like to think they are the dogs' favourite. And who does it really belong to? I bought it, feed it, look after it when it's poorly and take it for 99 per cent of its walkies, but the daughter still insists that it's her dog. Rubbish. And then the family members start to suspect that I love the dogs more than them.

My mother used to think so while she lived with us. To her it seemed that the dog was fed first, spoken to more and received more attention. There she was, mouldering in her bedroom, while I was out prancing about the park with the dog. 'You've spoken to that dog seven times in ten minutes,' she would shout jealously. 'I've been counting!'

Yes, I may well have done so. Because the darling does not answer back, or make offensive remarks, or tell me my bum's looking fatter, which my mother tends to do. But despite all these little problems and rivalries, the dogs definitely enhance our lives. They provide an outlet for all the feelings you couldn't otherwise express.

'Like many men, I can't do emotion,' my friend Whitwham admitted bravely, 'but I can with the cat. I can talk to him – about his girlfriends, tell him how beautiful he is. We have telepathy, we empathise, perhaps because we're lazy and we're both boys.'

In his household there's a big down on all forms of sentimentality. 'We don't allow ourselves any of that, we're too intellectual,' he says, 'but we can all be senti-mental and kitsch with the cat and talk widgy-woo language. And we're jealous. We all want to be the cat's favourite, to love the cat most. Without it the family would have split up years ago.' Same with dogs.

But perhaps jealousy is not so bad. It's at least based on love, rather than hatred. Love has rather gone out of the window for Mike and Linda's family. Their dog, a Jack Russell, has thrown the whole family into turmoil.

'It's loathsome and aggressive and it's nearly taken several people's limbs and noses off,' says Linda's sister Marilyn. 'My mother hates it with a passion, the cats hide on top of the cupboard, the vet can't get near it, the kennel won't take it, the neighbours are terrified of it. It causes awful family rows. When Linda, Mike and the dog come to stay we can't criticise, they're very defensive, they have no children, the dog is their baby. They still think there's nothing wrong with it, but we all want to kick it and run over it accidentally. I feel terribly guilty because I know it's not the dog's fault and I love animals, but I hate this dog.'

8: Ways to Lose a Dog

It is terrifying to lose your dog. There are too many ways that this can happen. The dog can run away, after a fox, a picnic, another dog on heat, and it can be gone in a flash. One minute your dog's fiddling around feet away, you're chatting to your friend, or admiring the trees, and suddenly it's gone. Over the hill, into the woods, into the pond. Sylvia's new little dog Alfie suddenly disappeared. Panic stations. He was too new to know his way home; we shouted, and called and ran around – no sign of him, but then we realised we'd just passed a large pond. We rushed back. There was his pointy little nose only just sticking out of the water, his short legs paddling like mad. This was his first swim, and a bit of a struggle. Quickly we pulled him out. Saved in the nick of time. Phew. But what if your dog never returns? You could be tormented by terrible imaginings for the rest of your life. Where was she/he? With someone kind? Cruel? Knocked over? You want to avoid this sort of worry, so you have to be very careful to whom you entrust your dog. Sometimes, disappointingly, some people can be a bit of a let-down. They are secretly not keen to look after your dog, but don't like to admit it. If they are aware of your anxieties, there are more subtle ways of making sure they never have to look after your dog again. Here are some tried and tested methods.

Do not tie that dog up outside a shop

Luckily, I now live alone with my dogs, but what use was my partner years ago, when I had one? None at all. Did I get any help looking after my dogs? No I did not. Foolishly I had presumed that a partner helps you with life, and takes your dog for a walkie when you're really busy. Don't count on it folks. I used to be really busy when I had a partner. I had my 90-year-old mother to look after, my teenage daughter, my work to do and I was taking a history degree, which meant lots of home-work and essays and general household tasks, so I asked the partner to take Lily for a walkie.

Since she came to us from the cruel breeder, Lily has always been a nervous dog, and terrified of traffic, shops and walking along any road which has either of these two things on it. In such a situation, she would have panic attacks, paw the ground, breathe heavily, and try to go home again. The worst, most terrifying thing that could have happened to her was to be tied up outside a shop on a busy street. So I warned my partner.

'Whatever you do, DO NOT TIE HER UP OUTSIDE A SHOP!'

He tied her up outside a shop. He walked her to the local shops, on the main road, and he didn't just tie her up outside the shop, but he tied her to a flapping metal sign standing outside the shop, which must have terrified her almost to death.

'I was only in the shop for one minute,' he said. 'Then I came out and she was gone.' There was the collar and lead, still attached to the metal sign. Panic stations. He knew it would be divorce and disgrace if he'd lost my dog. He ran home. No dog. He got into the car and started driving round the streets. No dog. He drove home in despair. And there she was, sitting on the door-step trembling, having luckily not been run over on the way home while crossing the busy road all by herself.

He need never have told me. I wouldn't have known, so why tell? The dog couldn't blab. No one else knew. I can't help but suspect that he knew that once I knew how close my dog had been to disappearance or even death when in his care, I would never dare put him in charge of her again. Absolutely right. I never asked him to take her for a walkie again. Lucky him. Did he do it on purpose? Subconsciously? I bet he did. Because he's not the only one.

Broken glass snack

Kath's son wanted a dog from the age of five. He staged what turned out to be a six-year campaign to persuade her to get a dog. When he was eleven his best friend moved hundreds of miles away to Penrith. He was desolate and his mummy ran out of excuses. They acquired a Labrador/Golden Retriever cross – 'the favoured breed of guidedog trainers'. Oscar. By the time Oscar was five months old and they'd had him for twelve weeks, the dog had worked its magic and the son had been transformed from unhappy to happy.

One morning, instead of taking Oscar on his usual walkie to school with her daughter, she had to leave him at home. Daughter had a class performance, to which dogs were not allowed. But that would be fine, she thought, because her husband, a lawyer, was working from home that morning, which he rarely did. A stroke of luck. He could look after Oscar. Kath didn't even need to put the dog in his cage to stop him wrecking the house, because her husband was there. In charge.

'I left him in pyjamas with the puppy in the hall,' says she. 'It was 10:15 by the time I got home (after celebratory coffee). Through the window I saw my husband putting the puppy in the crate. He must have been about to leave for work, I thought, so I went in, but as I entered the playroom that adjoins our kitchen I saw things strewn about – on the floor there was an empty carrier bag and my daughter's outgrown dressing gown, and on the sofa, her outgrown fleece. What was going on? When I left they were both in the carrier bag.

'I lifted up the fleece. Underneath were the remains of a smashed maple syrup bottle. I lifted up the dressing gown. Underneath that was a big sticky patch of floor from which syrup had clearly been licked. I looked up and saw the kitchen table covered in law books and a laptop and my husband peering round from the crate saying, "Oh no! The dog's just been sick. I wonder why."

'I could have told him. I'd worked it out, like Sherlock Holmes only much faster. Oscar must have taken the maple syrup bottle that I'd left on the kitchen table (he'd stolen from the table before), carried it to the sofa, spilt the syrup, licked it off the sofa, which was covered in hardened drips of syrup, pushed the bottle onto the floor and broken it, so that he could eat even more syrup along with some broken glass! My husband had negligently killed the puppy!'

Twelve years of Kath's life flashed before her. 'Twelve years of endlessly looking after the kids while he worked *all the time*, or him looking after them occasionally, but only if I'd sorted everything out first.' Now look what had happened the minute she left him to look after a new baby himself. So she had a scream.

'The dog's eaten broken glass! What the bloody hell were you doing?

'Husband looked rather scared. "I was in the bath," he said.

'You left the puppy uncrated in the kitchen, did not clear up breakfast and then went upstairs and got in the bath?' Living with a barrister for fifteen years had taught her to converse like this.

'Well yes,' he says.

'Didn't you see what had happened when you came downstairs?' Clearly he had sat at the table working. His books and laptop were a giveaway

'I was working!' he roars.

'Well why don't you just fuck off to work where you don't have any dependents you need to keep alive?'

'Right then, I fucking will!'

'Good. Fuck off!' Then Kath realised that the usually robust cleaning lady was trying to hide in the dishwasher. With trembling hands she put the puppy on his lead and took him down the street to the vet. She tried not to cry.

'They X-rayed him, and he had broken glass in his guts. "Feed him bread," they said, "it will wrap itself round the glass." We fed him cholla and chicken – the Jewish way through. The vet kept him in overnight to make sure.'

'Is he on the At Risk register? Ha, ha!' said the husband when they got home. His little joke. Then they all had a laugh about the husband's subconscious plot to murder the dog. Or was it just a plot to make sure he never had to look after the dog again? Have a guess.

A simpler method

Sonia used to ask her partner, Steve, to take the dogs for a walkie, while she was at work. But after a few days of this, she noticed that neighbours were glaring at her, and she'd come home and find crosspatch notices on her car saying 'Please pick up your bloody dogs' shit.'

Steve couldn't be fagged to pick up dog poo, so he left it lying about. But these were Sonia's dogs. The whole neighbourhood knew they were, they knew her address and they knew her car, so she got the blame. As with children, it's usually the mother who gets the blame. So that was the last time she asked Steve to walk the dogs. Clever chap.

Leaving your dog

When I grew up and wanted my own dog, my mother used to warn me. 'You'll never be able to go on holiday.' This isn't quite true. You can go on holiday if you have a dog, but your holiday won't be a real holiday, because you won't be able to relax. It's nothing like as bad as losing your dog, but a sort of half loss. How could you possibly have a carefree time, knowing that your dog is possibly suffering in kennels or at home? It's like leaving your mother in a care home or your little child with harsh relatives.

You can make all the preparation you like, but the person left in charge is not you. He or she may not love your dog as much as you do, or understand it as well, or feed it exactly right, or be as kind to it on its walkies, or let it sit next to them on the sofa. They will not put your dog first, as you do. They'll probably think your dog is pampered and spoilt, that you don't know how to bring a dog up, and then they'll subject it to their own comparatively brutish regime, and when you get home you will have a changed, or at least a resentful and sulking dog. I picked my dog up from a kennels and she just looked away from me. It wasn't a real kennels, but the home in which she'd been born, and where many of her relatives still lived, and every morning they all went out on a fun walkie to the fields behind the house to chase rabbits. More a holiday camp than a kennels. And she was loved and adored and slept on sofas. But she still looked snootily out of the car window all the way home, kept looking the other way when she got home, wouldn't play with her friends in the park and just trudged along looking straight ahead for a whole week. At least she survived and eventually returned to normal after her extended sulk. But will your dog even survive? Will it be alive when you get home?

I had left her once before, aged one year, to go to Center Parcs with my daughter, two friends and their children. Only for a weekend. I left a relay of people in charge. Naturally I planned to ring the relevant person morning and night to check on Daisy's welfare, but on the evening of my first night away, when my holiday had hardly begun, I remembered that I had left my daughter's toy farm animals on the living room coffee table. Help! The dog was bound to eat one, try and swallow it, it would stick in its throat, the darling baby dog would choke to death, so the minute I thought of it, I rang the dog-sitter on that shift. No answer. Where was she? I left messages. Still no response.

My holiday was ruined. I spent a sleepless, tormented night, weeping and worrying, woke at dawn and at last got hold of the minder. Was the dog still alive? Yes. Had she received my messages? Yes. Had she put the dangerous farm animals away safely? NO. They were still on the table within easy reach of the dog. What a fool and she couldn't go back and tidy them away, because she was stuck at work. The dog was at risk until the arrival of the next dog-sitter, due at lunch-time.

The dog lived. But what an ordeal. However don't let me put you off a dog or your holidays. Who knows, you may have an obliging partner, child, relative to take over the dog care. Or your dog may be more independent and carefree. Or you may be less of a worrier. Please get yourself a dog anyway.

Stolen dogs

Nicola Barlow suffered the worst sort of loss. She was at work one day when her friend phoned up with shocking news. She'd just driven past Nicola's house, she said, noticed that the front door was wide open, Nicola's car wasn't there, something must have been wrong, so in she went, and straightway noticed that Nicola's English Bull Terrier, Alfie, was missing!

'He was very, very handsome,' says Nicola, 'tan and white, a full male.' Just the sort of dog those bad boys in the park like to steal. 'We knew he'd been stolen because his collar and lead were gone. I never stopped looking for him for years, I went out searching. I made posters, saying, "If he's happy I won't ask for him back. Just let me know that he's well." It made me ill. I couldn't stop thinking about him. I have four stepchildren. They were all devastated. Our friends came out with us looking for him, we tried all the dogs' homes, all the vets. After nearly four years I went to Crufts and saw the Dog Theft Action stall. I went over and started telling them all about Alfie and started crying. A bit embarrassing isn't it? And then a month later they found him for me. HOW? Four years and twelve days after he'd been stolen.

'We live in Tamworth, Staffordshire, but Alfie was found in High Wycombe. He was very thin and under-weight, filthy dirty. We took him to the vet and found that he'd damaged his neck, probably by repeatedly running to the end of his chain and jerking it. We could tell he'd been chained up, because the fur on his neck was all worn away and the dirt was impacted in his ear, which showed he'd been kept outside for a long time.'

Probably he'd been used as a stud dog, and then just left in a yard. 'He was four when they stole him, and eight when we found him again. We had two lovely years with him after we got him back. And he died lying on the rug in our living room in front of our fire.

Once we'd found him, I decided to help Dog Theft Action, because what goes around comes around, doesn't it?

9: Food and Cooking

Many visitors object to my dogs begging for food at the table while we are eating a meal. Usually I forbid the dogs to do this, because I like a quiet life and can't be fagged to argue and explain to visitors the real reason for my dogs' behaviour. They are not just greedy and spoilt. They are working. Boxers, like many other dogs, originally had a specific work skill. In eighteenth-century Germany, Boxers herded cattle. They were also used in the darker areas of German Dog World for bull and boar baiting, and called Bullenbeissers. But apart from these specialised areas, a dog is an animal and in the natural world would work for its dinner, i. e. go hunting or scavenging.

That is what my dogs are doing at table. They have cleverly adapted to the modern world and are scavenging/hunting for food. Naturally they will go on and on doing so, even if they seem to us to be overdoing it, because their wild, natural selves are telling them that they must make the most of every opportunity. They don't know what's going to come along next. It could be famine or a row of tame chickens, or a human with a bowl of dinner, so they have to stock up. If they see food available, they must do their best to eat it.

To fit in with modern conditions and their current role as household pet, in which there isn't much of a hunting opportunity, they have perfected their scavenging technique. They have learned to sit patiently, looking as appealing and desperate as they can, while humans are eating. It has worked very well for centuries – they guard us, we feed them – and so they continue to do it, sometimes crying and dribbling to intensify the effect.

Convenience or home cooking?

Of course all this begging is in addition to their normal meals. They have two meals a day: breakfast and dinner, and naturally, I worry over them. Am I giving them suitable meals? Do they like them? It seems to me that their dinners are perhaps a bit samey. Perhaps they would like more variety. After all, what do they like most in life? Walkies and food. The walkies are already a bit of a struggle. At least the meals could be fun. And I've also noticed that the dried food doesn't seem to be doing their colitis much good. They still have it, usually in turn. If one dog isn't eating grass, vomiting or having holiday tummy, then the other is. So one day I asked Alistair the dog acupuncturist what he thought of dried dog food.

'How would you feel,' he asked, 'if the person in

charge of your dinners said to you, "Here is some human food. You are always going to get it in dried pellet form?"'

What a ghastly thought. If one of my main pleasures in life was eating – it is – then I would be browned off having to eat pellets, pellets and more pellets. I already had my suspicions about these pellets. The dogs weren't all that keen on them unless I perked them up with a little sprinkling of chicken or wet dog food or gravy, and even then the dinners still looked fairly dull. And crunchy, which was difficult for Lily, with her under-shot jaw and teeth that didn't meet very well or crunch effectively.

I had also noticed that if you soak the pellets, they turn into something like wet cement, which is frightfully heavy. I know this because I have often had to shovel up piles of it that the poor dogs had sicked up. And more terrifying still, I had picked up chilling anecdotes on my walkies about dogs who had unwisely galloped about with a stomach full of this food-cement and ended up with a twisted gut, horrible pain and of course another wallet-emptying visit to the vet.

Of course this is only hearsay, and if you took notice off all the scary stories you heard on dog walkies you'd be a gibbering nervous wreck in no time, but now the dog acupuncturist had given his verdict, that was it. I changed to home cooking. Of course it takes ages: boiling chicken, taking all the bones out and the skin and fat off, cooking the pasta, rice and vegetables, mixing it all up, when I could have just tossed a few handfuls of pellets into a bowl in seconds, and millions of people do, with no apparent bad effects on their dogs. But remember, my dogs are especially delicate and prone to colitis.

I don't care if people mock. I reckon it balances out: more time cooking, less time shovelling up sick and other stuff, which I won't go into.

Hand-feeding regime?

Hand-feeding was terrifically important at dog camp. It was the mainstay of Dima Yeremenko's method. This is how it worked. The dogs rarely, probably never, had a lovely big bowl of juicy dinner. Their dinners (usual dry food) were measured out and given to the dog by hand in small bits when, and only when, they were well-behaved. If the dog wanted its dinner, it had to do as it was told. The dogs did as they were told. But I had big problems with this method, because of my dogs' delicate stomachs and complex dietary requirements. I've already explained my concerns about dry pellet food, and on top of being dull, dull, dull, it also seemed to give them the squitters. They could not have too much protein. They needed lots of carbohydrates, and of course they much preferred their home-cooked dinners with gravy, and so did I, because the acupuncturist and the vet had recommended it, and that way I could be sure the meals were suited to their every need. And of course my cooking was delicious. They had their home-made dog chicken soup everyday, with sometimes a sprinkling of Pro-Soluble if their bowels were out of order.

How could I feed this by hand? How could I even make it on my camping cooker? I'd taken cooked supplies with me, but only for the first day and a half, then it would have to be tinned food and mixer and fingers crossed. But I had, as a token gesture towards the hand-feeding regime, brought some dried food. My plan was to do some dried food feeding as a pre-breakfast snack for my babies, then they could take part in the training, then go back and have their proper breakfast, and hopefully their digestive systems would cope.

So that's what I did. I reckoned that that way I could keep the luxury Jewish-mother dog-dinners low profile, and protect my dogs from this harsh regime, but still manage the hand-feeding training sessions. It worked on the first night. Phew.

I tried it the next morning. Hand-feeding session with dry food, then back to the tent for proper dog breakfast, but then a horrid surprise. There was to be another training session, almost straight away. 'Obedience workshop with Fran and Jennie.' But I was already knackered and Lily and Violet were full of breakfast. Dreary old dry snacks were the last thing they fancied. They would never behave like Fran's and Jennie's dogs: almost glued to their thighs, heads up eagerly looking at their owner, awaiting the next instruction. But did I really want that? No. I just wanted Violet not to pull and pounce. That was the sum of my aims. But I still had to attend the obedience workshop, and run round in a circle with Violet, and surprisingly she ran obediently to heel. Even without a crumb of tempting food. Why? Was she a) intimidated by the crowd of onlookers? b) By the presence of Fran, Jennie and DY? Or c) could it be my own brilliant dog-handling? Let's go for C.

Then another hand-feeding and training session. But we bunked off. That would be four in one day, and we were training-sessioned-out. We hid in our tent having pasta for me and gravy dinners for the girls. And then it was barbecue time. I admit that I am inconsistent and probably confuse my dogs, and dogs like to know who's in charge and what they're meant to be doing. Must try much harder.

Dog recipes

Some people don't use treats at all. As Barry the Dog Jogger said, his dogs follow him because they want to. He never bribes them with treats. But for those of us whose dogs occasionally don't want to follow us at all, treats come in handy, particularly, I have found, liver cake, so here are some recipes to help anyone who needs a bit of assistance with their recall.

Liver cake

Approx. 375g of liver, 2 eggs and 2-4 cloves garlic.

Whiz the above in a food processor – add 1 cup of self-raising flour. Spread out thinly on a lightly greased large baking sheet. Bake for 20-30 minutes in a moderate oven. Cool and chop. Freezes well.

Dave's dog birthday cake

Ingredients: minced beef, rice, steak. Vary the quantities to suit your dog.

Cook mince meat, mix with cooked rice. Press down into pudding basin, leave in fridge for a while to cool and solidify.

Cut steak into thin strips.

Take rice mixture out of fridge, turn out upsided-own onto plastic plate, decorate with strips of steak, meeting at a point at top of cake, so that every party-goer gets a strip.

Serve.

Mick's tasty treat

Boil liver (preferably lamb or chicken) for five minutes. (Be prepared. It stinks the house out.)

Cut into slices.

Dry in oven for hours. Take out. Add a dash of fish sauce for added smell and flavour.

Add small chunks of chicken. Freeze.

Jane's liver and garlic flapjacks

(for dogs allergic to wheat)

1lb liver
1 ½ lb porridge oats
2 tspns garlic paste
2 eggs

Put oats into large mixing bowl. Whiz liver in food processor until it looks like thick blood, add to oats, eggs and garlic paste, stir. It should be like sloppy porridge. Line a baking tray with baking parchment, pour mixture onto lined tray. It should be about an inch thick. Bake at 110 degrees for about 20 minutes.

We love Miniature Schnauzers

Jane often makes these divine flapjacks for Maisie, a Schnauzer who loves her nosh. She'll eat anything, even dead fish on Littlehampton beach. And she spins when it's tea-time – round and round at 4.30 to 5 p.m. Maisie has a lovely haircut, styled by Jane. 'As she's a girl Schnauzie, I thought she should have a girl's haircut, but they would only do the boy's – with eyebrows and beard. It didn't look right, so I cut it myself. She's very pretty, but she's not just a pretty face. She's small but not yappy. She has a wazzy bark, because she's a tiny dog who doesn't know she's a tiny dog. She thinks she's a Doberman. She's not frightened of anything.

'She doesn't need a walk every day. If I'm ill and not up to it, she doesn't nag and make a fuss. She's happy just to go round the block. She's a bit lazy, doesn't pull on the lead, loves going to the pub. They give her her own water and she lies in the hearth for hours, and she sits with me while I go fishing, for two and a half hours.

'You can cuddle her, she'll lie in your arms, she's very stubborn, but I love it – she's got so much character. She carries the biggest stick. If she's not very well, she's an absolute angel. She taps on the door till it opens (it will if you tap it enough), she'll have her 'mistakes' on the lino. She stays on her black towel when she comes in if it's been raining and she'll give me all her feet in turn to dry. She never runs away, always comes back and doesn't really have a typical terrier temperament. She's kinder, calmer, easier to train. Good-natured, undemanding, calm in the house, feisty and up for some fun outside.' Perfect.

My need to cook dog food

There is another benefit to cooking for dogs. It fulfils a need. Well it does for me. A few years ago I expelled my partner from the house. He had failed dismally to live up to expectations. Soon after that, my mother died, aged 98. I suspect she may have been clinging onto life because she didn't want to go until she was sure I'd got rid of him. I did, and she died a happier woman, free of anxiety. Well at least that bit of anxiety. Then my daughter went travelling the world for months on end. I had no one left to look after, hardly any shopping or cooking to do, nothing to rush back home for. I was free at last, but it felt rather odd. After all those years, it is difficult to kick the habit. I love staying at home in the evenings, but I no longer had an excuse: 'I can't leave my poorly old mother.' And I still longed to wander the supermarket and cram my trolley with delicacies, bargains and three-for-two of anything going, but what for? Just me?

So thank heavens for the dogs. They saved my bacon. They couldn't be left alone for long, they needed tons of food, and they had health problems, usually in turn. If one didn't have the runs, the other did, so they needed their delicate, home-cooked diet (or a colossally expensive special health diet from the vet), so naturally I decided on home dog-cooking, which does have its problems, because you may find that other people know better than you and like to tell you what you're doing wrong: no potatoes, says one, or wheat, or even rice, or porridge, so you have to decided who you're going to listen to.

'Oh no wheat!' says Phillipa. 'Dogs can't have wheat!'

'And no rice!' says Sonia, horrified. 'Amira's on a raw food diet. I get it delivered. It's only what humans can eat. But no rice or wheat. Carbohydrates are bad for dogs.'

'Not too much protein,' says the vet. 'Food high in carbohydrates for dogs with colitis.' I've gone with the vet. But despite all the worry, decision-making and extra hours at the cooker and sink, it has been worth it. Because once again I've had something to flap over, rush home for, cook for, argue about, stay in for, shop for and spend a fortune on. Soon I was bankrupt, anxious, worn out and happy again.

Herbie the squirrel eater

Whatever you feed some dogs, it will never be enough. Herbie the Working Cocker Spaniel is one such dog. He was out on a walkie with his owner Maureen, when he suddenly came out of a wood and appeared before her with a dead squirrel hanging out of his mouth, with its big, fluffy tail dangling. Maureen got a frightful shock. Perhaps he hadn't killed it, she hoped. Perhaps it was dead already, or poorly. But Herbie was thrilled with his squirrel. He wanted to hang onto it, so he ran away from Maureen and hid behind a tree.

'Come on Herbie, drop it,' said Maureen strictly, but Herbie defied her. Then along came a smartly dressed woman, spotted Herbie and the dangling squirrel and screamed. 'That is absolutely disgraceful!!'

'Try telling him that,' said Maureen, who may have looked calm, but was feeling frightfully agitated. Along came another woman. 'Jolly good,' she said, looking at Herbie and his squirrel. 'There are far too many of those damn things about.'

Both the women strode off, but poor Maureen was too embarrassed to carry on walking, because if she had, Herbie would have followed her with the squirrel in his mouth for everyone to see, and no doubt she'd have come in for more criticism. 'So I had to hang about, looking casual,' she says, 'as if I didn't have a dog with me, and was just looking at the trees and birds. It was a real dilemma. When the coast was clear I shouted, "Drop it, drop it!" again, but he took no notice, he just stayed behind the tree and ate it. Every bit of it. Then when he'd finished he followed me to the car, sat next to me in the front, and I kept looking at him and thinking, Inside that dog is a squirrel. I was mortified.'

Herbie would often run away from smaller parks. He'd get bored if Maureen was chatting to other dog walkers and he'd go cruising around looking for takeaways – there are always plenty scattered around – he once got into a high bin and found an almost whole Easter cake, with icing and marzipan eggs on it. 'It looked as if someone had bought it, tasted it, not liked and chucked it. I couldn't stop him. He ate the whole cake. I think I'll let him have a bit, then I shout to stop him, he takes no notice, he ate it all. I'm like a really bad mother, sounding cross and not actually doing anything.' Herbie would disappear for ages, but he always managed to get home somehow, and sit outside barking. 'But he was never sick. He just used to fart a lot.'

But outdoors or indoors, Herbie was always on the lookout for a snack opportunity, and one day, luckily for him, Maureen had left a whole ham in the middle of the kitchen table, ready for a family lunch, beautifully baked, stuck with cloves, mustard and demerara sugar, and wrapped in foil. For a few foolish moments, Maureen and her family were all in the hallway chatting. 'We went back into the kitchen and Herbie had the ham behind the telly. He'd got the tinfoil off and was tearing at it.' But poor Maureen couldn't get behind the telly, so she got a broom and whacked it all around Herbie – not hitting him of course, just the floor next to him, and tried to poke the ham away from him, shouting 'You

bastard, you bastard!' but Herbie just growled protectively and went on eating it, ripping at it ferociously.
'And it cost about sixteen pounds! We were just distracted
briefly, and he had it, and he'd shredded it, so it wasn't
really worth rescuing.' She still loves Herbie.

Why Spaniels?

Why? 'Because he's so amusing, cosy, podgy and cuddly,
but he's so disobedient, which stops it feeling too soppy.
Pam in the park has another Spaniel called Wendy. I
once gave them a lift home in the car, because it was cold
and rainy. Now whenever Wendy sees me, she stares at
me, wanting a lift. She lies down flat on the floor and
won't move. None of the other dogs do things like that.
It's classic Spaniel. Enthusiastic, a bit barmy, great character. And oh my God, Herbie is so handsome, he really
is. Pam calls him College Boy, because he has that fringe
over his eyes. You could part it, which made him look
very sophisticated and dignified. How you can call him
dignified, I don't know, but he was, if you didn't know
him. He wasn't remotely aggressive, not an ounce of
aggression in him, but he did bark and bark and bark
when he got outdoors. Some woman said to Pam, "That
damn black dog. I'm going to throw a bucket of water
over him." But it was just the initial excitement. He
stopped eventually.'

10: Dog Health

There is one particularly horrible thing about having a sick dog. It can't tell you what the problem is or describe how it feels. Sometimes the problem may be evident. Your dog will vomit or have a horribly obvious bowel disorder, but it can't explain anything less obvious. It can only look heartbreakingly glum, or cry, or lie on the ground shaking with pain, or refuse to eat or drink. It may hold an injured foot up, but what bit of the foot is injured? Is it a sprain? A hidden thorn? A pulled muscle? A fracture? Is it pretending or exaggerating because it knows that if it holds its paw in the air and cries it may get an extra biscuit, like it did last time? You don't know. And you won't know until you take it to the vet.

And that's the next horrible thing. Vet's fees. Especially if one has a pedigree dog prone to certain illnesses. Boxers (substitute here the breed of your particular dog) are prone to cancer, tumours, heart disease, eye ulcers, and colitis. In fact I find that whenever my dogs have an illness, the vet or someone or other will be bound to say, 'This sort of dog is prone to that.'

Whatever it is you can bet your life 'Boxers/chosen breed are prone to that'. Most prone to stomach upsets, from drinking dirty water in puddles, ponds and gutters, or eating some form of excrement (Boxers are prone to that – they don't mind which sort, anything will do, particularly fox, which smells the strongest and clings the longest), or a bit of left-behind picnic or chicken bone, or curry, or once some rotting mussels (found in a local park). That upsets their stomachs, and then, because Boxers never do anything by halves, it will turn serious, the dog will start passing slime and blood, and will have to be taken to the vet.

Mr Greedy, the vet

I have visited numerous vets. Some are worse than others. But a few years ago my friend Hannah found the worst one. Her dog Bonzo's stomach had gone haywire for the nth time. It was gurgling away like a main sewer and heaven knows what was swilling around in there. The vet rang with some test results and told Hannah that she should go and collect some antibiotics. She didn't need an appointment, she'd already had the consultation, all she needed to do was collect a second lot of the pills. She rushed to the surgery, and sure enough, the pills were waiting at reception.

Twenty pills for the dog – *EIGHTY-FIVE POUNDS!!* Hannah's jaw dropped open and stayed there. She had a little shout, clung to the counter for support and asked for an explanation.

'Your dog is a big dog (a Ridgeback), it needs double the quantity, and these pills are very expensive,' explained the receptionist politely. She was spot on. Those pills were very expensive. But Hannah was insured, so who cares? I'll tell you who cares. Not the insurers. They'll just put up my premium, together with the premiums of all their other clients, and so you and thousands of other dog-owners will care. It was March. This dog had cost Hannah one thousand pounds since Christmas. She could have bought or rescued several new ones instead, but of course she loved her dog. If she had to bankrupt herself to save his life, then she would do so.

But when people have a shock like that, or feel that there's something not quite fair going on, they tend to tell everyone they meet all about it, to let it all out, which is what Hannah did.

'Which vet do you go to?' the people ask. So Hannah told them. Many, who knew that vet, screamed with laughter. Others almost cried, recognising the experience. Hannah was in the supermarket doing her shopping one day, when she bumped into a couple who she used to meet a few years ago on her walkies, so she told them about the robber vet. At once they knew exactly who the vet was, even before she told them, and became very distressed, because they'd been there too.

'We took Molly in,' they said, as the chap's eyes filled

with tears. 'And we couldn't get her out again.' They took her in with one problem, then the vet found another ailment, then another until they felt they'd never be able to rescue Molly from the vet's clutches. Even the tiniest ailment ended up costing them half the Royal Mint. What was going on?

Hannah thought she ought to find out, so she rang the maker of the antibiotics. How much do they sell them for? 'We do not answer this sort of query,' said the spokeslady. But why not? This made Hannah even more curious. Something tremendously naughty must be going on if the price of doggie pills was a secret.

But for once she was in luck. She was chatting in the park about the price of dog pills, and discovered that our friend Dave's father was a professor of pharmacology. Dave owns a rescue German Shepherd/Lurcher mix and makes my dogs' birthday cakes. His father looked up the antibiotic prices for Hannah in the *British National Formulary*. And *quelle surprise*! Twenty of a similar human version of these pills cost £6.79! A generic brand costs £2.09! Chemists charge about three times the price. Let's not quibble about people making a living, but Hannah always thought three times £6.79 made £20.37. And there are even cheaper remedies available. So why eighty-five pounds?

Then Hannah's friend Audrey rang excitedly, because naturally Hannah had told her all about the vet's staggeringly overpriced pills. 'Quick!' she shouted. 'It's on the radio. Vets are overcharging for medicines!' What's more, those vets always fail to mention that you can have a prescription, then buy dog drugs for a more modest price at the veterinary chemists, *if the chemists can get them*. Because veterinary suppliers aren't keen on supplying chemists. At the time of writing this I heard that our Government had just promised to stop this racket in a few months. We are still waiting to hear of vets cheerily and voluntarily handing out prescriptions. With the exception of my own darling vet, whose charges are so reasonable, that I don't even want, or need, a prescription.

Luckily, lots of vets are not robbers, and I would trust mine with my own body on the operating table. But however reasonable your vet, a poorly dog can cost you thousands. Which means insurance, which can also cost you thousands.

Mr Even-Greedier, the insurer

Over the last couple of decades, since I have had dogs, insurance costs have rocketed, and as your dog grows older, the insurance costs rocket off into the stratosphere, because if there's one thing an insurance company knows, it's that another insurance company will not take on an elderly dog because it is very likely to be seriously poorly, and the older your dog gets, the more of a pariah you will become, as far as insurance companies are concerned, unless you are prepared to shower them in money. Which means that your insurance company knows you're struck with them, and they can raise your premium as high as they like, because you have nowhere else to go.

You can, of course, choose to have no insurance at all, but it's odds on that once uninsured a dog is bound to develop a vicious disease costing thousands in vet's fees and medicines.

When my insurance reached the size of a rajah's ransom, I asked the vet what I should do. 'Don't bother,' said she. 'Just try and put some money aside every week in a separate dog insurance account.' Good idea. I cancelled my insurance policy.

Then guess what? A couple of weeks later, the dog grew two tumours. Bad luck, but her operations cost less than half the insurance, so I was still quids in. Ha ha.

Swanky dog hospital

No wonder dog insurance and treatment costs a fortune. A modern dog hospital can be a very swanky place. Violet had been to this dog hospital when she was only one. My friend Jennifer and I left her there to have a monster leg operation: metal plates were put in her ankle and foot; bone sliced off her shoulder and stuck across her ankle. I blubbed all the way home. Would she live? Would she ever bounce around again?

Yes she lived, yes she would rush about, but only after six weeks in plaster, months of short walkies, then back for the same palaver for the other leg: cost about £2, 500 per leg and what luck that I had dog insurance.

The next night the nurse on dog ward rang with an update: Violet had her own bed, central heating, radio on, nurses day and night, eight dogs on the ward, plenty of diversion and personalised diet. And Dog Hospital was super-clean and swanky. Even her grubby old lead was rejected and the patient led away in a germ-free new one. And the waiting list was only one week. Beats the NHS.

I rang my daughter, who was in Australia at the time, with the details. We were thrilled to bits with Violet's progress. But other people were sickened.

'I know what I'd do,' said Whitwham, getting rather hot under the collar. 'A bullet through the skull. You could have bought ten new dogs for that money.' This is the trouble with having a sick dog. People without dogs tend to mock and disapprove, especially if they're acquainted with nine-mile waiting lists, galloping MRSA, crappy hospital dinners, exhausted and underpaid staff, and general filth.

I went out to dinner to take my mind off bone grafts, but there were more jokes at table. 'Are the nurses dogs? In uniform? Do they wear little hats? Which radio station?' Olivia's critique was the most harsh. 'Wouldn't it be kinder to put her down?' she asks with a steely look.

'There's nothing like a nice mongrel. That's the next one for you I hope. Forget your horrible dog fetishism with Boxers,' she banged on. 'It's just conspicuous consumption. And now you're throwing money at it. Like people in olden times who had very long fingernails to show they didn't have to work.'

The bitch. I took absolutely no notice and when darling Violet got home, I planned to sleep downstairs on a mattress next to the poor little crippled creature for six weeks. Mad or what? I don't care.

While Violet was in hospital, the house was very odd without her. My other dog Lily was twelve. She slept most of the time. She didn't seem to miss Violet, and just snoozed all day and seemed very chilled out. But what would life be like without Violet? She was the perky one. She's up first, she's hungriest and thirstiest, she plays with her squeaky duck more, she rests her darling velvety chin on my wrists to stop me practising the piano, and I thought it was a nuisance, but now I wanted the velvety chin back. She could rest it on my wrists for as long as she wanted. Boo hoo. What if Violet wasn't here when my daughter eventually came home? Unbearable. I couldn't help thinking of her running about in her carefree days of good health, galloping round in the long grass like a mad lamb. Violet was a white Boxer. Suddenly her funny way of running was tremendously endearing. Would she ever do it again? How do you stop a Boxer with bad legs from jumping about?

But Violet was doing very well in hospital. She had to stay for five days. Phew. Things were looking up for her, but down for Lily. I notice that she'd lost her appetite during Violet's absence. She had a little taste of dinner and then lay down again. She was much glummer than usual. Could she be missing Violet? I bet she was. Poor Lily was eating less and less. Would she last the five days?

Dog nurse

It is not easy nursing a dog. When she returned from dog hospital Violet had a postoperative Frankenstein leg that would not bend properly. It was full of metal and stitch marks. It was rather a sweat living in a three-story house with a four-stone crippled dog which had to be carried up and down stairs. Lily had perked up since Violet's return, kissed her repeatedly the minute she got home, started eating like a horse again, and wanted to play with the cripple.

'Keep it calm,' the dog surgeon had ordered, 'and take it for gentle walks.' Oh ha ha. How was I to do that? How about some sedatives? Not allowed. How was I to clear the neighbourhood of all cats, squirrels, frogs, dogs, birds, bees, joggers, window cleaners or any other dog-stimulants?

What an exhausting carry-on this dog nursing was, both physically and mentally. I had to sleep on the floor in a sort of dog nest, on night watch in case the sick dog had a chew at her injuries. On the first morning after Violet's return, the dogs squabbled over their chewies and squeaky chicken, threw their toys out of bed and cried in a heart-rending way for Marmite on toast. And what a performance it was to get them to kip in unison: first wear them out with a walkie for the cripple, then a walkie for the healthy dog, then breakfast, then more play-squabbling and diddling, and then you could bet your life that the minute they both lay down and I lifted my pen, the postman or the canvassers or the pizza leaflet people would pop something through the letter-box, or ring the bell, and it would be wakey, wakey, bark, bark all over again. I barely had a life.

Next day there were no leaflets, but a large fly zoomed in and got the dogs jumping. At every jump or pounce I feared the metal leg would crack again. It's much worse than having a sick child. At least you can tell a child why it mustn't jump about, and tell it that one day its leg will get better, but I couldn't explain anything to poor Violet. I could only hope and pray that no surprise squirrels came along and that the leg didn't crack again.

'I have never known a time when there wasn't something wrong with one of your dogs,' said Whitwham harshly. 'They're either under surgery or attacking something.'

He was exaggerating like mad. Probably because he's a writer. That is the trouble with writers. They tend to exaggerate. Being a journalist and writer myself, I tend to do it, and highlight the ghastly episodes. You have to. There's nothing interesting about perfectly behaved, healthy dogs. And that's what my dogs are, a lot of the time. These are just the highlights. Anyway, that morning, as well as the fly, a note arrived from a reader of a newspaper in which I write, begging me to write about something pleasant. My mother (whom I often used to write about when she was alive) would never have moaned so much wrote this lady strictly. 'She had character.'

So here is a short paragraph on the pleasant side of our lives, to show that however ghastly the difficult times and the nursing periods are, it is all worth it. Because every morning I wake to see two divinely beautiful creatures beside me. They never sulk, they always finish their dinners, their range of vowel sounds is so extensive that one day, I swear, they will speak to me, and the crippled dog will gallop over the Heath again. Aaah. Happy days.

Hector's mystery bad back

Andrew has a Golden Retriever called Hector. Hector was all right on their morning walkie, he ate his breakfast normally, then suddenly he was standing in the hall by the front door crying. What for? Had he a tummy ache? His tummy seemed a bit tense. Perhaps he wanted to go out for another poo, and would prefer not to do it in the back garden.

But then there was a sudden mouse alert. Sylvia, the older dog, had spotted one in the garden. Out she went like a bomb, and Hector followed, forgetting what was wrong with him for a moment and pouncing among the flowerpots. Then a sudden ghastly scream and Hector came back in, cringing and trembling.

Whatever could it be? He tried to lie down. Another dreadful scream. Andrew asked him what was the matter, but of course he couldn't say. Was something jabbing into his stomach? Had he swallowed a stick or bone? Andrew took Hector round the block. He seemed fine, he did another poo, but when he got home he started crying again. He tried to lie down, screamed with pain again, and then seemed so frightened of lying down that he stayed standing, crying again. He stood crying for most of the afternoon. He ate his dinner, he cried, all evening and all night. Andrew could just manage, very carefully, to get him onto the sofa to lie on his side. For a couple of hours, then he was up again crying until morning.

Off they went to the vet at dawn. It was his back. 'It could be a muscle spasm,' said the vet, 'or a slipped disc.'

Help. Poor Hector. He was given morphine and anti-inflammatories and sent home. Made no difference. He cried all day. It is terrible to watch a dog crying. His eyes kept closing and his legs kept sagging

and giving way from exhaustion, but he still wouldn't
let himself lie down. Even on the sofa. Back to the vet,
for methadone and tramadol. That should knock him
out. It didn't. Hector cried all the way through another
night. He had now been crying for more or less two
whole days and nights, sagging, and then jerking up
again. Torture for everyone. Even the morphine and
valium had failed to knock him out, so it was back to
the vet again in the morning, but they could do nothing
more. They'd tried everything they had. They hadn't
the equipment for the next stage. Hector must go to the
dog hospital, which meant that poor Andrew had to
drive him up the ghastly M1 and he'd had barely a
moment's sleep. More anxiety, because what if he were
to fall asleep at the wheel and crash? But Hector needed
an X-ray and MRI scan, and possible spine operation.
They didn't do spine operations at Andrew's vet.
Andrew doesn't believe in God, but he did thank him
on that occasion, for Hector's pet insurance. 'What if
someone has no insurance?' he asked the vet.

'Then they have a very difficult decision to make.'

Off they went, Hector crying non-stop in the back of the
car, huge traffic jams at Henlys corner, then they got lost in
Luton, both cried, Andrew prayed again, more thanks for
the insurance, and another prayer that they might both get
to the hospital to use the insurance. They were both in a
terrible state, Hector exhausted and whimpering, Andrew
exhausted and panicking, but they got there.

The vet examined Hector. 'It could be an infection, or a slipped disc,' said he, 'or a tumour.'

A tumour! On his spine! Andrew's blood ran cold. And there was he thinking a slipped disc was almost the end of the world. Now he knew there was a far worse possibility, and was hoping for *ONLY* a slipped disc.

He left Hector in hospital and drove home blubbing.

'When my father had a slipped disc,' his neighbour told him, 'he had to lay motionless and encased in plaster for months.'

Bloody hell! thought Andrew. How can you do that to a dog? But the neighbour's father's disc slipped in the Fifties. Hopefully methods had improved since then. Another bad night for Andrew. But in the morning the vet rang from hospital. A miracle. It wasn't a tumour, it was a slipped disc, and Hector was much better. He could lie down, and he hadn't even had any painkillers since he got there. The darling vet would keep an eye on him over the weekend, and then see how he was on Monday morning. But how could that be? Had the disc gone back into place? The vet couldn't say. Andrew had to wait till Monday.

Monday dawned. At last he could bring Hector home. He had mysteriously recovered. No one quite knew how. Perhaps the anaesthetic he had for his scan and X-ray knocked him out, allowed his back a bit of a rest, and when he woke up, he'd forgotten that he had a lying-down problem. It wasn't the slipped disc, says the vet. A disc can apparently stay slipped and not bother the dog. Hector was better, he might stay better. He might not. What was it all about? Nobody really knew. Hector was suddenly in terrible pain and then wasn't. A mystery, despite the scan, X-ray, consultation and five days in dog hospital. Which all cost £2000.

Plague of fleas

Tom has two Lurchers: Helen, who is smooth-haired and a pale sandy colour, and Eric, who is a bit fluffier and nearly black. One day some suspicious little black dots appeared around Helen's bottom, which he realised, with a sinking heart, was flea poo. Or really dried dog's blood, excreted by fleas, the vet explained. And perhaps Eric had them too. His coat looked rather dull and dandruffy, but as he was dark, it was more difficult to spot the dots. Annoyingly Tom had run out of anti-flea medication. So it was off to the vet again. It wasn't his usual favourite lady vet, who was sympathetic, knows his dogs personally and thinks them especially charming. This vet was rather stern. He examined Eric's bottom.

'This one is riddled with them,' said he. Tom felt like a neglectful parent, with whom Social Services have finally caught up. And it was 'Eric', not 'This One', but the vet didn't really care about that. Tom was told to not only treat the dogs, but to spray his whole house, said Mr

Vet. 'By the time you've finished I want this whole can to be finished.' The can was enormous.

Why so many fleas all of a sudden? The unusually warm October weather had apparently brought them out. Tom took his poor dogs home. He applied Frontline. It comes in little plastic vials which he had to squirt onto the back of their necks. But the fleas wouldn't all go straight away, the vet had warned him. They should be gone by Sunday. It was Friday. On Saturday Tom stroked Eric's tummy. He'd been standing close to Tom looking rather dejected. His tummy felt rather scabby, so Tom made Eric lie down and had a look. Horrors!! The tummy was covered with a writhing mass of fleas!!! Now Tom knew what 'riddled' meant. He'd never seen anything like this before. Yes, the odd few fleas, but not a whole swarming ants-nest-type mass of them. Poor Eric. And Tom had thought that Eric's recent odd jumping and scuttling movements, with collapsing legs, was old age and arthritis. No. It was the ghastly fleas, which must have been driving him mad for weeks.

Help! Tom felt even more neglectful. How could he not have noticed? He checked Helen as well. She too had a swarming stomach full of fleas. The little bastards. What was he to do? Surely the fleas should have been dying off by now. And it was Saturday night, all vets were shut. Why do emergencies always happen on a Saturday night? But Tom did have some medicated shampoo. So he washed the poor dogs' bottom/stomach areas, which surely couldn't interfere with the Frontline on their shoulders. Crowds of fleas were drowned. And Tom's own head was tickling and itching. Did he have the fleas? Were fleas host-specific? Was he just neurotic? He washed his own hair in nit shampoo. He hoovered the whole house, threw away the old hoover bag and sprayed flea-killer inside the new one, as he'd been told, to murder the fleas on their way in. He washed all dog bedding, and all his sheets and towels, and every garment recently used, at 90 degrees. He sprayed the whole house, but only halfway through he'd already used one whole giant can of stinking poisonous spray. What could it be doing to their lungs and general health? He started on the second one, locked the killer spray into each room separately, then opened all doors and windows and aired them. This took the whole weekend. Completely knackered, Tom returned to the vet on Monday, because three days had passed and the poor dogs were still crawling with fleas.

Luckily it was the darling lady vet who knew him very well. She sprayed the dogs with more killer spray – the instant sort which they use on stray cats – and as she sprayed the bottom end of Eric, fleas started popping out of his head, clearly visible against the pale fur and anxious to escape the hostile area of the rest of his body. What a nightmare these fleas were. And then Tom went home and realised he hadn't fumigated the basement. It was probably clogged with desperate fleas escaping the upper floors. More spraying of poison, and at last, by Tuesday, the fleas seemed to have disappeared.

Five days of hell. Tom felt dizzy, he had probably poisoned himself and his dogs, but at least his home was clean and no longer pestilential. Tom's girlfriend Tanya came to visit. What luck she'd been away over the weekend. 'My house has never been so clean,' Tom told her rather boastfully. 'You've never seen it like this before. I've been cleaning everything for three days.' He was tremendously proud of himself. It had been such a gruelling and massive effort. But then Tanya pointed to the lino between Tom's fridge and butcher's block. 'There's a dead mouse on your floor,' said she.

I know I said this book wasn't an instruction manual, but I think it might be wise to use Tom's story as a cautionary tale. Yes, he got rid of the fleas, but it was a tremendous palaver and a whole weekend of rigorous housework, and that dead mouse was a bit of a worry. Then he found another dead mouse, and suspiciously, no mice appeared in his house for several months, whereas pre-flea-spraying, he had been plagued by them. So heaven knows what's in that spray, if it murders and scares off mice. Can I therefore advise that you always keep your dog flea medication up to date?

How much can you love a dog?

Marge and Jed got Caspar the Weimaraner by accident. 'I suppose it was meant to be,' says Jed. 'It was
like a scene from *The Exorcist*. My friend arrived at the
door with a suitcase and Caspar. His wife had thrown
him out.' So they kept Caspar. He was a young dog,
only about seven months old, from a broken home.
What else could they do?

Then tragedy struck. Marge was out with Caspar on
his evening walkie in the park across the road, when a
boy threw a stick for him, but he threw it upwards instead
of forwards. It had been raining, the ground was muddy
and slippery, Caspar jumped up in the air, came down,
slipped, his paw bent backwards, his tendon snapped and
his bone broke. Somehow he got up and ran home on
three legs. He must have been in shock and not felt it.

Marge phoned Jed at work and he got home to find
poor Caspar lying down, shaking. 'I phoned some vets,
but none of them would come out. That surprised me.
Not even the RSPCA would come out. Then I tried the
Royal Veterinary College, and they sent an ambulance
and took him away. We went to see him the next day,
they told us what had happened, and that they needed to
put pins in his leg. They'd never done such an operation
on a dog this size, only on small animals. They had to
drill through his bones – there was smoke everywhere
while they were drilling – put in two pins, staple the

tendon back together, then put a cast on to keep the leg the right shape, then they built a cage over the whole leg to keep everything in place. Then Caspar came home.

'He was only allowed to do a little very careful walking, (into the garden), he wasn't allowed up onto the bed or sofa. So we slept on the floor with him. On a mattress. If we'd got on the sofa he'd have wanted to get up there with us.'

'These dogs are lucky,' says Marge. 'We treat them better than kids. I slept next to him all night, and Jed slept next to him all day, because he was working nights.' What devotion. Did they get enough sleep?

'Yes, Caspar was doped up, so he slept for a lot of the day. He could just about hobble into the garden. This went on for three months, and one day he got behind the sofa and pulled one of the pins out. We found it with blood on. We took him back to the hospital and they were very good. The kept him for a week to give us a rest. Because they knew what it was like for us. It was very hard. We felt terrible. It's like a kid – you know they're ill, they're looking at you all the time. If you're not with them and touching them, they're lost. They don't understand. They don't know what 'ill' is. You're watching them all the time – strangers or friends visiting couldn't really stroke him, because you didn't know what he'd do. He was feeling bad so he might snap at them.'

'We were exhausted, but we had no choice in the matter,' says Jed. 'It was that or him being put down. He was only two. People rang the bell and he wanted to get up and bark, so we had to stop everyone doing that. I paid fifty quid a week for ages to pay off the bill. We weren't insured. You don't expect that sort of thing, do you?

'After three months he was allowed out for ten-minute walkies in the park. Other dogs came up to see, because he looked very unusual in his plaster. They wanted to smell it. That got him excited too. We had to be very careful. But he was lucky. The operation worked, he didn't even have a limp afterwards. He lived until he was twelve. He had to wear nappies at the end. Dog nappies, but he didn't like them, so Marge just washed the bed every day instead.'

Eleven years later I went to see how they were, shortly after Casper died. Jed came to the front gate, eyes red from blubbing. They'd buried Caspar in the back garden.

'Perhaps you could go away and have a little holiday?'

'No! We can't leave him! We couldn't leave him when he was alive. We can't leave him now he's dead.'

They have a rather grand grave in the back garden: paving slabs on top to keep him safe from the foxes, his toys have been buried with him, there are pots of plants around it, a ring of solar lights. 'We said we'd never leave him in the dark.' There's a bowl of water in the centre, decorated with a pattern of biscuits, two tree stumps the shape of his favourite Markies biscuits.

Months later they have a new dog. Another Weimaraner.

'I'm trying not to let myself get too close to him,' says Marge. Will she manage it? Probably not. The grave and whole memorial site in the back garden are surrounded by garden canes, so that the new dog can't get in. There are reminders of Caspar indoors too. There's a shrine on the wall – with lots of photos of lovely Caspar, decorated with red fairy lights, there's special Caspar-print mugs of Caspar in the park with Jed, snow-globes with handsome Caspar sitting in the snow next to a giant snowman. Turn it upside down and the snow falls on the both, and all the family each have a silver locket with Caspar's fur in it. Marge shows me a Caspar charm bracelet: a bone, a mini-Caspar, a heart etched with 'My Dog'. 'We're terrible with these dogs. We're crazy, aren't we?' says she, 'but Caspar was a lovely dog. A stately gentleman.'

Goodbye dog

It may seem odd to the non-dog-owner that anyone could be so terribly upset when their dog dies, but nearly all dog-owners can understand it. Even the thought of it can set me off blubbing. I don't want to sound wet, but dogs are such divinely beautiful and loving creatures, that once you've lived with a dog, you wonder how you could ever have managed without one. Some people say, when their dogs die, 'I'm never getting another one. I couldn't bear to go through that again. I could never love another dog as much as I loved Bonzo,' or whoever. But I always find another dog as soon as possible, because I can't stand having that weird gap in the house where a dog ought to be. Although I dread 'going through that again', I dread the gap even more.

Nothing makes it easier. One day, just as some friends were visiting for coffee and croissant before we all went for a bracing walk over the Heath, we spotted my old dog Daisy busy vomiting and doing other awful things in the garden. I examined everything. Something was seriously wrong. I had a cry in the kitchen. But the dog still wanted her walkie. We took her out for a short stagger but had to turn back. The dog loomed about looking desperate.

I took her to the vet and had another cry in the surgery. Was this the beginning of the end? No. The dog recovered, but for how long? Boxers only last about ten years and she was ten and a half. I was wandering about the Heath the next day, thinking about this and weeping in the usual way to myself, when another dog-owner passed by. Her daughter also had an elderly Boxer and walked about crying. She assured me that I was normal. For a Boxer-owner. Or any dog-owner.

What a relief. I returned home feeling more cheerful and cast the Reaper to the back of my mind. At that time my mother was still around. She was at the kitchen table. 'What if the dog and I die in the same week?' she said, while rolling out some pastry.

In the end, the dog beat her to it. Along came the dreaded day when Daisy wouldn't get up. She had a stomach ache on Saturday, went to the vet, perked up and then on Sunday seemed to have had it. She didn't wag her tail, she couldn't lift her head. Perhaps she was dehydrated. I spooned water into her chops and wept. I ran about the house blubbing and told my mother the tragic news. She remembered the death of her own beloved Boxer dog forty years ago as if it were yesterday and started to cry.

The dog lay motionless. I spooned in more water and stared out of the open kitchen door into the garden in a desolate way. A squirrel appeared just outside. Suddenly the dog rose from the dead and bolted into the garden. The hated squirrel had revived it. Briefly.

A few streets away Sylvia was at it too. Her dog was all right, but her sixteen-year-old cat was very poorly. It staggered about with its head on one side but it still liked its dinner and sitting in the sun. Sylvia knew it hadn't got long to go. She was pampering it shamelessly with all sorts of treats, wrapping its pills in delicacies. Neither of us could go on holiday in case the cat or dog expired in our absence.

And how would I ever manage without the dog? One day soon it wouldn't be there in the back of the car, or snoozing on the sofa, or barking in the garden, lying in the sun, dribbling at the table or waiting and wiggling when I came home or playing with its squeaky. I planned to rush out and buy two more puppies immediately, probably sisters. Sylvia agreed. At least we'd be busy looking instead of crying at home in our empty kitchens.

Friends and advisers were beginning to give me odd looks about all this. 'You must give yourself time to grieve,' they said looking serious. No I mustn't, thank you. 'Yes you should,' shouted Jennifer, 'so you can pay some attention to me for a change!' That clinched it. A dog would never behave like that.

Never again

Most of us get another dog in the end. Holly never thought she would. She got such a terrible shock when her Bichon died in three days of leukaemia. 'I had no time to prepare myself. I was crying every day, everywhere. I cried walking along the street. The neighbours asked me what was the matter, I told them, and they told me to go to dog bereavement counselling, so I did. They were lovely people. Mine was a veterinary nurse and a counsellor. She listened to me and I cried and sobbed, and told them how much I loved and missed my Lucky. I felt so empty. I missed hugging him. He was my baby, friend and companion and left a big gap. I remember it burned my chest. Burning, burning pain. I can't describe it. I don't have a child and Lucky was the first dog I had. Their love is so pure. It's purer than relatives, than people. The counsellor told me not to get another dog until I felt ready.

'Lucky died in November. I got Daisy on Valentine's Day. That's three months.' Daisy is the most adorabubble little white fluffy, another Bichon of course, sitting on a turquoise armchair, in front of pink cushions and playing with her pink rubber squeaky. Aaaah! Holly kisses her head, nose and paws.

'I love you, I love you, I love you. Once you've had a dog, you can't live without one. Kiss kiss. I've kept her teeth, look.' And there's a tiny, perfectly white back molar. 'I washed it with salt and water. I collect them and save them. I've got two bottom front and one back. Last night I told Daisy to go and do her wee-wee in her wee-wee area (in the hall, covered in newspaper). She's only sixteen weeks old – but just as she was doing it, the neighbour's dog barked – a sort of warning bark, as if an intruder was coming in. She ran back to her bed, peering out, looking fearful. So I played her some soothing sounds: water falling, birdsong, ocean waves. It took about fifteen minutes to calm her down.

'She has dry food for dinner, with a bit of chicken, beef, salmon or turkey to make it more interesting – and vegetables. Her favourites are broccoli and peas. She loves apple, and iceberg lettuce – the crunchy bit in the middle, and she loves orange – just half a segment. She throws it about, plays with it, and then eats it. Kiss, kiss.'

Happy again with the new baby.

11: Grooming

There's a rather swanky grooming parlour in Harrods. The Pet Spa. Through a floor-to-ceiling glass wall you can see the dogs being groomed in a spacious salon. A grey-brown Toy Poodle is lying relaxed and motionless, being brushed and blow-dried on a table. The public are watching through the wall in clusters.

'He's been here before, hasn't he, that one?' says one woman observer. 'He's enjoying that.'

There's a ginger cat on the next table, perhaps not enjoying it quite so much. It has one person blow-drying and one holding it in place. Great tufts of ginger hair are flying about the room.

The Poodle groomer lifts her client up cradling it like a baby and carries it out of sight. In runs a brown Cocker Spaniel. 'Ooh look at him now! (The cat.) He's getting his hair done. Isn't he beautiful! Laughter. 'He's absolutely hating it!' 'Ha ha! It's being blow-dried.' Groups of shoppers come and have a stare and a laugh.

The dog and cat may be having a wash and bluff-dry. 'For the busy pet who is always on the go . . . [including] dead hair removal, two shampoos, a warm blow-dry, and a luxury finishing cologne spritz.' Out comes the Poodle looking fabulously fluffy, in goes a French Bulldog, which I meet at the reception desk with its owners.

'It's her birthday,' says the mummy. 'We're treating her!' On the desk are some plates of rather enticing doggie treats: popcorn, dog cherry-bakewell-look-alikes, and biscuits.

'Look. Treats,' I say to the Bulldog Mummy.

'Ooh no! She's on a strict diet.' Digestive problems.

In goes the little Bulldog for its birthday wash and fluff-dry, from £55.95. With such short hair? Is it worth it? 'Oh she loves it!' If she fancied it, she could also have a 'relaxing pedicure [including] a vanilla and milk-thistle paw soak, nail trim, between pads and paw trim . . . and gentle paw massage', or a 'blueberry and vanilla facial scrub to cleanse, soothe and balance . . . [with] a natural and gentle exfoliating effect, helping to remove dirt and unsightly tear stains around the eyes and mouth . . .' A snip at £19.95. Lucky doggie. Even luckier if her mummy goes shopping in this department.

Round the corner is a huge array of dog snacks: dog beer in brown bottles – Bowser Beer, dog petit fours, £17.95 for eight, chocolate yoghurt hearts £12.95 for four, gold medal biscuits, a comparative bargain at £4.94 for 4. Recession? What recession?

Nearby, behind some more floor-to-ceiling glass, are some dogs for sale. Three Toy Poodles, £1,700 each.

One's asleep, the other two are sitting gazing rather poignantly at the door at the back of their enclosure. They have a green carpet and large sheets of brown paper with a couple of puddles on them. Small crowds gather and gaze at them. A young woman points at one of the Poodles. She advises her mother. 'I think you should get him. That one right there. What do you think Dad would say?'

'Puppies,' says another. 'Isn't that sad? They're waiting by the door to get out.' It does look sad. In the next glass-fronted enclosure are two sleeping King Charles Spaniel puppies. I didn't think this was allowed anymore – puppies being sold in shops. But this is Harrods. They absolutely promise these puppies are not from puppy farms. Only from reputable breeders. They have vets and handlers on the premises, the puppies are taken for walk-ies round the shop-floor, and yes, they even get to go outdoors.

Outside the spa's window a lady groomer is chatting to the voyeur customers: 'We use a high-volume blaster to get the hair out. It's air-conditioned out there.' But what about the shampooing? They do that further along, out of sight, otherwise you'd be getting spray all over the windows. 'He's mine,' says she, pointing to a black Cockapoo (Cocker Spaniel/Poodle mix). Three groom-ers' dogs are scampering around happily inside the spa, now that the cat's gone. The Cockapoo, a grey-blue Staffie and a Chihuahua.

That must be heaven, being able to bring your dog to work. 'We're never going to earn a fortune being pet-groomers, so we've got to have some perks. Bringing the dogs to work is one of them. You don't do this for the money. You do it for the animals.'

'Dog grooming is a huge industry,' says she. 'Massive – from extreme to normal. It provides employment for thousands. We do it for the comfort of the dogs – take out the dead hair, dirt, debris. And at least these people can afford to look after their dogs. Or pay someone else to look after them.'

Or buy them some Procare Dental Gel, £24.90, mint flavour. They don't have chicken, liver or beef flavour. I know it exists. So that's a bit disappointing. I would have thought that a dog, given the choice, would go for one of those. Perhaps the owners prefer gales of minty dog breath, to go with the chic outfits round the corner: a doggie duffel coat, £47.95, or a pink-and-white-striped baby vest £52.95, or a pink Breezy Yodle Pet Sling for carrying your mini-dog, £175.00, or a navy blue doggy dress with ruffles, £97.95, or a doggie angora jumper, £125.00.

'Jesus!' says a passing shopper. Or are they just sight-seeing?

Back in the puppy pen, all three Toy Poodles are sitting longingly by the door. But don't worry, you can't have one unless you have a tenant's agreement and vet's references. All puppies have been thoroughly health checked. What could go wrong?

I don't know what to think about all this. Obscene extravagance or a colossal, thriving industry employing thousands, including the lovely groomer, earning a living.

'You're meant to be writing about how lovely dogs are,' says my friend Whitwham. 'This is about how horrid some humans are.' Perhaps not horrid. More bonkers, with more money than sense, or just needing something to love.

Groom Dog City

In a more modest groomers in the East End, Groom Dog City, the whole place is open-plan, so that owners can see everything that's going on, even the washing and shampooing, and there's a sofa for them to sit on. But today there's a darling little pink dog on the sofa. Pink! It's Molly, the Bichon. A beautifully sculpted powder puff of a dog, chilled out with its friend, Maggie, a Maltese Shih Tzu cross. At the back of the shop in its cage is a huge, perfectly white, exquisitely groomed Standard Poodle, Ralph.

These dogs all belong to Stuart, the proprietor and chief groomer. 'I like it open-plan,' says he. 'The dogs don't get so stressed, the owners can sit over there [on the pink dog's sofa] and watch. But sometimes I have to tell them not to talk to their dog. If it's wriggling or trying to bite me, and they're saying 'Good girl!' I don't want that. That's praising bad behaviour. Before I did this myself, I took my dogs to a groomer who wouldn't let you watch, so I know what it's like.'

He's right. I've heard several horror stories of groomers who whisk your dog away, won't let you watch, send you packing, then back you come for your dog and out it comes, traumatised, a nervous wreck with the wrong haircut.

This grooming salon has a fairytale beginning. Stuart had been an actor for 20 years, working in the dreary box office when there was no acting work, when he suddenly won £66, 000 in a Capital FM competition. He wanted to change his life, so he trained as a dog groomer and opened his first salon.

Now here he is, whisking my older dog up into the bath. He puts on a special collar and lead, attaches her to a bar on the wall, so that she can't jump out of the bath and off we go. Shower, shampoo, more showering. Both my dogs have always hated baths, so I've given up on them, but she's bearing up quite well. 'What the hell is this?' she's perhaps thinking. 'Who is this man?' turning her round and round and drenching her. She prefers to be looking in my direction.

'Some people only want their dogs to look like the breed standards,' says Stuart. 'Approved cuts. But I like to do what the owner wants.'

Do they want outrageous styles?

'They do, especially since Molly's been pink. She's not usually pink. She was just modelling for *Bride* magazine. I thought she'd be with the bride, but she was just on her own.'

My doggie is transferred to the drying table. Whatever will she think of that? The dryer is ferocious, rather like a plane taking off, but she doesn't seem bothered. I never would have thought it. Her hair's flying off, Stuart is brushing her rigorously with a Furminator. I must get one. Great chunks of fur are coming out. Fabulous. A lovely clean dog.

'Most dogs walk differently afterwards. They look proud. Particularly Poodles. They like a bath. It all depends on the owners. If they get stressed, the dogs get stressed. Some owners sit there and cry. They don't realise how much work it takes to clean a dog. Sometimes their coats are so matted I have to shave them short. I get a lot of Cockapoos (Cocker Spaniel/Poodle cross). A fashion breed, really in at the moment. People buy them and don't realise how much work it will be to keep them clean. Like Bichons and Poodles, they can get very matted. And that can be very bad for their health. It's very uncomfortable for them – imagine having a tangle that just keeps getting bigger and bigger – and they chew at themselves, they can't walk properly, the poo gets caught round their bums. It's very important to keep grooming them properly.'

Then Lily's off the table and into the drying cabinet.

It's a big see-through box with a warm breeze flowing through and a thermostat to make sure the temperature stays suitably low. She's not that keen. Who would be?

'They've had a mixed press, these drying cabinets,' says Stuart. 'A puppy was killed in one. I'd never put a puppy into one. The groomers went to lunch and forgot it was in there.' Cripes! But Lily's only in there for a few minutes. Stuart keeps looking and checking, and so do I. My poor baby looks rather baffled. Then out she comes looking rather fluffy. Then it's the other dog's turn. Same again. She does rather well too. Stuart chats while she goes through it. He's had some ghastly clients.

'One woman phoned saying her dog needed grooming. "It's got fleas," she says. "It's got thin because of the fleas."

'Perhaps you should go to the vet,' I say, but she says, "No, I'm too embarrassed. It needs to be de-flead first." So I agree to do a flea treatment, and she turns up in her dressing gown and slippers and puts a black plastic sack on my table. I ask where the dog is. It's in the sack. I look inside and there's a little Yorkie in there called Star. It was skin and bone, one of its eyes was a terrible mess. I took it out and gave it a big cuddle. I thought, I bet you've had no love. "I'm not treating it," I told her. "It needs to go straight to the vet." I booked a taxi, sent her to my vet with it, and asked them to tell me how it got on. They had to put it down.'

How does he stay cheery? Because that was an exception. Stuart gives both my dogs a little red, white and blue 'well-done' bow for having their bath and blow-dry and stay in the Box. They both seem perky after their experience. I saw everything, both dogs were well-treated and adored. But it's a bit of a worry to know that it's not always like this and that there's no real law about dog grooming.

'You don't need proper qualifications. There are lots of courses online which give you no practical experience. And you're using scissors and sharp instruments. It's very dangerous. Anyone can do it, and set themselves up as a dog groomer. I think that's terrible. If they're not trained with a City and Guilds qualification, then they won't have learned enough about dogs, they may not recognise the signs of stress – tongue going blue, eyes going red, restlessness and the rest of their body language.

Stuart is about to train to do extreme grooming. He hasn't done any so far, just a Mohican on a Bichon. 'People are against it. They think it's cruel. But as long as the dog's not on the table for too long, and you use the proper products, it's fine. Products must be specially made for cats and dogs, no human dyes, because they can affect the dog's immune system.'

Off I go with two fragrant-smelling dogs, looking rather pleased with themselves. Stuart was right.

Bad dog-hair day

There is one big advantage to having short-haired dogs. They don't really need to go to the hairdresser regularly, but Bichon Frises do, like any other curly-haired or fluffy dog. They're supposed to go every eight or ten weeks, but Holly took Lucky, her Bichon, every three months. 'You know how much hairdressers can cost. If you ask for a typical Bichon, they'll do that – the dog will come out, when it's been washed and blow-dried, with its head looking like a beautifully fluffed-up round powder puff on top of a white, sculptured fluff body. They dry it in a machine – a box with just its head sticking out, and air coming from every direction. In just a few minutes it comes out with an Afro. And they'll do her nails, anal glands (I don't allow that. I take her to the vet instead), they clean her eyes and ears.

'One day I rang up for an appointment. "What is your dog?" the woman asked.

'A Bichon.'

"I don't know how to do Bichons," says this woman, "but my colleague will be in on Monday and she's done a course on Poodles and Bichons. Bring him in on Monday."'

Holly took Lucky in on Monday. Unfortunately it was one of these places where you're not allowed to stay and watch. She collected poor Lucky a couple of hours later. 'He looked like a tiny donkey. All his fur had been shaved off. After a bit he began to look like a small lamb.' She's never going there again.

At least Yorkies and Bichons don't shed fur, but hairdressers become very important. You can, of course,
groom your dog yourself. Jill Dawson went on a grooming course: Learn how to groom your own dog in a day.
'I went along there armed with Hugo. Julie Lalou was
the teacher. It cost quite a bit – the cost of the course,
plus the instruments and equipment. She took me
through all the equipment: razors, slickers, matt-breakers
– I bought it all for £2-300. I do it every six weeks, but
it was such a useful course for me, and Hugo has to put
up with me as his coiffeur these days. In fact, I am keeping a bag of his squeaky-clean white marshmallow fluff
ready to make into yet another cuddly pillow for him
when we have enough. Not long now!'

Drive-in doggy wash

There could be an easier, and cheaper (£4-£9 according
to size and hairiness) way of keeping your dog clean,
fragrant and smart. The drive-in doggy wash. We have
one near us in a charming old pub called The Spaniards.
'Proud to be dog-friendly,' says the pub notice. 'Treat
your best friend to a doggy-wash and bag of hand-made
treats.' Why not? You just drive into the car park with
your dog, past the charming wooden benches out in the
pub garden, and there, in a small outhouse is the dog
wash. Inside it's rather dreary, with two old and empty

lavatory cubicles on your right, but your dog won't mind that. It may mind its wash.

There are four stages to the wash. You lift it up into the waist-high metal bath, attach its collar to the chain and clip provided, pull up an adjustable screen, and away you go.

1) Apply the shampoo and conditioner. (Do not leave dog unattended on machine.)
2) Rinse, I think from a black spray-gun thingy. Or was that the shampoo dispenser? ('Do not direct nozzle into eyes or mouth of dog or owner.)
3) Dry off with cold air from the blaster – like a hoover tube, 'to remove heavy moisture'.
4) Use warm dryer to fluff-dry your doggie.

And lastly, but very important. 'Disinfectant cycle 1 minute after wash has finished. Please remove dog from table promptly.'

It looks easy enough. I can't really say. I've never tried it. But it could be a godsend if your dog has just rolled in fox shit. One day I might have to have a go, hopefully with an assistant and a lovely sit-down at one of those tables first, with a big, stiff drink.

A sniff too far

Sometimes, very rarely, something so pointless and barmy turns up in Dog World, that I wonder whether there is any point to human life, and one of those things has appeared: perfume for dogs, at £38 a bottle, a *mélange* of 'sweet vanilla bourbon, with grace notes of French blackcurrant and Tunisian neroli'. A large Bassett called Shirley was modelling it. In case that isn't enough grand folly for one decade, Harrods also planned to introduce their own dog perfume: Sexy Beast. My Marxist chum Clayden promises that when the revolution comes, some of the first persons up against the wall will be the dog perfume and luxury goods sellers.

Anyway, who is it for, this perfume? The dogs or the owners? After my dogs' bath, our home did smell, for a few days, like a courtesan's boudoir, and my daughter adored it. She is not keen on the usual dog-stench *chez nous*. But I feel that a person who truly loves dogs will like, or at least not object to, their smell. Wet dog is not too pleasant, I admit, but I find that the inside of my dogs' ears smells fairly heavenly. I thought that dogs were meant to connect you to what's left of the natural world. They are not here to accessorise airheads. And as for the dogs, they don't even like perfume. They didn't seem to mind their own shampoo stink, but usually the stench of other people's makes them wrinkle up their noses and back off, whimpering and sneezing. Nor do my dogs care for the smell of alcohol, air-freshener or vanilla. I've just tested them to make sure. They ran away into the garden with their noses screwed up sideways.

In my experience a dog's absolute favourite perfume is excrement. They like to spread the aroma about when they've just done some, or roll in it when they come across it, or even snack on it. My dog's particular favourite is fox shit – a fabulously long-lasting aroma. They're also dead keen on duck, cat and human excrement, and small animal corpses lying about the parks, or if they're in luck, some dead fish tossed aside by fishermen, and they are mad keen on other dogs' bottoms. Try bottling some of that.

Bespoke tailoring for dogs

I must say, despite my Marxist friend's terrifying predictions, that Pugs look particularly good dressed up. I used to know a Pug and a Dachshund who wore rows of pearls (pretend) resting on their lovely full chests, and they did look pretty fabulous. A jewelled collar usually suits them, and you can get them jewelled – only semi-precious stones – or covered in charms, or boho, which is a bit hippy with dangly beads and bits and pieces, in a shop in Bermondsey: Holly&Lil. But perhaps that's not for every dog, and if your dog is rather more butch, like a Bulldog, then they also stock union jack-patterned, or patriotic stripes, or if you're not keen on nationalism, just plain old animal-print leather, with an attractively coloured surround, all handmade in England, all their own designs. I don't know what to think of all this. Dog World can easily throw you into moral confusion. We have people staggering around in rags even in this country, so it's a bit much having dogs swaggering around in jewels and beads and bespoke collars, leads, harnesses, waistcoats, woollies and raincoats, but when I get into the shop I find that it is much cheaper than Harrods and I am annoyingly charmed by it.

It has sensible slate floor tiles, a white wooden gate, so doggies can run about without escaping into the dangerous street, there's a bowl of water, dog's bed for the resident dog, and visiting dogs may run about freely off the lead. It's a rare shop in which you can do that. Paradise for dog-owners. And dogs – it sells doggie treats: carob and honey biscuits, cinnamon, ginger and clove bites, crunchy peanut-butter fingers, handmade treats from Devon – doggie toys, squeakies, chewies, doggie mugs, dog-shaped lamps, doggie cards, doorstops and food bins. Anything you fancy for your doggie, they have it. In come two chaps with a Spaniel. Rapturous greetings from the shop owner. 'Oh look at that Spaniel! How old is he? He's so good-looking!'

The shop is named after Holly, the owner Elaine's own dog, and her partner's dog, Lil, a Flat-Coated Retriever. Lil sadly died of cancer last year. 'We're thinking of getting another dog, but it'll have to be a puppy – so it gets used to this environment.'

The place is filling up. We have Holly, a big, black, fluffy mongrel, Barney, a Westie, and the Spaniel shopper. 'The only time I put Holly away is when a Bulldog comes in. I think she's frightened of them. Bulldogs get more cuddles than any other dogs. Perhaps she's jealous. She's a bit of a Princess. She likes to be the centre of attention.' But now she's fine with the visiting Spaniel and then a Sealyham.

Assistant Alex is sitting at the desk with a Schnauzer on her lap. 'Is he yours,' I ask. 'No, but he loves me. His owners, in a shop across the road, don't have a gate, and he knows his way to the café, and likes to run there if he gets the chance. So he comes to stay here instead.' His haircut is immaculate – perfectly neat and matching eyebrows, beard and short coat. His owners are immaculate, so he always looks immaculate too.

In come two women with another little foxy-looking dog, who rushes round the shop exploring, even into the back kitchen. No one minds. That makes five dogs in the shop, and no fights. Miraculous. There's a clamour as it arrives, as there is every time a new dog comes in. 'Oh this is so sweet!! What is it?' 'We don't really know.' Mongrel? This is a sensitive subject. You can only call a dog a mongrel if both parents are cross-breeds. If both parents are breeds, it's a cross-breed. If both parents are cross-breeds or mongrels, then it's a mongrel.

The owners of the Spaniel are worried that he's a little bit fat. He still gets a chewy and some dog shampoo. His fur gets very matted. 'We've got a Furminator.' 'We've got one too,' say the women with the foxy dog. 'They're amazing, look like a clipper blade. You can get them for long or short hair.' Furminators seem to be all the rage.

'We do ours once a week. It should be more,' say the Spaniel owners. 'And we take him to the groomer three or four times a year. He sheds fur. He's been to Harrods. It took two and a half hours!'

Olivia, the Sealyham, is trying on a new collar, soft leather, pink and cream, with leather bow. 'I like the nice width,' says the owner.

'You get the beauty of it. And she's got such a lovely neck,' says Elaine. The little Schnauzer comes up for a sniff. 'Go away.' Elaine opens two drawers full of dog collars. A fabulous selection.

'Washable, waterproof.' The collars which are encrusted with jewels or charms are sewn with high-tensile wire, which doesn't rot. 'No collar should stop a dog having a good life,' says Elaine. 'If a dog wants to roll in shit, you can clean it.' These outfits may be glamorous, but they're also practical. 'When Holly comes home, she runs upstairs and jumps in the bath. She was trained as a puppy to have a bath, and now she jumps in herself and waits. The first time she did it herself, the dog walker had just brought her home, the dog disappeared, I thought, where's my dog? and she was up there waiting.

'Holly's only ever been bitten once in six years. This man came in with his dog, a Staffie, he didn't want to let him off, but we said, go on, go on, it'll be all right, so he did, and he attacked Holly. It wasn't the man's fault.'

This is a good street for dogs altogether. They can go in the pub, the restaurants and the hotel. 'As long as they're well-behaved.'

The next Saturday is the day of the dog show, which is just down the road, the shop is even more packed out with local dog persons, the atmosphere is vibrant, Elaine is offering free wine, and it's even more of a crush because two elderly local ladies are there with their dogs in push-chairs, one a double. Why is her little Schnauzer in that?

'It's got a bit of arthritis,' says she. And the Westie at the back? 'She just felt like a ride.' And the other lady's Schnauzer? 'She's getting on a bit.' What a good idea. What else are these ladies to do with their arthritic and elderly dogs? Every dog needs daily outings, and the pushchairs are perfect. I'm hoping that when my dogs need transport, they won't be too big for a buggy.

Human grooming

It's not only dogs who find going to the hairdressers a bit of an ordeal. I dread it. I can't be the only one. It could be rather scary going into Taylor Taylor London, a fabulously glamorous hairdressing salon in London's uber-trendy Shoreditch, but it isn't. Why not? Because there are doggies in it! In you go, there's a swanky bar in reception serving coffees and drinks, and organic dog treats for resident and visiting dogs. The décor is fabulously glamorous, luscious flowery wallpaper, elegant chandeliers, but what's that on the floor? A doggie water bowl, and who's that on the vintage, brightly striped velvet *chaise longue*? It's a dog. Yes, on the velvet sofa. Which still looks immaculate – no mud, no hairs. 'We put a towel on it in winter,' they say.

Three of the dogs belong to joint owners Sarah and Cameron. 'I wanted to invest in something and be able to bring my dog to work,' says Cameron, 'and this was it. I'd been working in the restaurant industry and was often on the road.' Not the sort of life that suits a dog. 'It's one of the reasons I left my previous job,' says Sarah, 'because I couldn't have a dog at work, and I couldn't leave one at home for seven or eight hours, it seemed really mean. In the corporate world you can't even mention your dog, never mind bring it to work. It would be "Don't be ridiculous". So as soon as I had my own business, in came the dogs. We've been open since 2003 and we've always had a relaxed dog policy here. That's the whole point of the salon – very glamorous, but still feels like home from home.'

It's heaven for the staff and customers. Because going to the hairdresser can be a fairly grim experience, I find, particularly for the self-conscious or body-dysmorphic, but with a charming doggie snuffling about, snoozing next to you, or even sitting on your lap, the whole experience can be so much more relaxing. Someone loves you and wants to kiss you, whatever your hair looks like.

'We only have the smaller dogs – you couldn't have big ones – but I'm amazed at the number of people who like it. If we've got meetings all day here, we leave them in one of our homes together. Normally we have one or two dogs in. If someone's frightened of them, we take the dogs out for walkies, or down to the kitchen. Here everyone's fighting to take them out for walkies in their breaks. They don't even mind poop-scooping. They have pooed in the shop, but only when they were puppies. We have a wipe-clean floor. Customers can bring their own dogs in. One brings her Chihuahua. Very glamorous – their hair is colour co-ordinated.'

Today it's baking hot and there are four dogs pattering about in reception. Four dogs, in a workplace? Isn't it chaotic? Don't people trip over them? Are there dog hairs everywhere? Does it smell of dog? No to everything. It's calm, fragrant and mellow. There's Lily, Cameron's golden Cocker Spaniel, George, a Pug–King Charles cross belonging to Anna the stylist, and Sarah's two dogs – Yuri, a black English Cocker, and another Lily, the King Charles spaniel, who is madly in love with Stephanie the receptionist. She's on Stephanie's knee behind the desk, fondly flattening herself up against Stephanie's face and chest and kissing her face.

'She always licks my make-up off,' says Stephanie, not minding at all, and gives Lily a little snack. (There's also a snack supply at reception.) Lily likes to follow Stephanie around and often sits right behind her on the windowsill. But not today, because the sun's blazing in and the sill's boiling hot. Is she Stephanie's dog? 'No, but she loves me. I haven't got a dog, unfortunately, so I have a cuddle when I arrive. It's the first thing everybody does.'

'The dogs change the whole atmosphere,' says Sarah. 'It's much more relaxed. It's the English and their dogs – you go down the street, and if you're with a dog people stop for a chat and say hallo. Especially people who don't have dogs because they're in London. So they come here and have a dog for an hour. They can have a drink, cuddle a dog. Dogs put a smile on people's faces. People who are stressed about coming to the hairdresser relax. We should introduce dogs at dentists. I heard that because King Charles were royal dogs, no one was allowed to refuse them entry. I'd like to believe that was true.

George is only half King Charles, 'but he's perfect,' says Anna. And he is. After pattering about for a while, he's having a lovely snooze in his little cream, fluffy bed, by the wall near Anna's customer's feet. 'Last time I came he spent the whole time on my lap,' says the customer, 'but today it's a bit hot for that.'

It's cooler downstairs, where there's a tranquil, bronze-tiled massage room. Mile-long chandeliers hang elegantly the whole way down the spiral staircase. Busy upstairs, tranquil downstairs, but the dogs prefer it upstairs, perhaps because there are more snack opportunities. 'Yuri!' He's snuffling around a customer's handbag. 'There's a ham sandwich in there,' says she, stroking him. 'Oh he's so clever!'

'We need to have a level of being reasonable,' says Sarah. 'Not too many dogs at once. But we're open seven days a week, 9. 30 till 8 p. m. That's a long time to leave your dog. This makes life much easier for the stylists to be able to bring their dogs in. A couple more are thinking of getting a dog.'

Why not? These dogs seem pretty chilled. Lily and Yuri are kissing each other. 'Lily has eye problems,' says Sarah. 'Yuri keeps them clean. If you're poorly he'll come and lick you. I have arthritis in my fingers. He licks them, and now that I'm pregnant, he licks my belly button. He's a bit jealous. We call him my other boyfriend. They both sleep on the bed – Yuri on the pillow, Lily in the crook of my legs. We are a bit worried about what will happen when the baby arrives, in four months, so we're doing a few rules in advance. We're trying to prepare them.

'I look at them and think they have such a nice life. Lily, Yuri and Lily all go to the same holistic dog centre for massages, facials and grooming – together. They get very excited when we mention "Michele's house!" I used to hate traditional groomers – they'd put them in a cage. A cage! But Michele has a lovely dog chalet in her garden where they have their full-on massage every six to eight weeks, as a special treat.'

12: Best in Show

I'm not sure what to think about Crufts, our most famous and most gigantic dog show. Crufts is run by the Kennel Club, which sets the breed standards, and the breed standards seem to be getting more and more bonkers. So keen are the breeders to meet these standards, they sometimes tend to overdo it, which can make a dog's life rather grim.

I once met a Bulldog on my walkie which had had a face-lift. I know it was true, I could still see the stitches. This owner had sensibly decided to get rid of the wrinkles, but said that the poor dog's brother still had its wrinkles and was blundering around unable to see. Because the breed standards demand wrinkles, the breeder had gone rather over the top with the wrinkles, and here was this poor Bulldog blinded by the wrinkles tumbling over its eyes, which made the face-lift vital. And also, nasty things can happen between wrinkles: skin problems, infections, build-up of filth, a path worn by tears. And the modern Bulldog has been bred to have short legs and a tubby body – so short and so tubby that

a) they're bandy and can't walk very well, and b) can't clean their own bums, because they can't twist their stumpy bodies round and reach. And they can't give birth unaided, and go for an elective Caesarean, because the babies' heads are so big. Surely this isn't what the Kennel Club wants?

'We love dogs,' say the darling young girls and press officers in the Kennel Club offices, and it's true. They do love dogs. Look, they even bring them into work. I can see one snoozing under a desk. 'We were so upset when that programme came out,' they say. 'We cried.' Because the telly had exposed a wicked breeder, whose King Charles Spaniel had won Crufts, although it had syringomyelia, the terrible skull and brain disease, and she'd pretended it hadn't and gone on breeding from it, even though the Kennel Club forbids such a thing. But why have breed standards anyway? Why does a dog have to have its nose at such and such an angle, its wrinkles, ears, colours and shape just so? Who gives a toss?

Luckily most dog owners don't. There must be lots of sensible breeders and fabulous dogs at Crufts, and dog equipment, and dog activities. How can anyone keen on dogs not want to have a look at Crufts? But it's held at the Birmingham NEC. This makes the trip more difficult. On top of my usual moral scruples and worries there's also my loathing of the Birmingham NEC. It's too big for me. It's vast. It's like Westfield, on day one of the sales, with dogs. I wouldn't go to Westfield to save my life, but here I am at Crufts among the milling crowds. Everything seems like a mile walk away, across furry carpet floor tiles. There are endless shops, events, show rings, and breeds in endless rows of stalls.

I've come on the Working and Pastoral Group day, because it includes Boxers, my very favourite dogs. They're a half-mile trek across the NEC next to rings 35 and 36. Suddenly I see them after a long tramp across the acres of floor. There they are! Rows of stunningly handsome Boxers in their stalls. For a while I forget my scruples, because to be gazing at Boxers is heaven for me. What a jolly scene, with owners and their families clustered around their darling dogs, more or less camping there for the day, picnicking, chatting, waiting for their turn to show off their dog in the ring and see if it's going to win. Although I can't help but notice that some Boxers have had their tails docked. I thought that was illegal. Even the winner of Best in Breed has a docked tail. How come?

'It's an Irish Boxer,' explains the owner. In Ireland you can do what you like. No rules seem to apply. Why doesn't the Kennel Club just say 'No docked dogs may win, not even Irish dogs'? It can't be that difficult. That would stop people chopping off tails straight away. But they won't. Heaven knows why.

But I can't just stare at Boxers. There are hundreds of other fabulous dogs here. Whatever are these huge white dogs as big as ponies with white dreadlocks down to the ground? They're Hungarian Komondors. Here are three in a cluster, with owners on their knees busily pulling at the dreads – waterproof corded coats. Pulling, parting, fiddling, separating. One dog has the dreads on his head tied up in a topknot with a blue ribbon. It looks like a lifetime's work, forever hairdressing.

Beyond the Komondors are the Mastiffs, and the huge Dogues de Bordeaux, with enormous chests and enormous heads, some looking almost too big for their bodies. Here's one with its owner in a smart, dark grey suit. Owner also has a massive chest and bald head. I fancy them on guard outside my home. No robber would dare even approach. I pass another ring and see a small, thin boy in a smart grey, pinstripe suit with his Corgi.

'This is Tommy from Saffron Walden,' says an announcer. 'He is twelve years old.' He looks tremendously grown-up and professional. But I can't stop to see what Tommy is about to do. I'm in a hurry on my way to 'Heelwork to Music'.

Heelwork to Music is an hour late. Blast. What next? Too much to choose from. This is the hypermarket of Dog World: stalls for bedding, leads, foods, vitamins, clothing, accessories, bath products, indoor equipment, outdoor equipment, décor, dog kitchen-wear, dog bedroom equipment. And dog massage. A lucky Greyhound is lying on the ground among the milling crowds having a massage. The Greyhound is completely chilled out. I am not. I am overwhelmed by Crufts. Brain scrambled, feet burning. I don't feel I've seen a fraction of it.

So I go back to Crufts the next year, 2012, with a chum. One visit isn't really enough to take it all in. This time it's Gun-dog day. Loads of Setters fill the rings, roam around or flop in their stalls. But it's not just gun-dogs and assorted hounds and hunters. There are over 200 breeds of dog here, in over 200 stalls or enclosures, which is a lot of dogs to look at. But it's easier with a friend: you have support and you can branch out, split the burden of looking, linger over different favourites and compare notes. We walk round staring at all the different varieties of dog. I like the squash-nose ones: Boxers, French Bulldogs, Pugs and Bulldogs, and my friend likes the pointy-nose dogs. She falls in love with a long-haired snoozing Dachshund. There's a small pile of them on cushions on a table in their pen. Aaah! So sweet!

The owners sit in the pens or beside their dogs' stalls, chatting away. 'She was in hospital on a drip,' says a Terrier-owner. Some other ghastly dog had attacked her dog and pinned it down. 'Better than picking her up and shaking her. She went all floppy in the afternoon. Then she was in hospital on a drip. It was just shock.'

What odd little faces the Affenpinschers have. 'They're fun. Very mischievous,' says the owner. 'She just had my sandwich this morning. She looked up, she thought "She ain't watching," and she had the cheese, the ham and the top layer of the bread. I'm still going to eat the rest. She's left the lettuce.'

Because not many people know much about Deerhounds, and the owner was perhaps exhausted with describing them, he had put helpful little notices up on the walls of the booth. 'A soft look in repose, dignified, aloof, but keen faraway look when roused.' 'Docile, good-tempered, never suspicious, aggressive or nervous.' 'Jaws strong, with a perfect, regular and complete scissor-bite.' Sounds perfect.

But the Husky lady likes to chat. 'They chase chickens – and they'll get them. I keep chickens too. I had fifteen in my living room the other night. The chickens are a bit thick – they'll come and walk on the kennel roof, then they'll come down into the kitchen, and I tell them, "If you come in the kitchen, you won't go out again."'

'Don't they?'

'No they don't. But the cockerel's still here. He doesn't come in the kitchen.'

These Husky-owners seem rather laid back about the chicken killing. My neighbour Pike has a Husky. It also chases chickens, which is unfortunate, because his mother keeps chickens. Special and very attractive old breeds of chicken, and every time he takes the Husky to visit his mother down in Sussex, bang goes another chicken, or two. His mother got rather browned off with this and ordered him to do something about it, so he muzzled his

Husky, Smila. Off they went to visit his mother again, off shot the dog again after the chickens. She couldn't bite them, so she just battered one to death with her muzzle. Which wasn't a good outcome. Why are these people so keen on Huskies?

Why Huskies?

'They're brilliant escapologists,' says Pike. 'It's quite amazing. My last one was in a kennel with a 10ft-high metal railing. He escaped. I didn't know how, so I put him back, kept watch and filmed him. He climbed up, paw over paw, like a person, and jumped over the top. If you need to keep a Husky in, you need ten-foot railings that curve over inwards at the top, and they need to go three feet below ground. I like their freedom of spirit. Huskies don't bark, but Smila sings brilliantly. I had friends round – one was a specialist in medieval choral music – we were singing, a cappella, and Smila joined in. She was soon singing in tune, and definitely resolving blues riffs. My medievalist friend could tell.

'My wife Rita had both our children at home. Smila was present at both births and was incredibly concerned, and licked Rita on the head to make sure she was all right. When the children were very small, she'd position herself under the sofa, so that if they rolled off, they'd fall on her, not the floor. And if we were putting a nappy on or something, and the baby was screaming, she'd rush up and put herself between us and them, as if to say "Are you sure you know what you're doing?"

'Huskies can run all day for fourteen days, which is what they do in the Arctic, then they can lie about for another fourteen days while you sit by your hole in the ice waiting for fish. So translating that into our modern English life – you don't have to take them for a walk every day. So long as you take them for long walkies on the other days.

'She's also wonderfully good at murdering anything that comes near. She's worked out how to get out of the cat flap, the wrong way, and then brings home chickens and pheasants. But she's not territorial and probably wouldn't attack a robber.'

Sounds marvellous, except for the murdering and escaping.

Obedient doggies.

Perhaps Huskies are not for me. But back at Crufts there are squillions of other dogs to choose from. Up and down we go, past all the hundreds of breeds, hours have whizzed by and we still haven't seen any performances. An obedience and heelwork to music demonstration is just about to start. Phew, a chance to sit down. Here comes Janet with her dog and uniform blue top. And they're off! Janet throws the dumbbell, the dog must go and pick it up and bring it straight back to her. He stops en route. Whoops! There's a smell distracting him – no – he's going to pick it up – no, he's dropped it, says the commentator excitedly, and then explains why he looks a bit sluggish. 'He was doing heelwork to music yesterday.' He's obviously knackered today.

'Here's Sian. Throw! He's straight to it. A nice clean pick-up. Well done Sian!'

On comes Sophie. 'Another nice clean pick-up. Give! Finish! Well done Sophie. How about that? Only perfect!' This looks like a pretty heavenly pastime – playing with your dog all day, keeping it entertained, seeing how clever it can be, both getting exercise.

What a confusing place Crufts is – an odd mixture of charming, brilliant, bizarre, eccentric and horrid. I'm still worried about the breed standards and docking. I once asked a breeder why they do it.

'It's the shape of the dog,' said she. How barmy. I thought it was the shape of the dog with a bit cut off, which seems fairly pointless and cruel. Like having a finger chopped off two days after birth. Because that's when they do it. So to make sure I got a dog with a tail, I had to race down to Bournemouth the day after my puppy Violet was born, pay cash in advance, and then they promised the tail would stay on. And those were the kind breeders. None of the rest would even contemplate it. Because there are even more vital reasons why it should have its tail amputated: the tail will knock things off your coffee table, or whack your small children, they told me, and once a tail is injured, which happens frequently, it will never heal. What rubbish. I have no small children or coffee tables and after eight whole years, the dog's tail is still intact.

Jethro Magical Gay Guy

'Next week, my daughter's jumping out of an aeroplane, for charity,' says Sonia. 'You can take dogs, if they're not scared of aeroplanes.' So she'll be taking her Salukis. She takes them everywhere. They're used to travelling about the country, because they're always off to shows. She was about to take them to Greyhound Extravaganza the following Sunday, but bad luck, her Saluki, Jethro, was bitten on the thigh by a neighbour's dog, and has to stay at home with his Comfy Collar on (soft version of the plastic see-through bucket things) to stop him licking at his scar.

Greyhound Extravaganza isn't just for Greyhounds. It's also an All Breeds Fun Dog Show, including Lurchers and cross-breeds. What a disappointment, because it was the first show Jethro ever went to and he won First, Second and Third, and since then he's won over and over again. There are the rosettes to prove it – stacked along Sonia's mantelpiece and sideboard: red, blue and white (First, Second and Third) on the right side, yellow and green (Fourth and Fifth) on the other. The house is crammed with photos and paintings of the dogs, Jethro and Amira. Two boxes of two dogs' ashes are positioned neatly in the fireplace. Amira is snoozing on the floor next to a toddler playing with her toys, Jethro is snoozing on the sofa between us, all rather soothing. And here is Jethro's portrait in a flashy booklet from The Dashing Dog Show at Kensington Palace. There's a red rosette attached to the booklet and inside is his portrait, in an ornate gold frame, with his full name beneath it – Jethro Magical Gay Guy. Wow! Very grand. And doesn't he look elegant? He's an unusual, smooth-haired, 80% Saluki ('I had his DNA done') with a feathered tail and ears. 'And he got a certificate and a huge goodie bag, for the Prince Charming event.'

'But it was uproar,' says Sonia, 'because people were walking by shouting, "Disgraceful! Disgraceful that dogs are allowed on these premises!" But they were raising money for the palace's refurbishment. It's just a bit of fun. Every show I go to is raising money for charity. Anyway, at this Kensington Palace one, a woman comes up and says to me, "Are you entering yours?" I say yes, and she says, "Well I won't bother then," because she knew she didn't have a hope in hell of winning. Some people get very competitive, they take it very seriously and they don't like to lose. Then another says, "You could hardly call that a smooth dog, with those ears and tail!" Just jealous. She probably knew she wouldn't win either.

'I'd never say things like that. We all take the best dog home, don't we? We all have the best dog. I'd go again, but they might not hold it this year, because of all those people moaning last time. Jethro did a scurry there.' A what? 'You know – you're at one end of the track, someone else holds your dog at the other end, you call it, they let go, and they're meant to run to you. And he did, but then he ran away. Vooomph! Straight past me. Everyone was chasing him and in the end, the man from the Dogs Trust caught him.

'It all started when I went to a local dog show at the Mayhew [rescue centre]. Jethro came joint first with a Rottweiler. Marc Abrams, the vet, was there, and he said "You should show that dog." So I did.

'It's not a bit of fun for everyone. Some people take it very seriously. They go for the day, bring tables and chairs, and special grooming tables for the dogs. If somebody new comes and doesn't know what to do, they can be a bit sniffy.

'I said I'd come from London, and this woman says "You've come a long way," [we're in Luton] as if I was an alien. Then she says, "I'm a registered child-minder." I said, "So am I." She's got two Shih Tzus and a tent, and while we're talking, she's got one of them, a white one, up on the table for two hours, then she gets out the dog make-up – a big tin of white face powder and a big powder puff – I'm not kidding you – and she's powdering the dog all over, people are passing by and staring, thinking she's mad. Because this is just a fun show. It costs two pounds entrance per class, but one of the classes wasn't a Companion Class (registered by the Kennel Club) and it was meant to be. So she asked for her money back. The two pounds!

"It's for charity," says the organiser, but she still wanted it back. She wasn't my kind of person,' says Sonia.

How does Sonia know where all these shows are going to be? 'I buy *Countryman's Weekly*. It has a chart called Weekly Show Planner, so you can see what's on every week all over the country. I'd never go to the Suffolk Day Show again. There were fifteen hundred dogs! That's a hell of a lot. There were so many in the ring, they couldn't do it. One old lady got knocked over and trampled by big dogs – Great Danes, Pyrenean Mountain Dogs. She was badly hurt. Honestly, it wasn't funny.

'But I love it. Over the years I've met lots of people, made lots of friends. And it is exciting. Last year Jethro won best in show at Greyhound Walks near Braintree. When I got that I had tears in my eyes. The judge said, "Don't, you'll make me cry too. I saw you as you were coming in, and I was hoping you'd entered him."

'Then I dropped the plate (silver with gold edging and gold motif), I was in such a state – and I won a great big bag of food. Afterwards I couldn't believe it. It's so silly!'

A toddler walks past Amira's nose waving a bread stick. The dog takes absolutely no notice. A perfect child-minder's dog.

13: Worst in Show

I've never shown my dog Lily. What would be the point? She is a mutant. This is why I feel rather bitter about shows and breeders. We rescued her from a cruel breeder. But we didn't know that until we got her home. I should have seen the warning signs, but I probably didn't want to, because I was desperate for another dog after the death of the saintly Daisy, my last Boxer. I went to Boxer rescue, who sent me to a breeder who had a puppy that she wanted to get shot of.

This breeder was famous. A Boxer judge. You were almost bound to find some of her dogs on any worthwhile Boxer's pedigree. How could a dog from such a prestigious breeder have anything wrong with it? But it had developed an undershot jaw, and a prestigious breeder does not need a dog with a deformed jaw.

'How deformed?' I asked. 'Only a little bit,' said Mrs Breeder. So off we went, my daughter and I, to see it, out in the countryside. The puppy was brought out. It scuttled about, cringed a little and weed. But wasn't it sweet? What a darling little face. Daughter fell in love with it. All puppies are sweet, with darling little faces, but they don't all cringe and wet themselves. We should have been warned by this, but we weren't. Did I sensibly ask to see the puppy with its mother, and where it slept and played, which is what you absolutely must do when you choose a puppy? No I didn't. What a fool. We just fell in love with this puppy. We probably would have fallen in love with any puppy we'd seen.

Was this puppy used to living in a house? Yes, said the breeder. Would it be all right in the car? Yes. Could it have puppies? Yes, said the breeder. It had had its injections, it was healthy. So we paid a deposit and would come back and collect it in three weeks, when it was five months old. Why the wait? Because it had a blind brother, which it was looking after, the blind brother was being collected then, Mrs Breeder wanted both puppies collected at the same time, so that the blind one would not be traumatised twice: once when its companion left, and again when its new owner took it away.

What a kind, thoughtful woman, I thought, being so concerned about her puppies. Who would have guessed that she wasn't kind at all? She just had no use for a dog with a crap jaw. But luckily for her, along came Mrs Muggins with her daughter, and bought it, without even looking at its jaw properly, because you cannot bowl in and wrench open a nervous puppy's mouth to examine its teeth.

Back we came, weeks later, to collect our puppy. The woman collecting the blind puppy was there too.

'Are you paying for that dog?' she asked.

Yes.

'How much?'

I told her. 'You're being ripped off,' said she strictly.

But it was too late. I'd paid. And it's difficult to argue with a bossy breeder, when you're still feeling a bit weedy about your last dog, and you have a darling little puppy all ready to go home with you. We took her home. What a little wreck of a dog she was: trembling and vomiting all the way, sitting in the back of the car with daughter. Once home, she was terrified of everything: the house, people, noise, traffic, clattering plates and men in particular. She weed, trembled and starved for three days, shot up to daughter's room and stayed there, until we took her to the vet.

The poor little dog had billions of fleas, a flea allergy, worms and the lump on its chest was a tumour.

'Take it back,' said the vet, furious. But we couldn't, because we loved her already, and how could we take her back to that cruel judge-breeder-monster?

'That's what she relies on,' said the vet, fed up, and gave us his bill. And his next bill and his next bill. But what else could we do with this wreck of a dog? We kept her, and hoped things would improve. And they did.

So take this as a cautionary tale. Even if you do love a particular breed, and your parents used to have them decades ago when they weren't quite so deformed and inbred, don't buy another. And never take your child to the dog breeder's house to choose a puppy, because you'll both fall in love with it, and want it. Just this once, do what I say, not what I have done. Stick to cross-breeds or mongrels.

Bad boy breeders

There are all sorts of breeders: good, bad, kind, greedy, unscrupulous ones, legal, illegal and accidental ones. But our neighbourhood is crawling with a relatively new sort who can't be bothered with Crufts. They have their own particular way of showing off. A rather alarming new cottage industry seems to be springing up around here: the breeding of mixed-Bull-breed-type dogs by local youths. Many boys are now attached to a dog, and it is never a Pomeranian. Why accessorise with a machete, stabbing knife, falling-down trousers, bling or self-muti-lation, when one can have a slavering, jaw-locking dog-slave, biting and bonking and giving people a fright? Better still, breeding gives you an income and brings joy to your chums, without you even having to leave your home.

Anyway, I'm in the park with my dogs when in come some large local male children with their ferocious mixture dogs. Last week they had two, now they have an additional darling puppy. I admire it. 'It's part Pit Bull,' says the owner with pride. Why worry? Three is nothing. Next day into the park comes a large pack of boys with a medley of Staffs, Pit Bulls, Mastiff/Staff/ God-know-what crosses and selection of gambolling baby dogs, many lead-free.

I am keen not to irritate this band of dogs and their owners, but I am with my own two four-stone fearsome bitches. I keep them on their leads, then bad luck, one of the puppies comes wiggling up to play. But my semi-crippled dog is a nervous, dominant bitch and would rather pin the puppy to the ground to show who is boss, before starting to play, and so it pounces on the puppy, which belongs to a youth who is attached to two hulking dogs, muscles bulging, hackles rising, jaws agape, big teeth showing.

'Your dog bit my puppy,' declares the youth fiercely. I deny it. My dog was just establishing who was in charge, before playing. The youth does not agree. 'Your dog bites my puppy, it's dead.' I announce our departure. Meanwhile, reports of Staffie-Bull-breed attacks pour in. There's a killer one on Hampstead Heath, two rogue Staffs roaming the neighbourhood, crapping and attacking any cat or dog in their path. Another savaged Holly's little fluffy dog while it's owner stood staring. Holly screamed for help, neighbours dashed to the rescue, blood drenched the pavement, and now Olivia's elderly cat's leg has been broken in a Staffie-chase.

I blame the parents. There is nothing wrong with Staffordshire Bull Terriers. They can be darling, cuddly softies, provided they are brought up by women who teach them manners. In the old days, before this mad craze, they used to be admired as family dogs and called 'nanny dogs', because they were so perfectly behaved with children, but sadly they now attract not-so-clever boys. These boys are thrilled by their sinewy, cannon-ball demeanour and teeth, which snap shut and cannot be prized open. Then they can be twirled around in the air by the boy owner – a big, solid lump of whirling dog with its jaws clamped to his rope or stick.

This new fad has spread all over town, every town. The streets are filling with boys and dogs, and my friend Whitwham is sick of being pursued relentlessly while jogging by ravening creatures snapping at his legs. I tell him that Peterborough Council is offering free lessons in how to talk dog.

'How d'you say fuck off?' he says rudely. He is still a boy at heart. But luckily without a dog.

Dog plague

Try as I might to look on the sunny side of life, I can't help but notice that the crappy side seems to be getting the upper hand. As the months pass by, our local youths-with-Staffs/Pit-Bull-type-dog plague is getting worse and worse, but I have struggled to see it in a positive light. Perhaps these boys love their dogs. Perhaps they look after them and through them learn altruism and responsibility.

Vain hopes. I was out on my walkie on the benign side of Dog World, when I heard the sort of news which makes me want to pull my own head off. The dog-plague boys have a new craze: dog fighting. They take their pets to the top of a high building, shut them into the lift, send it down to the bottom, then open the doors and spot the winner. There are apparently three fight venues round here, including blood-spattered lifts, known to the police, but the police have taken no action, so I hear.

Annoyingly, the bad-boy dog-owners' reputation is rubbing off on all of us. Non-dog-owners are beginning to think that all dog-owners are irresponsible and all dogs, especially Bull breeds like mine, are potential fighters and child-eaters.

I often feel like a pariah when I take my two dogs out for a walkie, because to anyone who doesn't know much about dogs, they could easily be taken for Pit Bulls. I noticed on one walkie that a lady walking by with her two toddlers looked rather nervous. No wonder. The week before this walkie, a five-month-old baby had been killed by two Rottweilers and a fourteen-month-old toddler badly mauled by a dog in Leicester, and every year, 3,000 people in the UK are injured by dogs. Since the first attack, Whitwham, now even more of a dog-hater, has been ringing daily and ranting about dogs and what he would like done to them: have them all put down. All of them.

Typical. He's doing what all dog-haters do – blaming the wrong species. He should really be blaming the parents/owners. And often the shaven-headed-half-mast-trouser-boys don't make very good dog parents. Perhaps they have poor role models.

So far, I've only spotted one boy with a Rottweiler. It started off as a playful puppy, spent hours on a short lead while its owner and other boys sat on a bench on a street corner opposite my house, and taunted it. Within months it had turned into a snarling monster. Not because it was a Rottweiler. A Rottweiler, if it's treated properly, like Barry the Dog Jogger's Rottweiler, will behave itself, like any other dog. But there's one big difference. A Rottweiler weighs from eight to ten stone. My dogs weigh four stone each, I weigh ten and a half stone, I'm a big girl, but I have a tough job hanging onto eight stone of dog, so I try to take a friend on walkies to assist, or remote control collars, plus delicious treats – liver cake, chicken frankfurters, biscuits – distract them. I never dare let them off the lead together, I take them to isolated areas of the Heath and I put them on the lead near toddlers and other weedier dogs. Not that I'm perfect. But if I have to be so careful, how can any human manage two Rottweilers? Twenty stone of dog. Especially if those dogs decide to go on a rampage, or see a cat.

Communist dogs

There is an answer to this problem, if only we were Communists. I know that the Soviet Union had its faults, but in Russia, Dima the dog whisperer tells me, you have to have a test before you're allowed to have a dog, or at least you used to when he was young, to make sure you were fit to look after one. What a good idea. Wouldn't it be heaven if we could have one here, like a driving test, and that would keep the terrible owners out of the parks? If they even bother to get that far. Some just walk their dogs round the streets or keep them at home, pacing up and down on balconies and terraces, in back yards and on chains, like caged lions. Imagine what these tormented animals are going to do if they ever get out? Yes. They're going to charge about in a fairly murderous way, discharging all that pent-up energy, and take a chunk out of someone.

A neighbouring family have a large Akita, which they promised to have castrated when they bought it. Then they decided not to. At least the husband did. He was not keen on cutting a chap's balls off. Perhaps he took it personally. Now, having had a go at every other dog in the area, this poor dog can never be let off the lead. Possibly it would rather have no balls. We will never know.

A grossly overweight Labrador sometimes lumbers by. I asked its owner whether it goes to the park.

'No,' says he. 'It's seven. It doesn't need the park anymore.'

How I longed to punch the lazy bastard, but of course one cannot. It wouldn't help. You could drive yourself mad watching all the idiot dog-owners in the country, but let's not be too negative. There are plenty of good dog-owners and pleasant dogs who never harm anyone – about 7 million dogs in the UK who never get into trouble. But no one knows that or believes it anymore.

Not surprising, after all the Pit Bull dramas and another startling story in the newspapers about a gigantic fat Labrador, fed almost to death by its owners not too long ago. It isn't just us with obesity problems. One can't help but think that the world is stuffed with idiots, but no – the idiots are in the minority. Even though the Labrador rescue lady says they've had one dog in a day since Christmas – it's about the beginning of March as I write this – and all their foster homes are full up.

Why is that? Are these dogs unwanted Christmas presents? No, says the saintly rescue lady. They've usually just annoyed someone over the festive period – licked the turkey, stolen a mince pie, trampled a new present. And Christmas being a fairly tempestuous time in some families, it doesn't take much of a straw to break the owner's back, and so the dog gets thrown out. Easily done.

14: The Rescuers

Thank heavens there are hordes of dog rescuers. My friend Jennifer has had to carry out a double dog rescue – difficult for her because she isn't that keen on dogs, and is not a real dog rescuer. But as she found two of them trapped in a house, one in a cage and crap everywhere, what else could she do? So I helped, as I am familiar with Dog World and have contacts, and once we got going, Jennifer almost wept with relief. Because the Dog World population isn't half as grim as she thought it was. As soon as we asked for help, a whole array of kind, generous, selfless people volunteered to foster and adopt the dogs, clear up the crap, and drive all over the place carting the dogs about the country to new homes.

All dogs matter

What a good job there are people around to pick up the pieces, which is what Ira and her team does. They run a dog-rescuing charity called All Dogs Matter, which tries to home Staffie crosses particularly, because they're the sort of dogs, often bred by bad boys, that nobody wants, and they're clogging up all the rescue centres, and when the rescue centres are full up, then it's goodbye dogs. The days are long gone when Battersea and other rescuers could keep dogs indefinitely. Now they're put to sleep at the estimated rate of 500 a week, and it's a heartbreaking business to be in. I'm not even sure if that's the right number. I suspect it's much bigger, but no one dares to say the real number out loud. People would be too upset. I couldn't do rescuing. So this is a hymn of praise to all the people who do, like Ira.

She was following her dad's example. He was always bringing home strays, so Ira started to volunteer at the Mayhew Centre, and eventually, with her group of trustees, she started rescuing dogs herself and started her own charity – All Dogs Matter.

'We've re-homed about 150 dogs a year – 220 dogs this year, and seventy per cent of them are staffie crosses. Yes I get upset, but they all become one – you have to cut off to a degree. This isn't for the faint-hearted. We get lists like this' – she shows me one online – 'from different boroughs all over the country. The dogs each get their picture and a little write-up, then seven days in the pound. The council has to take them in for seven days, by law. See this little chap? I think he's good-looking, but many people think he's scary. To them he's just a very ordinary-looking brown Staffie-cross. He doesn't stand a hope in hell. It doesn't matter if they're micro-chipped – the microchip stops when the owner doesn't want the dog anymore. The dogs on the borough's list all need homes in the next couple of days – but for the less desirable ones, it's often curtains.

'With Staffies it's straightforward. They're tested straight away with another dog. If they growl, if they're dog-aggressive, the big rescue centres put them to sleep, especially if they're Pit Bulls, whether they're nice or not. Some rescues may keep them, but it can be problematic, because they're nearly all crosses now, so you don't really know what they are. They can't re-home them and these dogs spend the rest of their lives there. We work with the local RSPCA, and take in as many Staffies as we can. In return, the RSPCA neuter them for us and give us free or reduced-price veterinary treatment.

'At the start of the crisis, about ten years ago, I could see what was happening. People were ringing up to have Staffies rehomed, the homes wouldn't take them, which made the situation worse, because they just went back to the kids who were breeding them. They breed a bitch at home and advertise the puppies on the internet, probably on Gumtree, which, along with other charities, we're trying to stop. Three years ago they were selling dogs for £300, then they started giving them away on the inter-net. Or they're dumped.

'There's a prejudice against Staffies. People cross the road when they see me coming with mine. They should be short and stocky. They're terriers really – ratters. A cross between a Jack Russell and a Bulldog. They have big wide mouths and look as if they're smiling, in my opinion. They're very good with people and children. They have tenacity, they're not frightened, but they can be aggressive to other dogs if they're not socialised when they're young. These kids that breed them take them away from their mothers at about four weeks old, which is much too early, and that's where the trouble starts.

Pure Staffies are dying out. They're all crossed with something or other. I've got this dog on the internet – it's listed as a Spaniel-cross-Staffie. Look.' It's nothing like a spaniel, not a hint, it just looks like a Pit Bull-type. 'The owner dumped it because "It snarled at my child". Why buy a dog off the internet if you're on your own with a two-year-old child?'

Billie is a volunteer at All Dogs Matter. She has an American Bulldog cross called Tiny. He is not tiny at all. He is huge. 'I've always loved dogs. My family used to run pubs and we had German Shepherds. Then my boyfriend bought me this dog. He's my life [the dog]. I love him so much. I couldn't ever bear to give him up. We rescued him from a backyard breeder. He was the smallest of twelve puppies. They were in a playpen in a horrible, scruffy house, and they were all jumping up, but Tiny just sat back down in the corner, as if to say, "I might as well not bother. I'm never going to be chosen."

'I chose him. He loves my mum's Lhasa Apsos and my

boyfriend's sister's Staffies. As long as it's not silly people buying these dogs, they can have a good life.'

While I'm there a nearby vet rings. They've had a stray handed in – a nine-month-old German Shepherd. Can Ira take it? Yes but not now.

Can they keep it overnight? Ira's kennel is out in Bushey, it's too late to take it there. The local warden has no space until Wednesday. Billie will collect it for tonight. She goes off to collect it, and take it home. Another emergency rescue. But the phones keep ringing, and ADM's kennels are full. Busting at the seams.

'All the nice fluffy dogs find homes. The Staffies don't. We had two eight-week-old Staffie puppies in last week. That means they're still breeding them. They're still breeding.' But we do still manage to rehome lots of Staffies. They go to fantastic homes. We've had people from the Channel Islands come here especially for Staffies, because they can't get them over there. Someone's just come over from Malta to get a Staffie, because they love them and can't get them there either. They're very popular in Essex, and the German Shepherd that Billie took home for the night, ended up living happily in Hampstead.

Secret mission

All over the UK people are doing their best to rescue dogs from puppy farms, mostly found in Wales. It sounds even more gruelling than rescuing Staffies, or perhaps there isn't much difference. One couple became involved after adopting an ex-puppy-farm dog that they found in a rescue. It was in a terrible state, covered in mange, and it just sat, staring blankly. They kept it, it recovered, and they were was so impressed with the rescuers, and appalled by this 'trade', that they started to help them, and now go collecting dogs from puppy farms together. I'm being very cagey about their names, because they have to remain anonymous.

'We mustn't tell anyone who we are or where the dogs are coming from or what we're doing. So we keep it very quiet. We have to keep everything low-key, it's all done by word of mouth. The farmers tell each other "these people will take the dogs, no questions asked," then we get more dogs. Sometimes the farmers know where the rescuers are, and they'll bring the dogs to us, sometimes they phone and we collect them. They bring them because once the dogs are six or seven, they don't want them anymore. They're too old to breed from. Sometimes they try and sell them online, a few ask the vet to put them down, but not many bother to do that, because it's expensive, so they do it themselves.

'Puppy farms are not full of puppies gambolling about happily. Last year a man and his wife applied to a council in Wales for a licence to keep 180 dogs, with no other staff. They'd be automatically fed. You'd think they'd be automatically refused, but they got their licence. One of my dogs had puppies once. She was already pregnant when we got her. She had four puppies and it was very hard work. A full-time job, so how can two people look after 180 dogs? There's no legislation governing how many people should be looking after what number of dogs, but there is a new law being proposed saying that it must be one person to thirty dogs. That's not counting the puppies. They're consulting about it in the Welsh Assembly.'

There aren't many puppy farms in England, thank heavens. There are quite a few in Scotland, and Wales is stuffed full of them, because there they can be out of the way, out on isolated farms. 'You can't see that there's anything there. They open these big doors, to a barn or outbuilding, and there are the dogs, sometimes kept in the dark. Some have purpose-built kennels with runs, which aren't so bad, some are just old buildings, with stone pens, or sheds with no windows.

'If the council licence them, then the RSPCA thinks the council is responsible, so it's up to the council. When they are inspected, the breeders should be given no notice, but they usually get a tip-off, so they just tidy everything up. Sometimes the dealers set up fake homes, with the dogs and puppies in them, because they know that people know, or ought to know, that you should only buy a puppy if you've seen it with its mother.

'There are different sorts of puppy farmer. Some aren't too awful. They're quite sweet, they offer you a cup of tea – they've lived in the Welsh hills for years, they and their families have been breeding dogs for generations and generations. They're just ignorant. They have no real awareness that they're doing anything wrong and they probably can't even read the instructions from the council, which are very complex. Then there's the dealer type, very hard, just in it for the money, don't care about the dogs at all. A lot look very respectable. They drive up in big, smart cars. Some sell to dealers, to pet shops, online. They'll even meet you in a motorway service station with the puppy, so you won't have a clue what or where it's come from. Most of them are very hard-nosed.'

In the Sixties, when the price of milk dropped and farmers were having a hard time, and the government were encouraging farmers to diversify, puppy farming was one of the suggested alternatives. Battery dog farming. There's been a rumour that they were going to recommend it again recently. 'The whole breeding system is now so skewed,' says Mrs X, 'we would need to stop breeding any dogs at all for five to seven years, in order to get the numbers down to a manageable level, and empty the rescue centres.'

How are we to do that? And what ever are our poor police meant to do? They could have a dog amnesty – give up your unwanted/out-of-control dog now and you won't get even a telling-off – or drive around in a big van, scooping up dogs with useless owners. Shouldn't be difficult, because they won't be on leads. But easiest of all, close all the puppy farms. Isn't it mad to have them? Absolutely barking mad? Here we are, overrun with dogs, putting down thousands a year, and all the while, thousands more dogs are pouring in from the ghastly puppy farms in Wales. How difficult can it be to close them down? Battery farming is generally disapproved of, and we could get the Queen on side. She's fond of dogs. But then what to do with all these dogs? Just pray that there are enough rescuers to take them in.

Why Greyhounds?

Every breed has its own rescuers. Angela and Martin rescue Greyhounds. Their first was Harry, a Galgo, or Spanish Greyhound. 'He was quite beautiful,' says Angela. 'Long legs, long neck, long snout, long tail. Chicken chest.' What's that? 'You know. When you turn a roast chicken on its back. They're calm dogs, not fighters – drip-dry designer dogs – never seem to get dirty. They're so high off the ground, and they have short coats. It's such fun to watch Greyhounds running. I love to see them run. Now we have Percy, also a Galgo. Every day I take him to the Heath and someone says, "What a beautiful dog!" I'm proud that he's mine. I bask in his reflected glory. They don't fight, don't bite, don't bark. They're little angels. Good for old people and children. Don't need exercise. You take them out, they rush about for twenty minutes. That's it. You don't need to muzzle them. They chase things, but they don't kill them. They never pull on the lead. Percy is affectionate in a very quiet way. He's not very demonstrative.'

The dog who licked clocks

It wasn't always Greyhounds for Angela and Martin. They have had a chequered dog career. 'Walking a friend's Basset Hound, Harry, one day, we met a woman called Grace, also out with her Bassett Hound, a bitch called Buggalugs.

'Do you want to mate your dog with mine?' she asked. I did.

'Ring me in six weeks.' I did.

'She brought Buggalugs round, but Harry didn't know what to do, so I rang Mrs Bassett – yes she really was called that – the Dachshund breeder, who knew all about that sort of thing. Round she came with her KY jelly, assisted the dogs fairly robustly, and there was a happy result – nine puppies.

'The puppies were born in Wales and the owner invited us up there to visit. "You must come and see them." We went. It was a magnificent house, but there was no one there – they'd all gone tripping up the mountain. It was the Sixties. We hung about, because the puppies were there, in a greenhouse. Eventually the husband appeared in high heels and a Kaftan and took us to see them.

'A friend of ours had one of these puppies, but didn't look after it, so we took over. This Basset ended up paralysed, but not until it was twelve, then we got a Lakeland Terrier, Lucy. The owner warned us. 'I have to tell you, she licks the grandfather clock.'

'Don't worry,' we said. 'We don't have one.' And then we found that she licked all furniture. The dog psychologist came and tried to cure Lucy, but couldn't – he called her Lunacy. She lived until she was fourteen, but drove us insane. We had to take a seven-year rest after that, but still used to walk on the Heath, then we met this tall woman with red hair and three Greyhounds – Charlotte Cornwell. She was working with Annette Crosbie, dedicated Greyhound rescuer, and told us about the Spanish Greyhounds, Galgos, and introduced us to a woman, Anne Finch, who founded Greyhounds in Need (GIN), and we thought – if we were going to get another dog, we'd better get one of those, and quickly, before we were too old. We asked Anne whether there were any available and she said there were three coming out of quarantine on Thursday. We chose a brindle and called him Harry. We were devoted to him. He was the love of our lives.'

Bad hunting

A few years ago a Greyhound track was about to close down. That meant scores of Greyhounds were no longer wanted, and I'd been asked to write a piece about it, in the hope of finding a bit of sympathy and some new homes for the poor discarded dogs. Grisly news had recently emerged about a man up north who'd been shooting Greyhounds for £10 a pop, and burying them in a mass grave in one of his fields. And this was how I first met Angela and Martin. (Martin's taken over GIN, from Anne Finch.) It's very brave of them, like many other rescuers, to plunge into these horrors and try and sort them out.

We met at Kenwood House for tea. What a heavenly setting – an eighteenth-century mansion house on the edge of Hampstead Heath overlooking grand lawns which sweep down towards the lake. Angela and Martin's Galgo Percy was with them and not keen on company. He sat behind Angela's chair, saved from death, found in a fox trap in Spain, caught while looking for food, having been thrown out by his owner at the end of the hunting season. But now here is lucky Percy safe in sunny Hampstead. Angela is keen to show me some pictures of the horrible things done to Galgos to bump them off when the short hunting season is over. Why bother to feed and look after a dog for the rest of the year? But I don't want to see them. I don't need to, thank you very much.

'No thank you. I can imagine.'

'You need to see,' says Angela strictly. She slaps the ghastly photos on the table.

I would rather not have known quite how cruel people are, but now I do. Please, everybody, rescue a Greyhound if you possibly can.

Angela and Martin's first rescued Galgo, Harry, swerved to avoid a tree while running round a meadow in his thrilling way one day, strained a ligament and never really recovered. 'And he also had Leishmaniasis – caught in Spain before he got here. All his hair fell out, he looked like a skeleton, but luckily a vet realised what it was and prescribed allopurinol. He took it for the rest of his life and lived another four years, but had to be put down because of his leg injury. He died one January. I cried every day for two months. But after Harry we were besotted with Greyhounds. Then we got Percy. He was super-nervous, he'd never been in a house before. Harry used to love lying on top of me, but Percy didn't. He was so traumatised. When we first got him his tail hung down straight like a piece of dead meat. He didn't respond to anything. But he needed a home and we needed a dog. Dima taught us to hand-feed him. Then he began to let us stroke him. Eventually he started to respond.'

'Spaniards who rescue Galgos are fanatical,' says Martin. While he, together with a GIN vet, was visiting a dog rescue centre in Spain, (which takes in Galgos), the girls who ran it were driving him about in their van. They stopped in a garage and saw a pile of dirty fur. It was a dog. The girls asked the garage owner about it. 'It's been there for seven years,' he said. It wasn't tied up, it had probably been abandoned, and made itself a home there, near the café, where it could get scraps of food. These two girls didn't mess about. They didn't ask permission. They just picked the dog up, put him in the van, said, 'He's ours now' and drove off. The vet examined him, said he was seriously malnourished, stick thin and had ticks and fleas. The girls gave him a big meal, he wolfed it down and adopted him. And now he's a fabulous, happy dog.

'We've set up Galgo education programmes in Spain. We teach them about the treatment of Galgos through the medium of teaching English in primary schools. The present generation you can forget about. Start with the children. They're more receptive.' Perhaps they could start one here, before little boys grow up into the bad-boy-breeder brigade.

Tea, cakes and holiday tummy

To keep everyone perky and donating, Angela and Martin hold tea parties in their house for various animal charities: Greyhounds in need, Moonbears, PDSA. You name it, they do it. There's a short appeal, then tea and cakes. So I go. Regularly. One day I get to the All Dogs Matter party rather late. A guest opens the door.

'I'm very sorry,' I say. 'I fell asleep this afternoon because I was up all night because Violet (one of my dogs) had the shits. At one thirty, four and six in the morning.'

Was this woman shocked and disgusted at talk of diarrhoea? No, not at all. Because this was a dog tea party.

'What colour was it?' she asked, quick as a flash and very concerned.

'Sort of mustard colour,' I said.

'That's not too bad,' said she, relieved, 'but if it's pink, that's when you want to be worried. Then go straight to the vet.'

'I will,' I promised. But pink? I'd never come across that before. Later, thinking over our chat, I think she must have meant red, meaning blood. Groo. But I found this conversation rather refreshing. What other party could you go to and be able to speak freely about your worrying dog ailments in such a frank and helpful way? Nowhere. Only at a dog party, and I had no difficulty eating my cakes a little later on, after the appeal. I particularly liked the coffee walnut.

15: Sunny Side of Dog World

A beautiful, unseasonably warm and sunny March day, and the Southern Shires Bloodhound pack is about to go hunting in Windsor Great Park. Don't panic folks. They only hunt the natural scent of man. They don't hurt anything. They just sniff the runners before they run off. A group of riders, their horses, cars, trailers and dogs are getting ready to hunt. And two chaps and a woman all in shorts – the Quarry.

What a heavenly, peaceful scene! Endless acres of gently undulating parkland, magnificent shiny horses standing about, munching at the grass or the odd bag of hay, and some dogs – not the hounds, just along for the walkie.

'Hugo! Hugo, come! He's a horrible, hairy hound – a Blue-cross rescue Welsh Foxhound-cross-Harrier and he comes to work with me,' says Sarah. 'He sits under my desk. I'm in the RAF. I know they say dogs don't smile, but they do. Look.' Yes, Hugo is definitely smiling. And why not? He has landed in paradise. 'He'll come with me for a ten-mile hack and he'll still look at me at the end and say "What? Finished already?" Hugo! Hugo, come! You have to keep calling him. Hugo?'

Margaret-Ann has no dog with her. 'I arranged for this pack to come to Windsor,' says she. 'The Queen Mother used to terrify Marc. (Marc Winchester, Master of Hounds.) She'd come and she'd recognise all the Bloodhounds from the year before and wander about naming them. She was a wonderful hostess. She'd say, "Do have a sausage. Or a sausage roll."'

Two black Labradors are wandering about. 'Get in the car. In, in. Saffy, in!'

'Doggies on leads. Then they're under control,' says their owner, talking to no one in particular. 'That's the best way to be when you're a doggie.' What are their names? 'This is Poo-bear, because he's a dog of very little brain, and this one doesn't know what he is. He's just stupid,' said as if he's one of the loveliest dogs on earth.

The riders are getting dressed in hunt shirts and stocks, waistcoats, black jackets and hats, white and cream jodhpurs, and two Masters of Hounds in their bright red coats.

But where are the hounds? They're in the blue hunt lorry. On the top level. You can see a couple looking out of a barred window. All the equipment is kept on the ground floor of the lorry. Out they come, when all the riders are dressed, ready and mounted, and make their way over to Marc, on his horse in his red jacket, where they flop about in a rather chilled way, rolling on their backs, in their lovely loose fur: 'size 12 in a size 16 coat'. They mill around, staying more or less together. There's a bit of growling and pretend fighting. Noodle, one of this year's puppies, is being dragged along on a lead. She joins the pack. 'Her tail's wagging now. She's happy. Happy-ish.'

The plan is that the quarry run off twenty minutes ahead, the hounds have been shown a smelly sock from the runners to sniff. They'll follow that scent, the quarry will run to an allocated spot, and wait. That run is called a line. Then the hounds are laid on to the line of the quarry (released) and the riders follow. 'You'll hear them when they get the scent. The cry changes. They have wonderful scent. But heat is bad,' says Margaret-Ann. 'It makes the scent rise.' What happens when the hounds catch up with them? 'They'll come up and kiss them to pieces.'

What a perfect way to hunt. Everyone involved is cheery and polite. There are rules they must adhere to, including 'Always say thank you to someone opening a gate for you,' 'If you are riding a horse that kicks, please tie a red ribbon in its tail' or if your horse is a novice and 'you're unsure whether it kicks, please tie a green ribbon in its tail.'

A sudden shout 'Trailer!' Trailer, a hound, has disappeared behind one of the horseboxes. 'Who's upset Trailer?' There are twelve hounds – six couples, and quite a few of them are puppies. The hounds are all entire. Average age three and a half. 'Rhubarb's been red-carded. He chased the deer last time,' says Margaret-Ann, who knows this sport inside out. 'They used to be used for tracking deer. In the eighteenth and nineteenth centuries, many stately homes had their own Bloodhounds and deer parks.'

'Welcome to our friends from the New Forest Beagles,' says Marc. (You can tell these riders by the green on the reverse of their jackets. The Southern Shires Bloodhounds have a grey bit instead.) 'And we must thank Her Majesty the Queen! For permission to be here.'

'Her Majesty the Queen!' Everyone raises their glass of wine. 'And the rangers! We have three lines for you today. Keep off the mown grass! Keep off that or you're off to the Tower!' Marc is joined by his whippers-in, Miss Marshall and Miss Ball – fresh, English rose complexions, smartly got-up in black jackets, pale jodhpurs, smart white stocks (cravats). 'We'll be serving lunch when we get back. All jumps are optional. We'll give the quarry a few more minutes.'

Someone is criticising Hugo's owner. Very mildly. 'One word from you and he does exactly as he likes.' Hugo keeps away from the hounds. 'The first time he came he jumped out of the van, saw those huge hounds, and jumped straight back in the van again.'

Before the hunt sets off, wine and sausage rolls are handed round. Later, at the end of each line, there'll be jelly babies for everyone. For sugar to keep the energy levels up. Marc blows his trumpet. There's an immediate singing/calling/baying from the hounds. A magical sound. Charles, in a red coat is the field master, alongside another hunt member in a red coat. Margaret-Ann explains. 'They go at either side to keep the hounds within the allowable area, or they hold the hounds back. They and the Master wear red. It used to be called pink. It used to be only the landed gentry, lords and squires, who wore 'hunting pink' so that if they fell off they could be seen and got to first. It's no longer an elite outfit. It's practical. Very warm and waterproof, and you can see the red clearly at a distance. Everything to do with hunting is practical. The stock supports your neck – if you fall off, it protects your neck, and it can act as a handy bandage. It's quite a thick piece of cotton – some have padding. The whips aren't just a pretentious affectation. See that L-shaped part of the crop?' (The handle.) Yes. 'You can shut a gate with that. You crack the whip to get the attention of the hounds. You don't whip them with it. If you touch them they won't do what you want.'

What bliss it must be to ride across this vast park after the Bloodhounds, but not everyone has a horse or can ride well enough. So we're following in cars. We arrive at the edge of a wood, the end of the first line, where the quarry have stopped. The hounds have found them. A lady hands the quarry and riders another tray of jelly babies and wine gums. The hounds aren't taking much notice of the runners. They're not even kissing them. Why not? 'Because they've found them now. The scent is all around. They don't need to look for it anymore.'

'Did Trailer have his nose down following the line?'

'Yes. All the way.'

Margaret-Ann goes on explaining. 'Every call means something different. There are some wonderful calls.' The hounds all sit and lie around Marc. 'They love him dearly. Because he looks after them. It's all strictly under control. They don't leave to run after the runners until they're told to.'

Off they all go again. Quarry, hounds, cars. From the road we can see the hunt far away, across the great swathes of green, hounds first, the small horseback figure in red behind them, horn blowing, the black-jacketed followers on various shades of horse. 'See! They've come across the field silently, picked up the scent, started calling.'

We catch up with them in a field, at the end of the second line. The hounds are lying about or wandering around a little. 'They're Dumfries Foxhound Bloodhound crosses,' says Marc, pointing to a couple of black-backed ones, 'or Otterhound crosses,' [all over red]. Crossing them makes them healthier. Then you don't get eyes like that [pulls his outwards and downwards into slits], or droopy [pulls his bottom eyelids down] like that. It's always a bitch who's top dog, because they want to carry the genes forward. They will only have the alpha male.

She has the top dog because she's the top bitch. If I put a young one in, if it stayed there with her all day, she wouldn't have it. They're like lions. The head of the pride is always a male, but the lionesses do the hunting. If you have a pack of hounds and hunted only bitches together, they hunt better than males, they're more methodical. My hat! Someone's peed on it. [The poor hat had been on the ground.] We stop in summer because it's too hot and there's no scent.'

After a bit of a rest, and twenty minutes' wait for the quarry to get away, we're off to the end of the last line, passing through the deer park on the way. 'This business of going through the deer park always amuses me.' Margaret-Ann again. Do they chase the deer? 'Most of them are very good, but you'll sometimes get the odd one that riots.'

We end up at the very top of the Long Walk which is about two and two-thirds miles long and leads straight down to the George IV Gateway at Windsor Castle. It's a spectacular view, and at the top of the Long Walk, on top of a great pile of rock slabs, on top of grassy Snow Hill, is the Copper Horse, a huge and majestic statue of George III on horseback. We climb to the top of that, look away from the castle – a pastoral idyll, says the guidebook, and it is, then suddenly out of a wood into the open green expanse, come the great big, graceful, red-brown and black hounds, calling, followed by the red-coated Masters and the rest of the hunt. A fabulous sight, a tableau from the eighteenth century – a real live costume drama in front of your eyes. From a flat rock just beneath the horse's towering and massively impressive backside, I can see the hunt circle this hill, until they reach the end of their last line, at the top of the Long Walk. The hunt has been magical, harmless, thrilling, exhilarating, even for me just watching. Imagine being on a horse. If only all hunting with hounds could be like this.

Best of shows

Crufts was too big for me. My preferred size of dog show is the Bermondsey festival dog show. It's held in aid of a small dog charity on a circle of grass in a small Bermondsey park off Bermondsey Street. It's very crowded, we can barely see or hear the contestants, until we manage to get a seat on some bales of straw which are arranged around the ring. Marvellous – a ring-side seat, and in comes Martin the Whippet.

'Built for speed,' says the announcer, a chap dressed like John McEnroe in his heyday, but more charming. 'Look at the lines on that dog!' Then, 'Jouvert, the French Bulldog. Vive la difference! And Giules the Whippet. Another speed merchant! Now look at this relaxed dog! Number twenty-eight, Nero the Pug. He's not actually moving. Is he alive? And Spike, a Bulldog, only three months old!'

Crowd: 'Aaaaahh!!'

'We're asking the owners to walk their dogs around. We don't want any pile-ups here. We're looking for that connection between owner and dog . . . some chairs behind them, and . . . let's give them a big hand. There's a lovely Bulldog, oh sorry! A whippet. These are lovely dogs!'

And so are some of the owners. One in a frilly white skirt to match her fluffy white Tibetan Terrier. The audience cheers. We must cheer loudest for the dog we like best. This is the Pedigree Boys' class, and Manson the Bernese Mountain Dog wins. Hurrah. The losers are still cheerful. The sun's shining, we have a sudden early spring-summer. This is a mellow affair, with none of the tension and overwhelming effect of Crufts. And next comes the Loveliest Crossbreed Class. You wouldn't get that at Crufts either. We have Rango, a South London Bin-ends, a darling little black Pug/Chihuahua cross, Jackson the Chihuahua/Jack Russell cross. 'Who can do any tricks?' asks John McEnroe. 'Yes! Pirouettes and twirling!' It's the Pug/Chihuahua.

Audience: 'That is CUTE!!'

'Now here is Lexi.' She is elderly and a little over-weight. 'Lexi's just done a high five!'

Audience: Hooray!!

And she's just recovered from a brain tumour.'

Audience: 'AAAAHHHH! Huge round of applause.

A little ratty-haired, waif-like girl taps John McEnroe.

Her dog can do tricks. It's a medium-sized black raggedy dog of no fixed type. The girl is wearing fairly grubby boys' white football shorts and shirt which are too big for her. But her dog is very good at tricks. It gives its paws alternately, it stands up and puts its paws on the girl's chest, it sits, stands and lies down. The girl demonstrates repeatedly. She's good at this: strict but loving, consistent, totally focussed on her dog, patient, always rewarding the tricks. But nobody's really taking much notice. She just carries on quietly putting the dog through its paces. One day, she will probably be an excellent dog-trainer. This is the most impressive 'connection between dog and owner' so far. But the pasty girl and her dog are not very glamorous. She looks as if she doesn't have much else, beside her lovely dog.

Lexi wins the Special Survivor's award. The girl in white wins nothing. She quietly disappears into the crowd with her dog. I should have run after her and told her what a good trainer she was, but there wasn't time. I hope somebody else does and wishes her luck. She looks as if she needs it.

Meanwhile the show went on, with the Anything Goes class. Which seemed to mean dressing up. I suppose there are hard-liners who disapprove. You could see it as demeaning for the dogs, but they didn't seem to mind, and even if they did, it wasn't for long. We had Boris the Pug dressed as a pirate – red and white striped T-shirt, pirate's hat.

Audience girls behind me. 'Oh my God, that's hilarious!!

Homer the French Bulldog dressed as a matador, with a more or less all-over black velvet and gold outfit, with a little red flag attached and the appropriate hat. Owner was dressed as a bull – also head to toe in black velvet, but with horns and a nose ring. What an enormous effort they'd made. And what a laugh, which we could all do with nowadays.

Girls behind 'Oh bless him!!!'

'The human fashion show [which was going on up the road] doesn't have the warmth that this show has,' said John McEnroe. 'There's not the personality.'

He was spot on. It wasn't very competitive. I didn't notice any envy, bitterness or disappointment. But I do wish the little girl in white had won something. Or perhaps she didn't mind either. I heard later that she had a happy home life, with lots of pets, including a parrot, that her whole family was mad keen on animals, and she has plenty of clean clothes in her cupboard, but the show outfit was her favourite. You can never judge by appearances.

Dog's birthday

I'm in the local pet shop and notice a pink and white candy-striped large handbag thingy hanging from the ceiling. Is it for carrying a dog?

'Yes,' says the pet-shop lady, turning up her nose. 'We
have to have them in. People want them. Dogs have got
four legs haven't they? What do they think they're for?'

I don't expect she caters for puppy showers, either.
No. Does anybody do those?

'You're asking me?' And then a look of great distaste.
'It comes from America, doesn't it?'

Yes, but it's arrived here too. It's my dog's birthday
soon, so I'm wondering what's available. You need a
selection of toys, for the dogs to play with, water bowls,
grooming tools, for the humans to play with, snacks,
goodie-bags (cute paw-print pattern), your camera,
personalised doggy cake, invitations, decorations, and
an agility course, which all sounds a bit of a fag. You
can hold it in your garden or the park. Warning. Do
not invite dogs on heat. Dressing up is optional. And
then you need a pregnant dog, (and the groom, if possible) which I haven't got. So it'll have to be a more
modest affair.

My dog's been having fairly laid-back parties for
some time now. The regular group of dog walkers in
our local small park, have mostly chummed up, and so
have their dogs. We usually just have the regulars, and
it has been the custom for some years for Dave, owner
of Bissy – Greyhound/German Shepherd cross – to
make my dog a dog-cake on its birthday (the one
made of rice and minced beef moulded into a pudding-
shape and charmingly decorated with strips of fillet

steak). Dave brought plastic bowls to the park, all the dogs and owners present were invited, and had a fabulous time. One particularly magical birthday I brought along some Happy Birthday blue balloons, thinking they might last a couple of seconds. But the dogs somehow got the hang of playing nose-ball. They all jumped up and down, biffing the balloons into the air with their noses, for several whole minutes before bursting the balloons. One of the highlights of my life. I shall never forget it.

Dog café

Not far from one of the entrances to the Heath is the dog café. That is not its real name, but that's what we call it, because dog owners may sit in the outside bit of it, with their dogs. It is a heavenly place to meet your dog-friends, especially in the summer. There's some shade from the awning, and the winter isn't bad either, because they do lovely hot chocolate, cappuccinos, Italian cakes and continental and English breakfasts. Why go on holiday and bother with dog passports, when one can stay here and hang out in dog café?

This morning I went along there with my dog. The amenities are fabulous. A large bucket of water is provided for dogs, there are posts and railing to which you can secure your dog while you go in and buy your snacks and drinks, but the dog will not be alone. Other dog-owners will attend to it while you're away, so that it doesn't feel abandoned or upset in any way.

Today Clare is there with her Doberman, she is a regular at dog café. 'This is Alex,' says she, introducing me to her chum. 'Alex is a very good dog walker, if you need one.' I probably will sooner or later. Alex is with her Rottweiler Ike, who's wearing a red spotted scarf. This is the perfect place for dog-networking, and it was here that I came to find assistant rescuers when Jennifer needed help with the two abandoned dogs. The sun's shining, the dog are relaxing, and as I go in for my choc, Alex goes over to my darling dog, and talks to her. And there is my neighbour with her little brown dog, and another chum with her Retriever, all dogs sitting and flopping around in a mellow way. What a dreamy break-fast venue. While you're here, you could almost forget the world is going down the drain.

Not that dog café is always perfect. A wandering dog approaches a tied-up dog, infuriating the tied-up dog, which lunges at the wandering dog, tangling its legs in the lead, and there could have been a nasty accident, but luckily there wasn't. The wandering dog's mummy comes and pulls it away.

Mutterings from the seated dog persons. 'That dog shouldn't be off the lead here. Bloody silly woman. Oh! Back it comes!' Here you can hear the latest dog news. So-and-so's dog went for so-and-so's dog/a cyclist/

another dog minding its own business/the postman. 'And of course it wasn't her dog's fault. It never is. It's always the other person's fault. One rule for her, another for everyone else.' But it all spices up a coffee break.

Sadly, the more dogs there are in dog café, the more tension between the dog-owners and the non-dog-owners. Some people without dogs don't like a crowd of dogs sitting next to them. But they can sit elsewhere, say the dog people. There are large dog-free areas, and the inside of the café is entirely dog-free. But the non-dog-owners are winning. The atmosphere today is rather subdued. There is now a plan to make the dog-owners sit in a side outdoors area, with no shelter. Banished to round the side, in an enclosure. But today we're still in front in our usual place. Perhaps the move will never happen.

Blaze of glory

I'm entering my dog, Lily, for a local show, in the 'Most Appealing Eyes' category. She is thirteen and a bit. That makes her ninety-two in human years, and this may be her last chance. Will she be up to it next year? Even this year was a bit of a worry. She'd been feeling a bit ropey at the beginning of the week, but luckily she perked up in time. And what luck, after weeks of dismal rain, it was one of those perfect English summer days – big fluffy white clouds scudding across a blue sky, and a pleasant breeze. Just right for an elderly dog, who gets puffed out and knackered in the heat. Here's Dawn the dog-walker in the pub garden with her family and little Spaniel, in a red, white and blue rosette! 'She came first!' In the Medium Dog category! As well as its rosette, it has a lovely pink pretend flower in its collar. And her old dog Rodan has come sixth in the Large Dog category. Two winners! Dawn and her family are tremendously proud.

'See Mum,' says my daughter strictly. 'They made an effort. You didn't.'

Yes I did. Lily had a very thorough face wash with her special peach-scented wipes, with particular attention paid to in-between wrinkles.

Nearly time for Most Appealing Eyes group. We make our way to the show ring in the churchyard. It is jam-packed with audience, the show so popular that you can hardly get near enough to see the ring and competitors, and among the crowds are loads of dogs: plain, dressed-up, winners, competitors, observers. There goes a dog and its owner, both in matching pink fairy wings – another in an orange cardi, another reddish, fluffy Pomeranian with a yellow rosette. Isn't the owner thrilled? Not really. 'It's only third,' says she, a tiny bit disappointed.

I hear our category being called out from the ring. 'Dog with the Most Appealing Eyes?' In we go. A lovely big fluffy white dog is up before the judges. 'Look at those piercing blue eyes!' says the Master of Ceremonies. 'What is he?' A Husky cross. 'And who's this?' to a little girl with a small grey wispy dog. 'Now look at those eyes! He's definitely in with a chance.' Next up is a lady with an elderly white and brown dog. Very appealing! 'Who is this?' This is blah – fifteen years old!!! Roar of applause.

It's our turn. 'And what's your name? Lily the Boxer. Thirteen years old!' Loud cheers from the crowd. 'And she has a fan club!' How lovely to see the elderly appreciated. It's like the old days of Wilfred Pickles. 'Thirteen!! Give her a big hand Mabel,' and the same jolly atmosphere. We are quite caught up with the thrill of the show. But I don't think we have much of a chance. The compere didn't really praise Lily enough, in my opinion, and then suddenly her name is called. 'Lily the Boxer?' She has won! Only sixth place, but a fabulous pink rosette and enormous goodie bag. What excitement. Daughter adores pink, and the dogs adore what's in the bag. What a fabulous afternoon. My old dog, aged ninety-two, with her odd, sticking-out jaw, almost completely grey face, weedy back legs and arthritis, has won a beauty contest! I always knew she was profoundly beautiful, but it is heaven to have her beauty publicly acknowledged.

Back to the pub garden, to join some old neighbours of ours, with their creamy Sheepdog, sitting very politely and calmly, and at the next table is the woman with the first-prize-winning white dog, very cheery, naturally, but she's noticed some grumpy people about. 'There are some people out there,' she says, looking startled, 'moaning that there are too many bloody dogs!' Too many dogs? At a dog show? Dismal creatures. But they're not dog-owners, so they're having no fun. The sun, the cakes, the strawberry beer, barbecue tent, ice-creams, morris dancers, climbing wall, bouncy rope with squealing kiddies boinging up and down – it all makes no difference, and they are still pissy-faced, but if they had a dog, their spirits would lift. There are no glum dog-owners here, winners or not.

Is it worth it?

I can't pretend that owning a dog is no trouble. Hearing about the struggles, expense, squabbles, heartbreak, stolen Sunday roasts, accidents, emergencies, bad-boy dog-owners and knife-edge walkies, you may be wondering 'Why bother?' But those difficulties are only a tiny fraction of a life spent with dogs. For the rest of it you will have devotion, comfort, affection, loyalty, laughs, and a great blast of love. Fall down the stairs, nearly break your ankle, and the dogs are there, concerned and giving you a kiss. You're in bed and you feel safe and protected, because they're nearby, snoring reassuringly, but ready to jump up, bark ferociously and frighten away robbers. They can cheer up and comfort the sick and elderly, they're not put off by misery or personality disorders, they just pile in and carry on, to them no one is self-centred, self-conscious, defensive, unattractive, weird-looking, on the autistic spectrum or inadequate. They love us whatever. All we have to do is look after them properly. And even if we don't they are extraordinarily forgiving. They live in the here and now, and this way of being is catching. Why lie in bed feeling dreary and paralysed by fears of the future, global meltdown, wars and cancer? With a dog around, you can't. You must get up, face the world, get out into the fresh air and keep going.

I remember as a young child, waking up one morning feeling nothing in particular. It was school holidays with nothing much happening, and then suddenly in came the dog. He jumped up onto my bed, stood over my, looking down, chops drooping, tail wagging, saying 'Get up! Time to play.' It's an invitation no one can resist. When I grew up, left my parents' home, moved into a flat in town and worked full time, I could no longer have a dog. For 20 years. I missed it terribly. What a difficult couple of decades. A dog would have helped me through the ghastly bits.

Now over twenty years later I have dogs again. I wake up one morning feeling the usual existential dread and terror, but there is one dog lying on its back on the sofa-waving its legs in the air, and the other bouncing around throwing my sock about. Immediately, the world is a jollier place. And apart from all these emotional perks, everyone should know by now that dogs are good for your physical health. A dog's presence is good for the heart and general wellbeing. Remember my mother's constipation and last few months of life? The dogs cured the first and perked up the second. And that's nothing compared to what many dogs can do: guide the blind, warn and protect soldiers, help autistic children, help children to read, sniff out people buried in earthquakes, sniff out cancers and predict seizures.

A dog is the perfect companion for anyone, particularly the over-protective type of person. The dog does not want you to mind your own business. Its whole life is your business. You may be as intrusive and over-protective as you like, the dog won't mind. You can supervise its meals, tell it what to eat, choose its outfits, organise its day, tell your friends every detail of its private life and inspect its bowel movements. It will not grow up and accuse you of ruining its life. It will only love you.

But however hard I try, I can't convince everyone. Some people, who do not have a dog, will always disapprove of dog-lovers. They will say that your dog is your substitute partner or baby. They will say this as if you are a tragic and pathetic creature who has not managed to attract and keep a husband/wife/partner, or who cannot have, or cannot cope with, a real human child of your own, or more than one child, so instead you have chosen a dog. Ignore these people. So what if you have plumped

ACKNOWLEDGEMENTS

I would like to thank all the dog-owners, walkers, trainers and rescuers who have shared with me, and allowed me to write about, their experiences in Dog World: Martin and Angela Humphery and Greyhounds in Need, Nova White, Jill Dawson, Jed Reid and Marge Harris, Wei Tang and Adrian Phillips, Sonia Humphreys, John Clayden, Ira Moss and All Dogs Matter, Dima Yeremenko and everyone at Good Boy Dog school and Doggie Boot Camp, Karen and Dave Perks, Dawn and Mick Doran, Elaine Durack, Sue Scully, John Hayes, John Brown, Anthony Boyle and Ingela Thuné-Boyle, Catherine Bourne, Sara Keene, John O'Driscoll, Marc Winchester and members of the Southern Shires Bloodhounds, Mary Ray, Sophie Radice, David Gryn, Georgia Abrams, Suzanne Freed and Velo Mitrovich, Matilda Mahtab, Stephanie Isles, Jane Andrews and Claire Wynnick, Dave Spector and Chris Cloett, Maureen O'Leary, Zarah and Mark Wolf, Crufts, The Kennel Club, the Dogs Trust, Stuart Simons, Barry Karacostas, Tony Nevett, Danny and all the staff and pupils of Maplefields School, Elaine

Jones, Pike and Rita Galloway, Cameron Amos and Sarah Brass, Chris Hardwidge, Alex, Clare Tapply and all the regulars at dog café, and the other Heath and park wardens, and members of Dog World, who must be nameless. My friends Carol McNicoll, Jennifer Woolfenden, Hazel Pethig, Clare Moynihan, Monica Evans, Anne Munsie and occasionally even Ian Whitwham the Dog Hater, for bravely accompanying me on my dog walkies, my daughter Amy for her invaluable input and for sharing her mother with dogs, my vet Carol Hills, for her ideas, and together with all her colleagues, for keeping my dogs going while I wrote this. Thanks to the *Guardian* newspaper for giving me so many opportunities to research and write features about dogs, and to Kerri Sharp, for giving me the chance to write a whole book about them.